ICTS 144 Physical Education
Teacher Certification Exam

By: Sharon Wynne, M.S
Southern Connecticut State University

"And, while there's no reason yet to panic, I think it's only prudent that we make preparations to panic."

XAMonline, INC.
Boston

XAMonline, Inc.
21 Orient Ave.
Melrose, MA 02176
Toll Free 1-800-301-4647
Email: info@xamonline.com
Web www.xamonline.com
Fax: 1-781-662-9268

Library of Congress Cataloging-in-Publication Data

Wynne, Sharon A.
    Physical Education 144: Teacher Certification / Sharon A. Wynne. -2nd ed.
    ISBN 978-1-58197-989-3
    1. Physical Education 144.   2. Study Guides.   3. ICTS
    4. Teachers' Certification & Licensure.   5. Careers

Disclaimer:
The opinions expressed in this publication are the sole works of XAMonline and were created independently from the National Education Association, Educational Testing Service, or any State Department of Education, National Evaluation Systems or other testing affiliates.

Between the time of publication and printing, state specific standards as well as testing formats and website information may change that is not included in part or in whole within this product. Sample test questions are developed by XAMonline and reflect similar content as on real tests; however, they are not former tests. XAMonline assembles content that aligns with state standards but makes no claims nor guarantees teacher candidates a passing score. Numerical scores are determined by testing companies such as NES or ETS and then are compared with individual state standards. A passing score varies from state to state.

Printed in the United States of America

ICTS: Physical Education 144
ISBN: 978-1-58197-989-3

ILLINOIS CERTIFICATION TESTING SYSTEM (ICTS) – Physical Education

ABOUT THE ICTS
The ICTS tests are criterion referenced and objective based, meaning the test measures a candidate's knowledge and skills in relation to an established standard rather than in relation to the performance of other candidates.

Basic Skills test:
- Consists of 125 multiple-choice questions in reading comprehension, language arts, and mathematics.
- Also contains a constructed-response writing assignment.

Content-Area tests:
- Consists of 125 multiple-choice questions.

PASSING REQUIREMENTS
All test scores are reported using a range from 100 to 300 with a total test score of 240 or higher required for passing. Candidates who wish to retake a test must complete the registration process and make the appropriate payment.

Table of Contents

Domain/Competency/Skill #   *Pg.*

DOMAIN 1.0   **HEALTH-RELATED PHYSICAL FITNESS**

COMPETENCY 1.0 UNDERSTAND TECHNIQUES AND PROCEDURES
              FOR DEVELOPING AND ASSESSING HEALTH-RELATED
              FITNESS.. 1

SKILL 1.1   *Demonstrate knowledge of expected developmental progressions,
               ranges of individual variation, and levels of readiness for health-
               related fitness* 1

SKILL 1.2   *Identify and apply developmentally appropriate strategies,
               instruments, and technologies to assess and monitor individual
               fitness levels, to measure learner progress in fitness development,
               and to provide feedback to students* 2

SKILL 1.3   *Apply principles and techniques for designing and implementing
               individualized fitness programs (e.g., setting realistic, short-term
               goals, identifying risk factors, applying training principles to fitness
               goals)* 4

SKILL 1.4   *Demonstrate an understanding of factors and techniques that
               motivate students to enhance health-related fitness levels for
               overall personal well-being* 7

SKILL 1.5   *Analyze health-related fitness goal setting, activity selection, and
               personal health-related fitness programs for individual students* 9

SKILL 1.6   *Evaluate fitness and health-related services, products, and
               advertising (e.g., claims about fitness equipment, weight control
               products and programs, dietary supplements)* 11

SKILL 1.7   *Demonstrate an understanding of how to incorporate fitness
               concepts into various physical activities* 14

COMPETENCY 2.0 UNDERSTAND PRINCIPLES AND ACTIVITIES FOR
              DEVELOPING AND MAINTAINING HEALTHY LEVELS OF
              CARDIORESPIRATORY ENDURANCE 15

SKILL 2.1   *Understand the structure and function of the cardiorespiratory
               system and its specific adaptations to physical activity* 15

SKILL 2.2   *Identify and apply principles, skills, and activities for aerobic
               conditioning* 17

SKILL 2.3   *Apply techniques for assessing and monitoring endurance levels
               (e.g., measuring heart rate before, during, and after exercise)* 18

SKILL 2.4   *Recognize and select aerobic activities appropriate for various
               developmental levels and purposes* 19

SKILL 2.5   Demonstrate knowledge of a variety of methods for promoting students' use of self monitoring of exercise intensity (e.g., perceived exertion, pulse monitors, pedometers) 20

COMPETENCY 3.0 UNDERSTAND PRINCIPLES AND ACTIVITIES FOR DEVELOPING AND MAINTAINING FLEXIBILITY AND MUSCULAR STRENGTH AND ENDURANCE 22

SKILL 3.1   Understand the structure and function of the musculoskeletal system and its specific adaptations to physical activity 22

SKILL 3.2   Identify and apply principles, skills, and activities for developing strength and endurance in various muscle groups and parts of the body 24

SKILL 3.3   Identify and apply principles, techniques, and activities for promoting flexibility of the major joints of the body 50

SKILL 3.4   Identify and apply principles and activities for developing proper posture and efficient body mechanics 52

SKILL 3.5   Identify and apply principles, types of equipments, and safety practices for progressive-resistance and flexibility exercise (e.g., weight training, circuit training, stretching).....................................53

SKILL 3.6   Recognize flexibility, strength, and endurance activities appropriate for various developmental levels and purposes (e.g., increasing muscle mass, increasing muscular endurance, toning) 57

SKILL 3.7   Identify and analyze techniques for evaluating flexibility and muscular strength endurance 58

COMPETENCY 4.0 UNDERSTAND PRINCIPLES AND ACTIVITIES FOR DEVELOPING AND MAINTAINING LEVELS OF BODY COMPOSITION THAT PROMOTE GOOD HEALTH 59

SKILL 4.1   Identify and apply principles of nutrition and weight control and ways in which diet and eating habits affect physical development and health...59

SKILL 4.2   Analyze the relationship between body type and body composition and apply techniques for evaluating body composition (e.g., skinfold, girth measurements, BMI) 60

SKILL 4.3   Demonstrate knowledge of the relationship between physical activity and body composition (e.g., caloric intake and expenditure) 61

SKILL 4.4   Select appropriate activities and material for developing and maintaining healthy levels of body composition.............................62

SKILL 4.5   Identify and correct misconceptions related to body composition, dieting, nutritional needs, exercise, and training.............................63

DOMAIN 2.0   **MOVEMENT AND SKILL ACQUISITION**

COMPETENCY 1.0 UNDERSTAND PRINCIPLES AND CHARACTERISTICS OF MOTOR DEVELOPMENT.........65

SKILL 1.1   Recognize principles, critical elements, sequences, and characteristics of motor development during infancy, childhood, adolescence, and adulthood...65

SKILL 1.2   Demonstrate knowledge of appropriate developmental progressions and individual variations...66

SKILL 1.3   Identify principles of perceptual-motor development and components such as visual, auditory, tactile, and kinesthetic discrimination, and evaluate their relationship to motor development and performance 68

COMPETENCY 2.0 UNDERSTAND THE PRINCIPLES OF MOTOR LEARNING AND MOVEMENT SKILS ACQUISITION.......69

SKILL 2.1   Demonstrate knowledge of principles and stages of motor learning and concepts associated with skill acquisition (e.g., practice, self-assessment, readiness, observational learning, skill analysis) 69

SKILL 2.2   Apply knowledge of levels of readiness in motor learning 70

SKILL 2.3   Identify and apply appropriate instructional cues and prompts for basic motor skills 71

SKILL 2.4   Identify techniques for detecting errors in and providing corrective feedback for motor performance 74

SKILL 2.5   Identify developmentally appropriate instructional and practice experiences to promote acquisition of motor skills 75

COMPETENCY 3.0 UNDERSTAND MOVEMENT CONCEPTS AND BIOMECHANICAL PRINCIPLES.......................................76

SKILL 3.1   Identify critical elements of basic movement patterns (e.g., locomotor, nonlocomotor, manipulative, rhythmic) 76

SKILL 3.2   Demonstrate knowledge of basic movement concepts and ways to promote application of movement concepts 78

SKILL 3.3   Recognize biomechanical principles (e.g., those related to motion, balance, force projection and absorption, speed, acceleration) and apply these principles to various movement activities..79

SKILL 3.4   Apply movement concepts and biomechanical principles to the learning and development of new skills (e.g., catching balls while moving, throwing objects using opposition) 87

SKILL 3.5   Analyze various movement patterns for effectiveness...................87

COMPETENCY 4.0 UNDERSTAND METHODS FOR INTEGRATING LOCOMOTOR, NONLOCOMOTOR, MANIPULATIVE, AND RHYTHMIC MOVEMENTS INTO SKILLED COMBINATIONS...89

SKILL 4.1   Demonstrate knowledge of techniques and motor patterns for throwing, catching, dribbling, kicking, and striking skills and combinations of manipulative skills in gamelike conditions 89

SKILL 4.2   Select appropriate activities, materials, and equipment for development of combinations and sequences of locomotor, nonlocomotor, manipulative, and rhythmic movement skills..........92

SKILL 4.3   Identify techniques for assessing student performance on combinations and sequences of locomotor, nonlocomotor, manipulative, and rhythmic movement skills 96

COMPETENCY 5.0 UNDERSTAND TECHNIQUES, SKILLS, STRATEGIES, BASIC RULES, ETIQUETTE, AND SAFETY PRACTICES FOR INDIVIDUAL AND GROUP SPORTS 98

SKILL 5.1   Demonstrate an understanding of critical elements, skill progressions, strategies, and types and uses of equipment for individual and group sports...98

SKILL 5.2   Recognize basic rules, etiquette, and safety practices associated with individual and group sports 125

SKILL 5.3   Select and apply offensive, defensive, and cooperative strategies in group sports 135

SKILL 5.4   Identify and apply developmentally appropriate strategies and instruments to assess learner performance in individual and group sports 136

COMPETENCY 6.0 UNDERSTAND TECHNIQUES, SKILLS, STRATEGIES, BASIC RULES, ETIQUETTE, AND SAFETY PRACTICES ASSOCIATED WITH LIFELONG SPORTS, CREATIVE MOVEMENT, DANCE, NONCOMPETITIVE ACTIVITIES, AND COOPERATIVE ACTIVITIES 138

SKILL 6.1   Demonstrate an understanding of critical elements, skill progressions, strategies, safety practices, types of equipment, and basic rules and etiquette for lifelong sports and activities............138

SKILL 6.2   Recognize techniques, steps, sequences, activities, etiquette, and safety practices for creative movement and dance activities 141

SKILL 6.3   *Identify concepts, strategies, and safety issues in the development of noncompetitive and cooperative activities (e.g., challenge course, team-building activities, ropes course)* 144

SKILL 6.4   *Identify and apply developmentally appropriate strategies and instruments to assess learner performance* 146

DOMAIN 3.0   **THE ROLE OF PHYSICAL EDUCATION IN PROMOTING DEVELOPMENT**

COMPETENCY 1.0 UNDERSTAND THE ROLE OF PHYSICAL EDUCATION IN THE DEVELOPMENT OF POSITIVE PERSONAL BEHAVIORS 148

SKILL 1.1   *Identify developmental progressions in the cognitive and affective domains* 148

SKILL 1.2   *Recognize the relationship between physical activity and the development of personal identity and psychological well-being* 150

SKILL 1.3   *Evaluate the role of physical activity in fostering awareness and enjoyment of aesthetic and creative aspects of skills performance* 152

SKILL 1.4   *Demonstrate an understanding of the ways in which physical activities can promote positive behavior (e.g., confidence, honesty, personal self-control, competence, perseverance)* 154

SKILL 1.5   *Analyze the influence of performance expectations related to gender, physical appearance, and skill level on the development of self-image* 157

COMPETENCY 2.0 UNDERSTAND THE ROLE OF PHYSICAL EDUCATION IN THE DEVELOPMENT OF POSITIVE SOCIAL ATTITUDES AND BEHAVIORS 159

SKILL 2.1   *Demonstrate an understanding of socialization processes that occur through physical activity* 159

SKILL 2.2   *Recognize the ways in which physical activities can promote positive social attitudes and behaviors (e.g., teamwork, leadership, compassion, fairness, respect)* 160

SKILL 2.3   *Demonstrate knowledge of the socio-cultural benefits of participation in a variety of individual and group physical activities* 160

COMPETENCY 3.0 UNDERSTAND THE ROLE OF PHYSICAL EDUCATION IN THE DEVELOPMENT OF CRITICAL-THINKING, PROBLEM-SOLVING, AND DECISION-MAKING SKILLS 161

SKILL 3.1   Analyze techniques, strategies, and activities for developing higher-order thinking skills in the context of physical education activities 161

SKILL 3.2   Recognize the role of physical activity, sports, and games in the development of conflict-resolution skills 162

SKILL 3.3   Identify key elements and steps in self-assessment, goal-setting, problem-solving, and decision-making processes in relation to physical activity 163

DOMAIN 4.0   THE PHYSICAL EDUCATION PROGRAM

COMPETENCY 1.0 UNDERSTAND THE DEVELOPMENT AND EVALUATION OF PHYSICAL EDUCATION PROGRAMS 165

SKILL 1.1   Analyze and evaluate historical, philosophical, social, political, and economic issues that influence the physical education profession and their impact on instructional programs at the local, state, national, and global levels 165

SKILL 1.2   Identify and apply principles and procedures for organizing and administering a comprehensive physical education program for all student populations 171

SKILL 1.3   Recognize the value orientations, goals, and models of physical education curriculum design and analyze factors affecting curriculum design 172

SKILL 1.4   Establish appropriate criteria and select tools for the evaluation of a physical education program 175

SKILL 1.5   Revise a given physical education program based on a needs assessment or other appropriate evaluation 179

SKILL 1.6   Demonstrate an understanding of factors that affect the preparation of a budget to support the physical education program 180

COMPETENCY 2.0 UNDERSTAND PRINCIPLES AND PROCEDURES OF SAFETY, EMERGENCY FIRST AID, AND EQUIPMENT MAINTENANCE 181

SKILL 2.1   Recognize and apply managerial and instructional routines that create safe environments 181

SKILL 2.2   Identify procedures and issues related to the use, maintenance, and storage of equipment, technology, and other physical education resources 183

SKILL 2.3   Identify potential safety issues related to physical education activities and demonstrate an understanding of principles and techniques of injury prevention 187

SKILL 2.4   Evaluate physical and environmental factors and potential safety hazards associated with games, sports, and recreational and outdoor activities 189

SKILL 2.5   Demonstrate knowledge of first-aid principles and procedures for a variety of emergency situations 190

COMPETENCY 3.0 UNDERSTAND LEGAL AND ETHICAL ISSUES THAT INFLUENCE PHYSICAL EDUCATION PROGRAMS 193

SKILL 3.1   Demonstrate an understanding of legal responsibilities and issues associated with teaching physical education (e.g., Title IX, inclusion, safety, professional liability, negligence) 193

SKILL 3.2   Recognize state and federal laws and guidelines regarding gender equity, special education, religious issues, privacy, and other aspects of students' rights 196

SKILL 3.3   Demonstrate an understanding of the boundaries of professional responsibilities when working with students, colleagues, families, and community members 198

SKILL 3.4   Apply ethical, professional, and legal guidelines in making decisions in various physical education settings and situations 199

COMPETENCY 4.0 UNDERSTAND PRINCIPLES AND PROCEDURES FOR EFFECTIVE ADVOCACY, COMMUNICATION, AND COLLABORATION 201

SKILL 4.1   Recognize how to use community resources (e.g., YMCA/YWCA, Boyd/Girls Clubs, recreation departments, parks, health clubs) to enhance physical activity opportunities, and demonstrate an understanding of how to advocate effectively to promote physical activity opportunities within the community 201

SKILL 4.2   Demonstrate an understanding of strategies and mechanisms for communicating with a variety of constituencies (e.g., students, families, community members, public officials) 202

SKILL 4.3 *Identify strategies for communicating, consulting, and collaborating with teachers, counselors, special education personnel, administrators, and other colleagues* 204

SKILL 4.4 *Recognize the roles of state and national professional organization for physical educators* 205

SKILL 4.5 *Demonstrate familiarity with professional development opportunities associated with physical education, sports, and fitness, as well as related qualifications, educational requirements, and job responsibilities* 206

Annotated List of Resources 209

Sample Test..211

Answer Key 237

Rationales with Sample Questions 238

Sample Written Assignments 1-2 279

Great Study and Testing Tips!

What you study in order to prepare for the subject assessments is the focus of this study guide, but equally important is *how* you study.

You can increase your chances of truly mastering the information by taking some simple but effective steps.

Study Tips:

1. **Some foods aid the learning process.** Foods such as milk, nuts, seeds, rice, and oats help your study efforts by releasing natural memory enhancers called CCKs (*cholecystokinin*) composed of *tryptophan*, *choline*, and *phenylalanine*. All of these chemicals enhance the neurotransmitters associated with memory. Before studying, try a light, protein-rich meal of eggs, turkey, and fish. All of these foods release the memory enhancing chemicals. The better the connections, the more you comprehend.

Likewise, before you take a test, stick to a light snack of relaxing and energy boosting foods. A glass of milk, a piece of fruit, or some peanuts release various memory-boosting chemicals and help you to relax and focus on the subject at hand.

2. **Learn to take great notes.** A by-product of our modern culture is that we have grown accustomed to getting our information in short doses (e.g. TV news sound bites or USA Today style newspaper articles).

Consequently, we've subconsciously trained ourselves to assimilate information better in neat little packages. If your notes are scrawled all over the paper, it fragments the flow of the information. Strive for clarity. Newspapers use a standard format to achieve clarity. You can make your notes much clearer by using proper formatting. A very effective format is the *"Cornell Method."*

Take a sheet of loose-leaf lined notebook paper and draw a line all the way down the paper about 1-2" from the left-hand edge.

Draw another line across the width of the paper about 1-2" up from the bottom. Repeat this process on the reverse side of the page.

Look at the highly effective result. You have ample room for notes, a left hand margin for special emphasis items or inserting supplementary data from the textbook, a large area at the bottom for a brief summary, and a little rectangular space for just about anything you want.

3. Get the concept then the details. Too often, we focus on the details and don't gather an understanding of the concept. However, if you simply memorize only dates, places, or names, you may well miss the whole point of the subject.

A key way to understand things is to put them in your own words. If you are working from a textbook, automatically summarize each paragraph in your mind. If you are outlining text, don't simply copy the author's words.

Rephrase them in your own words. You remember your own thoughts and words much better than someone else's, and subconsciously tend to associate the important details to the core concepts.

4. Ask Why? Pull apart written material paragraph by paragraph and don't forget the captions under the illustrations.

Example: If the heading is "Stream Erosion", flip it around to read "Why do streams erode?" Then answer the questions.

If you train your mind to think in a series of questions and answers, not only will you learn more, but it also helps to lessen the test anxiety because you are used to answering questions.

5. Read for reinforcement and future needs. Even if you only have 10 minutes, put your notes or a book in your hand. Your mind is similar to a computer; you have to input data in order to have it processed. *By reading, you are creating the neural connections for future retrieval.* The more times you read something, the more you reinforce the learning of ideas.

Even if you don't fully understand something on the first pass, *your mind stores much of the material for later recall.*

6. Relax to learn, so go into exile. Our bodies respond to an inner clock called biorhythms. Burning the midnight oil works well for some people, but not everyone.

If possible, set aside a particular place to study that is free of distractions. Shut off the television, cell phone, and pager and exile your friends and family during your study period.

If silence really bothers you, try background music. Studies show that light classical music played at a low volume aids in concentration.

Music that evokes pleasant emotions without lyrics are highly suggested. Try just about anything by Mozart. It relaxes you.

7. **<u>Use arrows not highlighters.</u>** At best, it's difficult to read a page full of yellow, pink, blue, and green streaks.

Try staring at a neon sign for a while and you'll soon see my point. The horde of colors obscures the message.

A quick note, a brief dash of color, an underline, and an arrow pointing to a particular passage is much clearer than a horde of highlighted words.

8. **<u>Budget your study time.</u>** Although you shouldn't ignore any of the material, *allocate your available study time in the same ratio that topics may appear on the test.*

Testing Tips:

1. Get smart, play dumb. Don't read anything into the question. Don't assume that the test writer is looking for something else than what is asked. Stick to the question as written and don't read extra things into it.

2. Read the question and all the choices *twice* before answering. You may miss something by not carefully reading and re-reading both the question and the answers.

If you really don't have a clue as to the right answer, leave it blank the first time through. Go on to the other questions, as they may provide a clue as to how to answer the skipped questions.

If later on, you still can't answer the skipped ones . . . ***Guess.***
The only penalty for guessing is that you *might* get it wrong. One thing is certain; if you don't put anything down, you will get it wrong!

3. Turn the question into a statement. Look at the way the questions are worded. The syntax of the question usually provides a clue. Does it seem more familiar as a statement rather than as a question? Does it sound strange?

By turning a question into a statement, you may be able to spot if an answer sounds right, and it may also trigger memories of material you've read.

4. Look for hidden clues. It's actually very difficult to compose multiple-choice questions without giving away part of the answer in the options presented.

In most multiple-choice questions, you can often readily eliminate one or two of the potential answers. This leaves you with only two real possibilities, and automatically your odds go to fifty-fifty with very little work.

5. Trust your instincts. For every fact that you have read, you subconsciously retain something of that knowledge. On questions that you aren't really certain about, go with your basic instincts. **Your first impression on how to answer a question is usually correct.**

6. Mark your answers directly on the test booklet. Don't bother trying to fill in the optical scan sheet on the first pass through the test.

Just be very careful not to miss-mark your answers when you eventually transcribe them to the scan sheet.

7. Watch the clock! You have a set amount of time to answer the questions. Don't get bogged down trying to answer a single question at the expense of 10 questions you can more readily answer.

THIS PAGE BLANK

DOMAIN 1.0   HEALTH RELATED PHYSICAL FITNESS

COMPETENCY 1.0   *UNDERSTAND TECHNIQUES AND PROCEDURES FOR DEVELOPING AND ASSESSING HEALTH-RELATED FITNESS.*

SKILL 1.1   *Demonstrate knowledge of expected development progressions, ranges of individual variation, and levels of readiness for health-related fitness.*

A normal three-year-old should be able to walk up and down the stairs, jump from the lowest step, and land on both the feet without falling. They should also be capable of standing on one foot and balancing and kicking a large ball (though not with a lot of force). A three-year-old can jump on the same spot, ride on a small tricycle, and throw a ball (although not very straight and with limited distance). The large motor skills are more or less developed, but fine motor skills and hand-eye coordination need refining. For example, a three-year-old may not be able to dodge a ball or play games like badminton, which require greater hand-eye coordination, speed, and balance, but a three-year-old can catch a big ball thrown to him/her from a short distance.

A four-year-old is capable of walking on a straight line, hopping using one foot, and pedaling a tricycle with confidence. A four-year-old can climb ladders and trees with relative ease. A four-year-old child can run around obstacles, maneuver, and stop when necessary. A four-year-old can throw a ball a greater distance and is capable of running around in circles.

A five-year-old is capable of walking backwards, using the heel and then the toe, and is able to easily climb up and down steps by alternating feet without any outside help. Five-year-olds can touch their toes without bending at the knee and balance on a beam. They may be able to do somersaults provided it is taught in a proper and safe manner. A five-year-old can ride a tricycle with speed and dexterity, make almost ten jumps or hops without losing balance and falling, and stand on one foot for about ten senconds.

Early elementary school children have already acquired many large motor and fine motor skills. Their movement is more accurate and with purpose, though some clumsiness may persist. An elementary student is always on the run and restless. A child older than five finds pleasure in more energetic and vigorous activities. He/she can jump, hop, and throw with relative accuracy and concentrate on an activity which sustains his/her interest. However, concentration on a single activity usually does not last long. Early elementary students enjoy challenges and can benefit greatly from them.

When proper and appropriate physical education is available, by the time a child finishes the fourth grade he is able to demonstrate well-developed locomotor movements. He is also capable of manipulative and nonlocomotor movement skills like kicking and catching. He is capable of living up to challenges like balancing a number of objects or controlling a variety of things simultaneously. Children at this developmental age begin to acquire specialized movement skills like dribbling. When a child has finished eighth grade, he is able to exhibit expertise in a variety of fine and modified movements (e.g. dance steps). Children begin to develop the necessary skills for competitive and strategic games. Despite a lack of competency in a game, they learn to enjoy the pleasure of physical activity. By the time the children finish the twelfth grade they can demonstrate competency in a number of complex and modified movements with relative ease (e.g. gymnastics, dual sports, dance). Students at this age display their interest in gaining a greater degree of competency at their favorite game or activity.

SKILL 1.2   *Identify and apply developmentally appropriate strategies, instruments, and technologies to assess and monitor individual fitness levels, to measure learner progress in fitness development, and to provide feedback to students.*

Data from physical fitness assessments can diagnose an individual's level of fitness and identify the components of fitness in need of improvement. We compare data to fitness standards and norms.

Cardio-respiratory data identifies an individual's functional aerobic capacity by the predicted maximum oxygen consumption. This can partially explain natural leanness, running ability, and motivation.

Muscle strength data identifies an individual's ability to execute some basic skills, an individual's potential for injury, an individual's potential to develop musculoskeletal problems, and an individual's potential to cope with life threatening situations.

Muscle strength data identifies an individual's ability to exercise continually for an extended period of time and an individual's potential to develop musculoskeletal problems.

Flexibility data identifies an individual's potential for motor skill performance, an individual's potential for developing musculoskeletal problems (including poor posture), and an individual's potential for performing activities of daily living.

Body composition is an indicator of an individual's health status and potential to participate in physical activities.

The following is a list of tests that instructors can use to assess the physical fitness of students.

Cardio-respiratory fitness tests – maximal stress test, sub maximal stress test, Bruce Protocol, Balke Protocol, Astrand and Rhyming Test, PWC Test, Bench Step Test, Rockport Walking Fitness Test, and Cooper 1.5 Mile Run/Walk Fitness Test.

Muscle strength tests – dynamometers (hand, back, and leg), cable tensiometer, the 1-RM Test (repetition maximum: bench press, standing press, arm curl, and leg press), bench-squat, sit-ups (one sit up holding a weight plate behind the neck), and lateral pull-down.

Muscle endurance tests – squat-thrust, pull-ups, sit-ups, lateral pull-down, bench-press, arm curl, push-ups, and dips.

Flexibility tests – sit and reach, Kraus-Webber Floor Touch Test, trunk extension, forward bend of trunk, Leighton Flexometer, shoulder rotation/flexion, and goniometer.

Body Composition determination – Hydrostatic weighing, skin fold measurements, limb/girth circumference, and body mass index.

Agility tests – Illinois Agility Run.

Balance tests – Bass Test of Dynamic Balance (lengthwise and crosswise), Johnson Modification of the Bass Test of Dynamic Balance, modified sideward leap, and balance beam walk.

Coordination tests – Stick test of Coordination.

Power tests – vertical jump.

Speed tests – 50-yard dash.

After assessing an individual's fitness level, a personal fitness trainer or instructor can prescribe a training program. Prescription of a fitness program begins with:

1. Identifying the components of fitness that need changing (via assessment)

2. Establishing short-term goals

3. Developing a plan to meet the established goals

4. Keeping records to record progress

5. Evaluating progress of goals and making changes based on success or failure

For successful programs, the instructor and student should formulate new goals and change the personal fitness program to accomplish the new goals.

For unsuccessful programs, changing the goals, particularly if the goals were too unrealistic, is an appropriate response. Adjusting goals allows individuals to make progress and succeed. In addition, analyzing positive and negative results may identify barriers preventing an individual's success in her personal fitness program. Incorporating periodic, positive rewards for advancing can provide positive reinforcement and encouragement.

SKILL 1.3   Apply principles and techniques for designing and implementing individualized fitness programs.

BASIC TRAINING PRINCIPLES

The **Overload Principle** is exercising at an above normal level to improve physical or physiological capacity (a higher than normal workload).

The **Specificity Principle** is overloading a particular fitness component. In order to improve a component of fitness, you must isolate and specifically work on a single component. Metabolic and physiological adaptations depend on the type of overload; hence, specific exercise produces specific adaptations, creating specific training effects.

The **Progression Principle** states that once the body adapts to the original load/stress, no further improvement of a component of fitness will occur without the addition of an additional load.

There is also a **Reversibility-of-Training Principle** in which all gains in fitness are lost with the discontinuance of a training program.

MODIFICATIONS OF OVERLOAD

We can modify overload by varying **frequency, intensity, and time**. Frequency is the number of times we implement a training program in a given period (e.g. three days per week). Intensity is the amount of effort put forth or the amount of stress placed on the body. Time is the duration of each training session.

PRINCIPLES OF OVERLOAD, PROGRESSION, AND SPECIFICITY APPLIED TO IMPROVEMENT OF HEALTH-RELATED COMPONENTS OF FITNESS

1. Cardio-respiratory Fitness:

Overloading for cardio-respiratory fitness:

- **Frequency** = minimum of 3 days/week

- **Intensity** = exercising in target heart-rate zone

- **Time** = minimum of 15 minutes rate

Progression for cardiovascular fitness:

- begin at a frequency of 3 days/week and work up to no more than 6 days/week

- begin at an intensity near THR threshold and work up to 80% of THR

- begin at 15 minutes and work up to 60 minutes

Specificity for cardiovascular fitness:

- To develop cardiovascular fitness, you must perform aerobic (with oxygen) activities for at least fifteen minutes without developing an oxygen debt. Aerobic activities include, but are not limited to brisk walking, jogging, bicycling, and swimming.

2. Muscle Strength:

Overloading for muscle strength:

- **Frequency** = every other day

- **Intensity** = 60% to 90% of assessed muscle strength

- **Time** = 3 sets of 3 - 8 reps (high resistance with a low number of repetitions)

Progression for muscle strength:

- begin 3 days/week and work up to every other day

- begin near 60% of determined muscle strength and work up to no more than 90% of muscle strength

- begin with 1 set with 3 reps and work up to 3 sets with 8 reps

Specificity for muscle strength:

- to increase muscle strength for a specific part(s) of the body, you must target that/those part(s) of the body

3. Muscle endurance:

Overloading for muscle endurance:

- **Frequency** = every other day

- **Intensity** = 30% to 60% of assessed muscle strength

- **Time** = 3 sets of 12 - 20 reps (low resistance with a high number of repetitions)

Progression for muscle endurance:

- begin 3 days/week and work up to every other day

- begin at 20% to 30% of muscle strength and work up to no more than 60% of muscle strength

- begin with 1 set with 12 reps and work up to 3 sets with 20 reps

Specificity for muscle endurance:

- same as muscle strength

4. Flexibility:

Overloading for flexibility:

- **Frequency**: 3 to 7 days/week

- **Intensity**: stretch muscle beyond its normal length

- **Time**: 3 sets of 3 reps holding stretch 15 to 60 seconds

Progression for flexibility:

- begin 3 days/week and work up to every day

- begin stretching with slow movement as far as possible without pain, holding at the end of the range of motion (ROM) and work up to stretching no more than 10% beyond the normal ROM

- begin with 1 set with 1 rep, holding stretches 15 seconds, and work up to 3 sets with 3 reps, holding stretches for 60 seconds

Specificity for flexibility:

- ROM is joint specific

5. Body composition:

Overloading to improve body composition:

- **Frequency**: daily aerobic exercise

- **Intensity**: low

- **Time**: approximately one hour

Progression to improve body composition:

- begin daily

- begin a low aerobic intensity and work up to a longer duration (see cardio-respiratory progression)

- begin low-intensity aerobic exercise for 30 minutes and work up to 60 minutes

Specificity to improve body composition:

increase aerobic exercise and decrease caloric intake

SKILL 1.4   *Demonstrate an understanding of factors and techniques that motivate students to enhance health-related fitness levels for overall personal well-being.*

Finding intrinsic motivation for study is the main factor promoting the development of self-motivated learners. Helping learners become self-motivated is a process that revolves around connecting them personally with the material that they are studying, and instilling a belief in the their ability to control the outcome of their studies (if they believe they are not capable of mastering the material, they cannot become self-motivated learners).

This process begins with the cultivation of a positive attitude about the study of the subject matter in question. Instructors should emphasize to students that they are capable of mastering the material. Instructors can reinforce this belief by setting small, incremental milestones in the educational plan that show the students the progress they are making.

Having convinced the students of their ability to learn the subject matter and master their goals, instructors should teach the students to become increasingly goal-oriented. This begins with students setting their own short-term goals and, after they begin developing a pattern of meeting their goals, longer-term goals. As students set goals, instructors should teach students to accept and assume responsibility for their decisions, actions, and outcomes.

ROLE OF EXERCISE IN HEALTH MAINTENANCE

Possibly the best way to motivate students to engage in regular physical activity is to educate students on the many health benefits of exercise. The health risk factors improved by physical activity include cholesterol levels, blood pressure, stress related disorders, heart diseases, weight and obesity disorders, early death, certain types of cancer, musculoskeletal problems, mental health, and susceptibility to infectious diseases.
BENEFITS OF PHYSICAL ACTIVITY

Physiological benefits of physical activity include:

- improved cardio-respiratory fitness

- improved muscle strength

- improved muscle endurance

- improved flexibility

- more lean muscle mass and less body fat

- quicker rate of recovery

- improved ability of the body to utilize oxygen

- lower resting heart rate

- increased cardiac output

- improved venous return and peripheral circulation

- reduced risk of musculoskeletal injuries

- lower cholesterol levels

- increased bone mass

- cardiac hypertrophy and size and strength of blood vessels

- increased number of red cells

- improved blood-sugar regulation

- improved efficiency of thyroid gland

- improved energy regulation

- increased life expectancy

Psychological benefits of physical activity include:

- relief of stress

- improved mental health via better physical health

- reduced mental tension (relieves depression, improves sleeping patterns)

- better resistance to fatigue

- better quality of life

- more enjoyment of leisure

- better capability to handle some stressors

- opportunity for successful experiences

- better self-concept

- better ability to recognize and accept limitations

- improved appearance and sense of well-being

- better ability to meet challenges

- better sense of accomplishments

Sociological benefits of physical activity include:

- the opportunity to spend time with family and friends and make new friends

- the opportunity to be part of a team

- the opportunity to participate in competitive experiences

- the opportunity to experience the thrill of victory

SKILL 1.5   *Analyze health-related fitness goal setting, activity selection, and personal health-related fitness programs for individual students.*

SEE ALSO Domain 1, Skill 1.3

The following is a list of physical activities that may reduce specific health risks, improve overall health, and develop skill-related components of physical activity.

1. **Aerobic Dance:**
Health-related components of fitness = *cardio-respiratory, body composition.*
Skill-related components of fitness = *agility, coordination.*

2. **Bicycling:**
Health-related components of fitness = *cardio-respiratory, muscle strength, muscle endurance, body composition.*
Skill-related components of fitness = *balance.*

3. **Calisthenics:**
Health-related components of fitness = *cardio-respiratory, muscle strength, muscle endurance, flexibility, body composition.*
Skill-related components of fitness = *agility.*

4. **Circuit Training:**
Health-related components of fitness = *cardio-respiratory, muscle strength, muscle endurance, body composition.*
Skill-related components of fitness = *power.*

5. **Cross Country Skiing:**
Health-related component of fitness = *cardio-respiratory, muscle strength, muscle endurance, body composition.*
Skill-related components of fitness = *agility, coordination, power.*

6. **Jogging/Running:**
Health-related components of fitness = *cardio-respiratory, body composition.*

7. **Rope Jumping:**
Health-related components of fitness = *cardio-respiratory, body composition.*
Skill-related components of fitness = *agility, coordination, reaction time, speed.*

8. **Rowing:**
Health-related components of fitness = *cardio-respiratory, muscle strength, muscle endurance, body composition.*
Skill-related components of fitness = *agility, coordination, power.*

9. **Skating:**
Health-related components of fitness = *cardio-respiratory, body composition.*
Skill-related components of fitness = *agility, balance, coordination, speed.*

10. **Swimming/Water Exercises:**
Health-related components of fitness = *cardio-respiratory, muscle strength, muscle endurance, flexibility, body composition.*
Skill related components of fitness = *agility, coordination.*

11. **Walking (brisk):**
Health-related components of fitness = *cardio-respiratory, body composition.*

GOAL SETTING

Goal setting is an effective way of achieving progress. In order to preserve and/or increase self-confidence, you and your students must set goals that are frequently reachable. One such way of achieving this is to set several small, short-term goals to attain one long-term goal. Be realistic in goal setting to increase fitness levels gradually. As students reach their goals, set more in order to continue performance improvement. Keep in mind that maintaining a current fitness level is an adequate goal provided the individual is in a healthy state. Reward your students when they reach goals. Rewards serve as motivation to reach the next goal. Also, be sure to prepare for lapses. Try to get back on track as soon as possible.

SKILL 1.6   *Evaluate fitness and health-related services, products, and advertising (e.g., claims about fitness equipment, weight control products and programs, dietary supplements).*

There is generally a wide array of information available related to health, fitness and recreational activities, products, facilities, and services. It can be difficult for the untrained consumer to sort through it all to find information that is pertinent and accurate.

When evaluating information relating to fitness and sports equipment, consumers (for example, parents of students who are seeking to equip their home with training facilities for themselves and their children) should ask the sales staff about the differences between their choices; not just in terms of prices, but also in terms of potential fitness benefits and especially safety (Is the equipment in question safe to use? Is it safe for all ages? Is a spotter required for its use?).

When evaluating weight control products and programs, consumers should ask sales staff to explain the mechanism by which the program functions (e.g. does it limit caloric intake, maximize caloric expenditure, or function by means of some other process?). The word of the sales staff is not sufficient, however, and consumers should investigate further using the tools at their disposal, which include public and university libraries, the internet, and physical education professionals at their children's schools.

When evaluating fitness-training facilities, consumers should consider several factors. These factors are quality and availability of training equipment, hygiene of the facility, and overall atmosphere. You can determine the general quality of the equipment by its age and you can glean further information from a discussion with the training staff on-site. You can investigate the availability of the equipment by visiting the facility at peak training times (which vary depending on the demographics of the facility – again, you should ask the training staff for the appropriate times). If it takes too long for equipment to become available and lines seem to form, this may not be the best facility for your needs (unless you're not interested in visiting the facility during those hours). Most important, though, is the atmosphere at the facility. The best way to get a feel for this is to have some short conversations with some customers about their experiences there.

DENTIFY EXERCISE MYTHS AND GIMMICKS

Exercise myths and gimmicks include:

- drinking beer/alcoholic beverages is a good way to replenish loss of body fluids after exercising,

- women should not exercise while menstruating or pregnant,

- physically fit people will not die from heart disease,

- you cannot be too flexible,

- spot reduction is effective,

- children are naturally active and do not need to exercise,

- muscle will turn into fat with the cessation of exercising,

- fat can turn into muscle,

- women will develop large muscles by weight training, you should exercise while sick regardless how ill you are,

- cardiac hypertrophy developed by exercising is harmful to health,

- exercise increases the appetite,

- exercise gets rid of sagging skin and wrinkles,

- yoga is a good way to develop fitness;

- losing cellulite requires special treatment, body wraps are a good way to lose weight.

IDENTIFYING EXERCISE EQUIPMENT AS EITHER SOUND OR UNSOUND USING PHYSIOLOGICAL PRINCIPLES

Rolling machines, vibrating belts, vibrating tables and pillows, massaging devices, electrical muscle stimulators, weighted belts, motor-driven cycles and rowing machines, saunas, and plastic or rubberized sweat and sauna suits **are all ineffective exercise equipment because they produce passive movement** (no voluntary muscle contractions).

Sound exercise equipment produces active movement resulting from the participant initiating the movement of the equipment or the participant voluntarily producing muscle contractions.

The more you analyze exercise equipment on the market the more you may wonder who is actually creating it. For example, equipment that has weight increments measured as light, medium, or difficult, is unsound. Such ambiguous labeling depends on who is using the equipment and their level of proficiency.

Some advertisements claim that their equipment uses all muscle groups at once. Just three minutes a day is as good as a total gym workout. Such claims are certainly false.

But what is good equipment? Good equipment uses a safe range of motion, safe increments of weight progression, and is structurally sound. The components of good equipment are reliable and not likely to cause injury. Safe equipment can consist of a combination of pieces that, when used correctly, improve physiological processes by guiding range of motion.

FALLACIES AND DANGERS UNDERLYING SELECTED DIET PLANS

High Carbohydrate diets (i.e. Pritikin, Bloomingdale's) can produce rapid or gradual weight loss, depending on caloric intake. Usually requires vitamin and mineral supplements because protein intake is low. These diets may or may not recommend exercising or permanent lifestyle changes, which are necessary to maintain one's weight.

High-Protein Diets promote the same myths, fallacies, and results as high carbohydrate diets. High-protein diets also require vitamin and mineral supplements. In addition, these diets are usually high in saturated fats and cholesterol because of the emphasis on meat products.

Liquid Formulas that are physician/hospital run (i.e. Medifast, Optifast) provide 800 or fewer calories a day consumed in liquid form. Dieters forgo food intake for 12 to 16 weeks in lieu of the protein supplement. Liquid diets require vitamin and mineral supplements and close medical supervision. Dieters should gradually reintroduce food after the initial fast. These diets can result in severe and/or dangerous metabolic problems in addition to an irregular heartbeat, kidney infections and failure, hair loss, and sensations of feeling cold and/or cold intolerance. These diets are very expensive and have a high rate of failure.

Over-The-Counter Liquid Diets (i.e. Slimfast) are liquid/food bar supplements taken in place of one or more meals per day. Such diets advocate an intake of 1,000 calories daily. Carbohydrate, protein, vitamin, and mineral intake may be so low that the diet can be as dangerous as the medically supervised liquid diets when relied on for the only source of nutrition. Because of the lack of medical supervision, the side effects can be even more dangerous.

Over-The-Counter Diet Pills/Aids and Prescription Diet Pills (appetite suppressants) have as their main ingredient phenyl propanolamine hydrochloride [PPA]. Keeping weight off by the use of these products is difficult. Dizziness, sleeplessness, high blood pressure, palpitation, headaches, and tachycardia are potential side effects of these products. Moreover, prescription diet pills can be addictive.

Low Calorie Diets (caloric restricted) are the most misunderstood method of weight loss. However, restricting the intake of calories is the way most people choose to lose weight. All the focus is on food, creating anxiety over the restriction of food - especially favorite foods. These diets are also difficult to maintain and have a high failure rate. Like the other diets, once the diet is over, dieters regain weight quickly because they fail to make permanent behavioral changes. Side effects of caloric restriction include diarrhea, constipation, Ketosis, a lower basal metabolic rate, blood-sugar imbalances, loss of lean body tissue, fatigue, weakness, and emotional problems. Low calorie diets require dietary supplements. Those who choose **fasting** (complete caloric restriction) to lose weight can deplete enough of the body's energy stores to cause death.

SKILL 1.7   *Demonstrate an understanding of how to incorporate fitness concepts into various physical activities.*

One of the most important tasks for physical education instructors is to introduce students to strategies to incorporate physical activity into everyday situations. For example, instructors can recommend that students walk or ride a bike to school, rather than drive or ride the bus. In addition, there are a number of everyday activities that promote fitness including yard work, sports and games, walking, and climbing stairs.

COMPETENCY 2.0   *UNDERSTAND PRINCIPLES AND ACTIVITIES FOR DEVELOPING AND MAINTAINING HEALTHY LEVELS OF CARDIORESPIRATORY ENDURANCE*

SKILL 2.1   *Understand the structure and function of the cardiorespiratory system and its specific adaptations to physical activity.*

STRUCTURE, FUNCTION, AND REGULATION OF THE HEART

The function of the closed circulatory system (**cardiovascular system**) is to carry oxygenated blood and nutrients to all cells of the body and return carbon dioxide waste to the lungs for expulsion. The heart, blood vessels, and blood make up the cardiovascular system. The following diagram shows the structure of the heart:

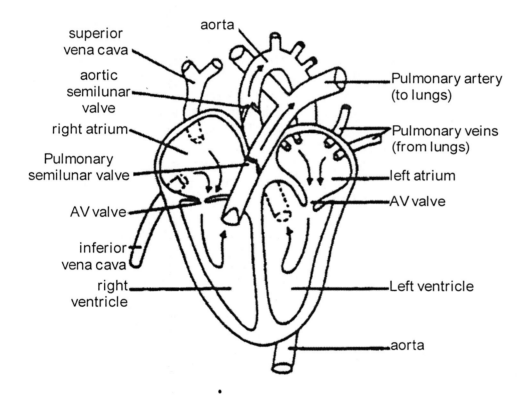

The atria are the chambers that receive blood returning to the heart and the ventricles are the chambers that pump blood out of the heart. There are four valves, two atrioventricular (AV) valves and two semilunar valves. The AV valves are located between each atrium and ventricle. The contraction of the ventricles closes the AV valve to keep blood from flowing back into the atria. The semilunar valves are located where the aorta leaves the left ventricle and the pulmonary artery leaves the right ventricle. Ventricular contraction opens the semilunar valves, pumping blood out into the arteries, and ventricular relaxation closes the valves.

The cardiac output is the volume of blood per minute that the left ventricle pumps. This output depends on the heart rate and stroke volume. The **heart rate** is the number of times the heart beats per minute and the **stroke volume** is the amount of blood pumped by the left ventricle each time it contracts. Humans have an average cardiac output of about 5.25 L/min. Heavy exercise can increase cardiac output up to five times. Epinephrine and increased body temperature also increase heart rate and, thus, the cardiac output.

Cardiac muscle can contract without any signal from the nervous system. The sinoatrial node is the pacemaker of the heart. It is located on the wall of the right atrium and generates electrical impulses that make the cardiac muscle cells contract in unison. The atrioventricular node briefly delays the electrical impulse to ensure the atria empty before the ventricles contract.

KNOWLEDGE OF PROCESS OF BREATHING AND GAS EXCHANGE

The respiratory system functions in the gas exchange of oxygen and carbon dioxide waste. It delivers oxygen to the bloodstream and picks up carbon dioxide for release from the body. Air enters the mouth and nose, where it is warmed, moistened and filtered of dust and particles. Cilia in the trachea trap and expel unwanted material in mucus. The trachea splits into two bronchial tubes and the bronchial tubes divide into smaller and smaller bronchioles in the lungs. The internal surface of the lung is composed of alveoli, which are thin walled air sacs. These allow for a large surface area for gas exchange. Capillaries line the alveoli. Oxygen diffuses into the bloodstream and carbon dioxide diffuses out of the capillaries and is exhaled from the lungs due to partial pressure. Hemoglobin, a protein containing iron, carries the oxygenated blood to the heart and all parts of the body.

The thoracic cavity holds the lungs. The diaphragm muscle below the lungs is an adaptation that makes inhalation possible. As the volume of the thoracic cavity increases, the diaphragm muscle flattens out and inhalation occurs. When the diaphragm relaxes, exhalation occurs.

ADAPTATIONS TO PHYSICAL ACTIVITY

The cardiovascular and respiratory systems provide the ability to sustain this movement over extended periods. When the body engages in exercise training several times, each of the physiological systems undergoes specific adaptations that increase the body's efficiency and capacity. For example, the heart beats faster during strenuous exercise so that it can pump more blood to the muscles.

SKILL 2.2   Identify and apply principles, skills, and activities for aerobic conditioning.

PRINCIPLES AND ACTIVITIES FOR DEVELOPING AEROBIC ENDURANCE

The term aerobic refers to conditioning or exercise that requires the use of oxygen to derive energy. Aerobic conditioning is essential for fat loss, energy production, and effective functioning of the cardiovascular system. Aerobic exercise is difficult to perform for many people and participants must follow certain principles and activities in order to develop aerobic endurance.

Slow twitch muscle tissue, fueled by oxygen, powers aerobic activities. For the body to sustain aerobic activity for an extended period of time, the heart must pump oxygen-rich blood to the muscles of the body. When the heart tires due to insufficient cardiorespiratory fitness, the quantities of oxygen delivered to the muscles decreases to levels that cannot sustain the activity.

Other physiological processes involved in aerobic endurance include the respiratory system (which must take sufficient air into the body and efficiently supply oxygen to the blood), the blood itself (which must efficiently carry oxygen), the circulatory system (that takes blood to the muscles and then returns it to the heart), and the muscles themselves (which must efficiently extract oxygen from the blood).

Tips that aid in developing and building aerobic endurance include working out for extended periods at the target heart rate, slowly increasing aerobic exercises, exercising for three or four times per week, and taking adequate rest to help the body recover.

Exercising in the target heart rate zone for 30-45 minute periods is the most important principle in the development of aerobic endurance. Submaximal intensity activities, such as walking and slow jogging, are effective aerobic activities that improve aerobic endurance without unnecessary strain on the body.

The following is an example of a **cardio-respiratory fitness** program design:
- **mode:** aerobic activities (e.g. walking, jogging, swimming, cycling, rowing)

- **frequency:** 3 to 5 days/week

- **intensity:** 60% to 90% of maximum oxygen uptake or 60% to 80% THR

- **time:** 20 to 60 minutes of continuous or interval (non-continuous) activity (time depends on intensity level)

- **progression:** instructor adjusts prescription according to an individual's fitness level and conditioning effects.

SKILL 2.3   Apply techniques for assessing and monitoring endurance levels.

PERCEIVED EXERTION

Perceived exertion is one method of monitoring intensity of aerobic activities. Participants describe how hard they feel they are working based on physical sensations such as muscle fatigue, sweating, heart rate, and breathing rate. The Borg Scale is a quantitative rating system of perceived exertion. The following is an example of the Borg Scale, which ranges from 6 to 20, with corresponding descriptions.

6	No exertion at all
7	Extremely light
9	Very light (e.g. walking slowly at own pace for several minutes)
11	Light
13	Somewhat hard
15	Hard (heavy)
17	Very hard (i.e. a healthy person can still continue, but with great difficulty)
19	Extremely hard (i.e. most strenuous exercise most have ever experienced)
20	Maximum exertion

TARGET HEART RATE ZONE AND HEART RATE MONITORS

The target heart rate (THR) zone is another common measure of aerobic exercise intensity. Participants find their THR and attempt to raise their heart rate to the desired level for a certain period of time. Students can use electronic heart rate monitors that constantly track heart rate during physical activity. Such monitors often alert students when they enter and leave their THR, allowing for adjustment of activity level. There are three ways to calculate the target heart rate.

1. METs (maximum oxygen uptake), which is 60% to 90% of functional capacity.

2. Karvonean Formula = [Maximum heart rate (MHR) – Resting heart rate (RHR)] x intensity + RHR.   MHR= 220 - Age
Intensity = Target Heart Range (which is 60% - 80% of MHR - RHR + RHR).

THR = (MHR - RHR) x .60 + RHR to (MHR - RHR) x .80 + RHR

3. Cooper's Formula to determine target heart range is:
THR = (220 - AGE) x .60 to (220 - AGE) x .80.

SPREADSHEETS

Physical education instructors and students can use computer spreadsheets to track progress in aerobic fitness development. Such programs help simplify data presentation and manipulation and allow for graphical representation of data.

SKILL 2.4   Recognize and select aerobic activities appropriate for various developmental levels and purposes.

Aerobics are a fundamental component of every physical education or training program. Aerobic activities are necessary for all because they are central to weight reduction, cardiovascular fitness, muscular strength development, and performance in all sports events.

Appropriate aerobic activities for various developmental levels vary from low and moderate intensity exercises to high intensity ones. Low and moderate intensity activities include doing household work, walking, playing with children, and working on the lawn. High-intensity aerobic activities include jogging, cycling, participating in sports like ice or roller-skating, downhill skiing, and swimming. Treadmills and other equipment help create strenuous aerobic exercises.

Instructors and students must take care while undertaking such high-intensity aerobic exercises, because they can be highly strenuous and taxing on muscles, especially during the initial stages. At this beginning stage, the exercise intensity must be low. With passage of time and development towards higher stages, the student can increase the level and intensity of aerobic exercises.

Whether the goal is to develop the body's ability to undergo high levels of muscular activity or just to remain fit, there are aerobic activities suited to every developmental stage and for every person.

CARDIOVASCULAR ACTIVITIES

Walking is a good generic cardiorespiratory activity for promoting basic fitness. Instructors can incorporate it into a variety of class settings (not only physical education instructors – for example, a Biology class might include a field trip to a natural setting that would involve a great deal of walking). Walking is appropriate for practically all age groups, but can only serve as noteworthy exercise for students who lead a fairly sedentary lifestyle (athletic students who train regularly or participate in some sport will not benefit greatly from walking).

Jogging or **Running** is a classic cardiorespiratory activity in which instructors can adjust the difficulty level by modifying the running speed or the incline of the track. It is important to stress proper footwear and gradual increase of intensity so as to prevent overuse injuries (e.g. stress fractures or shin splints).

Bicycling is another good cardiorespiratory activity that is appropriate for most age groups. Obviously, knowing how to ride a bicycle is a prerequisite, and it is important to follow safety procedures (e.g. ensuring that students wear helmets). An additional benefit of bicycle riding is that it places less strain on the knee joints than walking or running.

Swimming is an excellent cardiorespiratory activity that has the added benefit of working more of the body's muscles, more evenly than most other exercises, without excessive resistance to any one part of the body that could result in an overuse injury. To use swimming as an educational cardiorespiratory activity, there must be qualified lifeguards present, and all students must have passed basic tests of swimming ability.

There are many alternatives for cardiorespiratory activities, like **inline skating** and **cross-country skiing**. More importantly, instructors should modify the above exercises to match the developmental needs of the students – for example, younger students should receive most of their exercise in the form of games. An instructor could incorporate running in the form of a game of tag, soccer, or a relay race.

SKILL 2.5   Demonstrate knowledge of a variety of methods for promoting students' use of self-monitoring of exercise intensity.

SELF-ASSESSMENT

We can measure cardiorespiratory fitness in a number of ways. The simplest way is for the students to check their resting heart rate. To do this, the students should:

- Find their pulse in any point of the body where an artery is close to the surface (e.g., wrist [radial artery], neck [Carotid artery], or the elbow [brachial artery]).

- Count how many heartbeats they feel in one minute's time.

We usually express resting heart rate in "beats per minute" (bpm). For males, the norm is about 70 bpm. For women, the norm is about 75 bpm. This rate varies between people and the reference range is normally between 60 bpm and 100 bpm. It is important to note that resting heart rates can be significantly lower in athletes, and significantly higher in the obese.

Another way to measure cardiorespiratory fitness is by having students determine their Target Heart Rate (THR). The Target Heart Rate, or Training Heart Rate, is a desired range of heart rate reached during aerobic exercise, which allows a student's heart and lungs to receive the most benefit from a workout. Students should check their heart rates frequently during activity to ensure they train within their THR zones.

Finally, another useful technique for self-assessment, which instructors can combine with the pulse-rate monitoring mentioned above, is to instruct the students to keep a training log. The indicators tracked in the log may be very concrete (e.g. heart rate during exertion, duration of exertion, or resting heart rate and blood pressure), or more subjective (e.g. how students feel during and after their workouts). Instructors should also encourage older students to devise their own training benchmarks based on their knowledge of cardiorespiratory fitness training processes and their personal fitness goals.

COMPETENCY 3.0   *UNDERSTAND PRINCIPLES AND ACTIVITIES FOR DEVELOPING AND MAINTAINING FLEXIBILITY AND MUSCULAR STRENGTH AND ENDURANCE*

SKILL 3.1   Understand the structure and function of the musculoskeletal system and its specific adaptations to physical activity.

STRUCTURES, LOCATIONS, AND FUNCTIONS OF THE THREE TYPES OF MUSCULAR TISSUE

The main function of the muscular system is movement. There are three types of muscle tissue: skeletal, cardiac, and smooth.

Skeletal muscle is voluntary. These muscles are attached to bones and are responsible for their movement. Skeletal muscle consists of long fibers and is striated due to the repeating patterns of the myofilaments (made of the proteins actin and myosin) that make up the fibers.

Cardiac muscle is found in the heart. Cardiac muscle is striated like skeletal muscle, but differs in that the plasma membrane of the cardiac muscle causes the muscle to beat even when away from the heart. The action potentials of cardiac and skeletal muscles also differ.

Smooth muscle is involuntary. It is found in organs and enables functions such as digestion and respiration. Unlike skeletal and cardiac muscle, smooth muscle is not striated. Smooth muscle has less myosin and does not generate as much tension as skeletal muscle.

MECHANISM OF SKELETAL MUSCLE CONTRACTION

A nerve impulse strikes a muscle fiber. This causes calcium ions to flood the sarcomere. Calcium ions allow ATP to expend energy. The myosin fibers creep along the actin, causing the muscle to contract. Once the nerve impulse has passed, calcium is pumped out and the contraction ends.

MOVEMENT OF BODY JOINTS

The axial skeleton consists of the bones of the skull and vertebrae. The appendicular skeleton consists of the bones of the legs, arms and tail, and shoulder girdle. Bone is a connective tissue. Parts of the bone include compact bone that gives strength, spongy bone that contains red marrow to make blood cells and yellow marrow in the center of long bones to store fat cells, and the periosteum that is the protective covering on the outside of the bone.
A joint is a place where two bones meet. Joints enable movement. Ligaments attach bone to bone. Tendons attach bone to muscle. Joints allow great flexibility in movement.

There are three types of joints:

1.   Ball and socket – allows for rotational movement. An example is the joint between the shoulder and the humerus. Ball and socket joints allow humans to move their arms and legs in many different ways.

2.   Hinge – movement is restricted to a single plane. An example is the joint between the humerus and the ulna.

3.   Pivot – allows for the rotation of the forearm at the elbow and the hands at the wrist.

ADAPTATIONS TO PHYSICAL ACTIVITY

The structure and function of the human body adapts greatly to physical activity and exertion. When challenged with any physical task, the human body responds through a series of integrated changes in function that involve most, if not all, of its physiological systems. Movement requires activation and control of the musculoskeletal system.

When the body works, it makes great demand on every muscle of the body. Either the muscles have to 'shut down' or they have to do work. Muscles, also known as 'biochemical motors', use the chemical adenosine triphosphate (ATP) as an energy source.

Different types of systems, such as the glycogen-lactic acid system, help muscles perform. Such systems help in producing ATP, which is extremely vital to working muscles. Aerobic respiration, which also helps in releasing ATP, uses the fatty acids from fat reserves in muscle and helps produce ATP for a much longer period of time.

The following points summarize the process of bodily adaptation to exercise:

• Muscle cells use the ATP they have floating around in about 3 seconds.

• The phosphagen system kicks in and supplies energy for 8 to 10 seconds.

• If exercise continues longer, the glycogen-lactic acid system kicks in.

• Finally, if exercise continues, aerobic respiration takes over. This would occur in endurance events such as an 800-meter dash, marathon run, rowing, cross-country skiing, or distance skating.

SKILL 3.2   Identify and apply principles, skills, and activities for developing strength and endurance in various muscles groups and parts of the body.

The following is an example of a **muscle strength** program design:

- **mode:** weight training (isotonic/dynamic)

- **frequency:** minimum 3 days/week to a maximum of every other day

- **intensity:** 60% to 90% of maximum muscle strength (1-RM)

- **time:** 3 sets with 3 to 8 reps and a 60 second rest interval

- **progression:** increase workload (overload) when individual can perform 15 reps at 10 RM level

The following is an example of a **muscle endurance** program design:

- **mode:** weight training

- **frequency:** minimum 3 days/week up to every other day

- **intensity:** 30% to 60% of maximum muscle strength (1-RM)

- **time:** 3 sets with 12 to 20 reps, or until point of muscle fatigue with a 15 to 60 second rest interval

- **progression:** increase workload (overload) periodically based on number of continuous repetitions

Major muscle groups of the body that are benefited by exercise are the: traps, delts, pecs, lats, obliques, abs, biceps, quadriceps, hamstrings, adductors, triceps and biceps; gluts.

Muscular strength is the ability of the muscles to exert force during an activity. It also helps the muscles to perform without fatigue. The activities that can help improve muscular endurance include walking, jogging, bicycling or dancing. Muscle strength is a measure of how much you can lift one time in a maximal effort situation. Larger people tend to have an edge over smaller people in terms of pounds lifted. The exercises that can help build muscular strength are push-ups(keep body straight, one leg raised), back lunges(keep tummy tight, back straight, head up), and two-point oblique (lie on back with back pushed into floor, right hand behind right ear, right knee bent with foot flat on floor).

EXERCISES THAT BENEFIT THE MAJOR MUSCLE GROUPS OF THE BODY

Some of the major muscle groups of the body important to physical fitness are the traps, delts, pecs, lats, obliques, abs, biceps, quadriceps, hamstrings, adductors, triceps, biceps, and gluts.

Dumbbell Shoulder Shrug
(Trapezius)

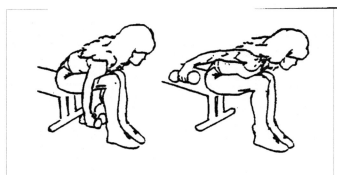

Seated Bent-Over Rear Deltoid Raise
(Rear Deltoids)

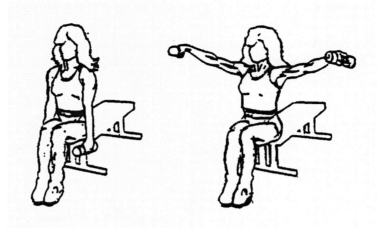

Seated Side Lateral Raise
(Front and Outer Deltoids)

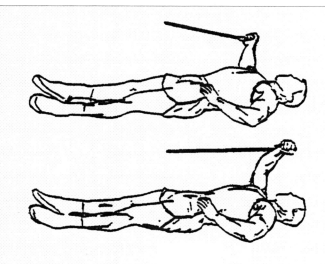

Lying Low-Pulley One-Arm Chest
(Lateral Pectorals)

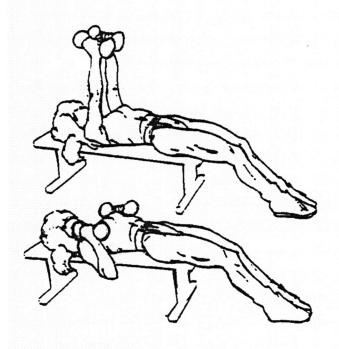

Flat Dumbbell Press
(Pectorals)

Medium-Grip Front-to-Rear Lat Pull Down
(Lats)

Straight-Arm Close-Grip Lat Pull Down
(Lats)

Dumbbell Side Bend
(Obliques)

Seated Barbell Twist
(Obliques)

Leg Pull-In
(Lower Abdominals)

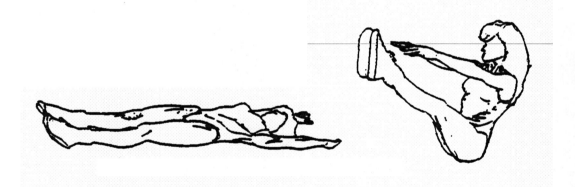

Jackknife Sit-Up
(Upper and Lower Abdominals)

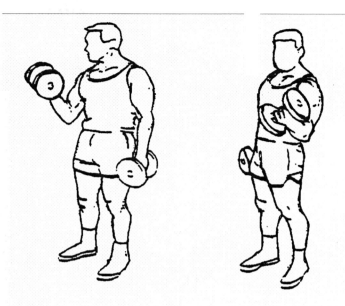

Standing Alternated Dumbbell Curl
(Biceps)

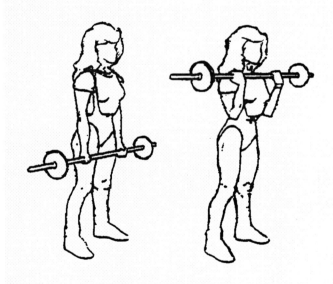

Standing Medium-Grip Barbell Curl
(Biceps)

Standing Close-Grip Easy-Curl-Bar Triceps Curl
(Triceps)

Standing Bent-Over One-Arm-Dumbbell Triceps Extension
(Triceps)

Flat-Footed Medium-Stance Barbell Half-Squat
(Thighs)

Freehand Front Lunge
(Thighs and Hamstrings)

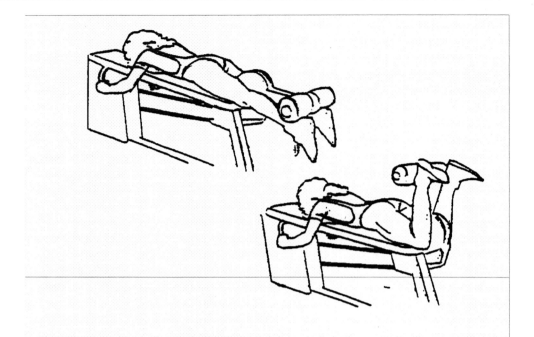

Thigh Curl on Leg Extension Machine
(Hamstrings)

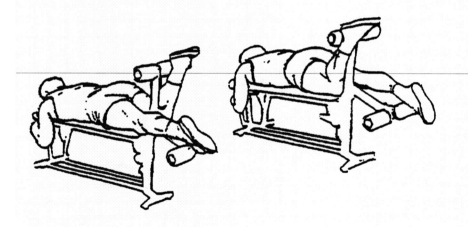

One-at-a-Time Thigh Curl on Leg Extension Machine
(Hamstrings)

Hip Abduction
(Hips)

Hip Adduction
(Inner Thigh)

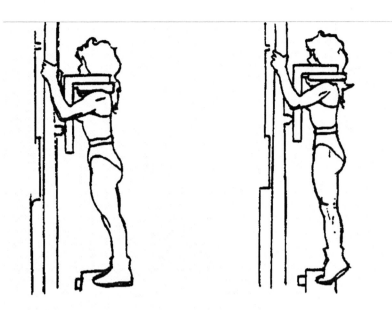

Standing Toe Raise on Wall Calf Machine
(Main Calf Muscles)

Main Calf Muscles

Standing Barbell Toe Raise
(Main Calf Muscles)

Hip Extension
(Hips and Thighs)

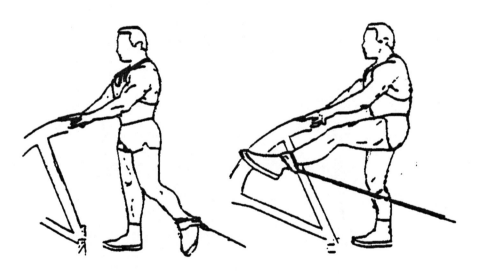

Hip Flexion
(Hip Flexors)

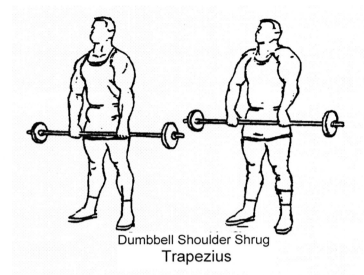

Dumbbell Shoulder Shrug
Trapezius

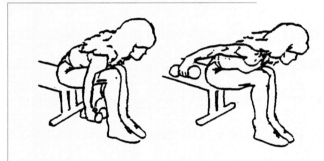

Seated Bent-Over Rear Deltoid
Raise

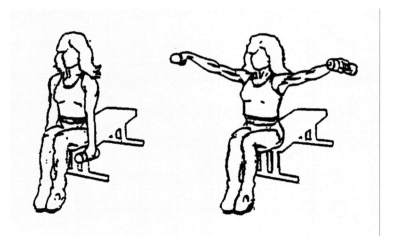

Seated Side Lateral Raise
Front and Outer Deltoids

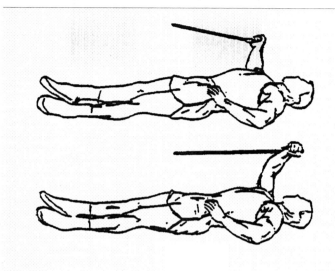

Lying Low-Pulley One-Arm Chest Lateral
Pectorals

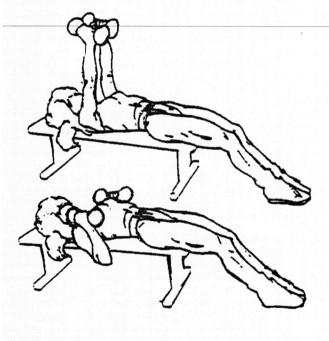

Flat Dumbbell Press
Pectorals

Medium-Grip Front-to-Rear Lat Pull Down
Lats

Straight-Arm Close-Grip Lat Pull Down
Lats

Dumbbell Side Bend
Obliques

Seated Barbell Twist
Obliques

Leg Pull-In
Lower Abdominals

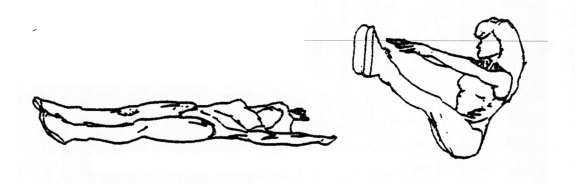

Jackknife Sit-Up
Upper and Lower Abdominals

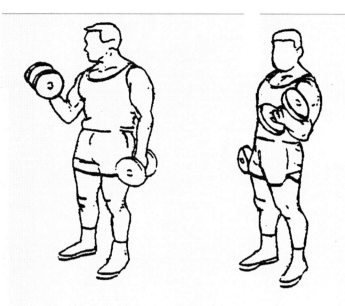

Standing Alternated Dumbbell
Curl

Standing Medium-Grip Barbell
Curl
Biceps

Standing Close-Grip Easy-Curl-Bar Triceps
Curl

Standing Bent-Over One-Arm-Dumbbell Triceps Extension
Triceps

Flat-Footed Medium-Stance Barbell Half-Squat
Thighs

Freehand Front Lunge
Thighs and Hamstrings

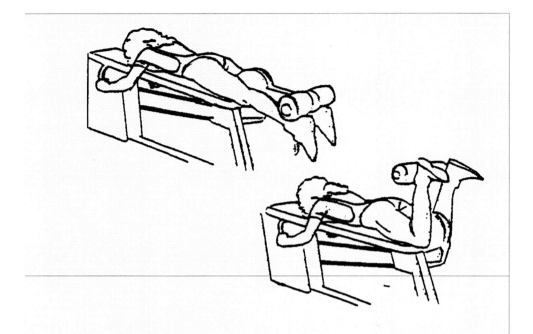

Thigh Biceps Curl on Leg Extension Machine
Hamstrings

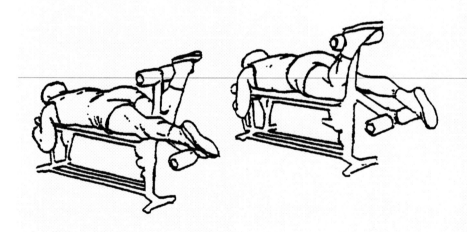

One-at-a-Time Biceps Curl on Leg Extension
Machine
Hamstrings

Hip Abduction
Hips

Hip Adduction
Inner Thigh

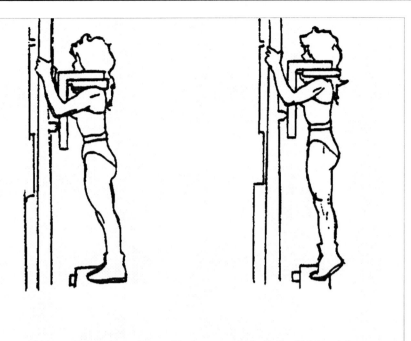

Standing Toe Raise on Wall Calf Machine
Main Calf Muscles

Standing Barbell Toe Raise
Main Calf Muscles

Hip Extension
Hips and Thighs

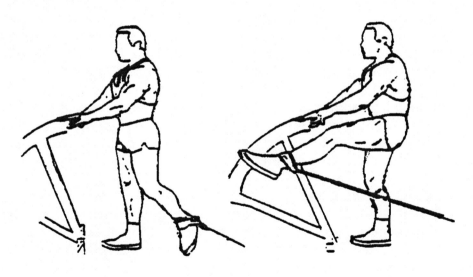

Hip Flexion
Hip Flexors

SKILL 3.3   *Identify and apply principles, techniques, and activities for promoting flexibility of the major joints of the body.*

Flexibility is the range of motion around a joint or muscle. Flexibility has two major components: static and dynamic. Static flexibility is the range of motion without a consideration for speed of movement. Dynamic flexibility is the use of the desired range of motion at a desired velocity. These movements are useful for most athletes.

Good flexibility can help prevent injuries during all stages of life and can keep an athlete safe. To improve flexibility, you can lengthen muscles through activities such as swimming, a basic stretching program, or Pilates. These activities all improve your muscles' range of motion. While joints also consist of ligaments and tendons, muscles are the main target of flexibility training. Muscles are the most elastic component of joints while ligaments and tendons are less elastic and resist elongation. Overstretching tendons and ligaments can weaken joint stability and lead to injury.

Coaches, athletes and sports medicine personnel use stretching methods as part of their training routine for athletes. They help the body to relax and to warm-up for more intense fitness activities.

COMPONENTS OF FLEXIBILITY

Muscles – Muscle is the body's contractile tissue. Its function is to produce force and cause motion (movement within the internal organs and, especially for our purposes, locomotion). Muscles are generally split into Type I (slow twitch) which carries more oxygen and sustains aerobic activity, and Type II (fast twitch), which carries less oxygen and powers anaerobic activity. Muscles that are too short can limit flexibility, and failing to stretch after resistance training can cause the muscles to shorten. The stretch reflex, whereby the opposing muscle will contract in order to prevent over-expansion, can also curtail flexibility (this contraction is generally premature, and part of flexibility training is to re-train the opposing muscle not to contract as quickly).

Joints – Joints are the locations at which two bones make contact. Their construction allows movement and provides functional mechanical support. We can classify joints as fibrous (connected by collagen), cartilaginous (connected by cartilage), or synovial (capped by cartilage, supported by ligaments, enveloped by the synovial membrane, and filled with synovial fluid). The limits of its range of motion, imposed by the joint's physical structure or, more often, by lack of flexibility of the muscles, ligaments and tendons, define a joint's flexibility.

Ligaments – A ligament is a short band of tough fibrous connective tissue composed mainly of long, stringy collagen fibers. They connect bones to other bones to form a joint. Ligaments can limit the mobility of a joint or prevent certain movements altogether. Ligaments are slightly elastic and under tension, they will gradually lengthen. Ligaments that are too short may curtail flexibility by limiting a joint's range of motion.

Tendons – A tendon (or sinew) is a tough band of fibrous connective tissue (similar in structure to ligaments) that connects muscle to bone or muscle to muscle. Tendons are composed mainly of water, type-I collagen, and cells called tenocytes. Most of the strength of tendons stems from the parallel, hierarchical arrangement of densely packed collagen fibrils, which have great strength, little extensibility, and no ability to contract.

EXERCISE PRINCIPLES

The basic principles of fitness training, overload, progression, and specificity, apply to flexibility exercises. These principles can help develop flexibility of major joints and areas of the body.

Overloading for flexibility:

- **Frequency**: 3 to 7 days/week,

- **Intensity**: stretch muscle beyond its normal length,

- **Time**: 3 sets of 3 reps holding stretch 15 to 60 seconds.

Progression for flexibility:

- begin 3 days/week and work up to every day,

- begin stretching with slow movement, as far as possible, without pain holding at the end of the range of motion (ROM) and work up to stretching no more than 10% beyond the normal ROM,

- begin with 1 set with 1 rep, holding stretches 15 seconds and work up to 3 sets with 3 reps, holding stretches for 60 seconds.

Specificity for flexibility:

- ROM is joint specific.

SAFETY

Safety and proper form are important considerations when engaging in flexibility exercises. The following is a list of rules that participants should follow when performing stretches:

- Always warm up before stretching: perform light to moderate cardiovascular activity prior to stretching to increase muscle elasticity – stretching while "cold" can cause injury because the muscles are tight and less elastic

- Stop if you feel pain: stretching should not cause acute pain, mild discomfort or a mild pulling sensation is acceptable

- Move into each stretch slowly and steadily – don't bounce

- Avoid "locking" joints by completely straightening them during stretches – always allow a small amount of bend when stretching

- Relax the shoulders, hands, and feet while stretching

- Maintain proper posture

SKILL 3.4   *Identify and apply principles and activities for developing proper posture and efficient body mechanics.*

Posture is the position of the body while standing, sitting, or lying down. Posture is extremely important as it keeps bones and the joints aligned ensuring proper use of muscles. When this is the case, a body will use less energy and fatigue will be less likely. Good posture allows the body to use the strongest muscles for the most difficult tasks, preventing undue strain on muscles and bones. Cornerstones of good posture include proper alignment of the vertebral column, and releasing unnecessary tension in the muscles of the body (e.g. tensed shoulders).

Developing a critical image of the body is one of the first steps in assessing posture. We need a comprehensive view of the body and how it moves as a result of posture to evaluate the body.

Here are some key points to look for while assessing posture:
- Slouching leads to neck, shoulder, and backaches as well as joint stiffness.
- First, you must exercise. To help your body stand straighter and taller, you have to strengthen the abs and back muscles.
- You can take a look in the mirror while standing. The ears, shoulders, hips, knees, and ankles should be in a straight line.
- Keep you knees at hip level when sitting.

- Sit as far back against the back of the chair as possible.

When sleeping, always sleep on a firm mattress on your side and never on your stomach. When bending to lift and carry heavy objects, bend from the knees, not the waist, and keep the back straight. Bending from the knees places the burden on the legs and reduces strain on the lower back.

CORRECTING POOR POSTURE

An imbalance of strength between opposing muscles can cause poor posture. An important step toward rectifying poor posture is to strengthen the muscles used to hold the body in the proper way. A lack of flexibility in key muscles can also cause poor posture (whereby the student would feel strain to maintain correct posture). In this case, the student must stretch the appropriate muscles.

Proper posture is also important during exertion, for example when lifting and carrying. You should utilize the strong muscles of the legs, rather than the weaker muscles of the lower back, when carrying heavy objects. Thus, instructors should teach students that when bending to lift something, they should keep their backs straight and bend with their knees. A helpful visualization tool for students is to have them imagine the spine as an arrow, with the arrowhead at the base of the spine. Bad posture tends to point the arrow backwards, whereas good posture will point the arrow down.

SKILL 3.5   Identify and apply principles, types of equipment, and safety practices for progressive-resistance and flexibility exercise.

PROGRESSIVE-RESISTANCE EXERCISE

The practice of progressive resistance is an integral part of individual physical development and training programs. As with all other forms of exercise, participants should always follow certain principles and safety practices when performing progressive-resistance exercises.

As a safety precaution, instructors should formulate a health or medical questionnaire for students to complete. This can serve as a screening tool before enrolling a student into a progressive-resistance program. When beginning a weight-training program, novices should not attempt to lift too much weight.

Other principles and guidelines that participants should follow include:
- Warm-up prior to performing resistance exercises
- Gradually increase the number of repetitions for each exercise
- Exercise at least two days and receive adequate rest to achieve proper muscle development
- Perform exercises in a controlled manner

- Perform each exercise through a functional range of motion
- Work in conjunction with instructors who provide adequate feedback and guidance

Apart from the aforementioned principles, other basic principles of progressive resistance training include careful monitoring of types of lifts, intensity, volume, and variety of lifts, and taking adequate rest for recovery.

The equipment used for progressive resistance training or exercise include fit strips, dumbbells or barbells, and weight machines. Circuit training involves engaging in a variety of fitness exercises to achieve a full-body workout.

Partner-Resistance Exercises

For partner-resistance exercises, instructors should instruct students to pair-up with classmates of comparable size and strength, to ensure that the activity is productive and both training partners can apply sufficient resistance. Safety procedures for partner-resistance activities include properly demonstrating the required activity and clarifying to students that excessive competitiveness (to the extent of risking damage to another student) is not acceptable. In partner-resistance activities, the paired students serve as spotters for each other.

Weight Training

Weight training involves the use of weights (e.g. barbells or dumbbells) to create resistance to physical motion of body parts. In the case of weight training, properly demonstrating the required activity is fundamental, as the physical weights can present a heightened possibility for injuries. Instructors should instruct students to err on the side of less weight when unsure how much to use. A spotter should monitor students at all times. For students to make educated decisions about weight training (always under supervision), they must understand the risks and benefits of weight training for personal muscular strength and endurance development.

Circuit Training

Athletes use circuit training to increase the efficiency and intensity of a training routine by alternating exercises that target different muscle groups instead of alternating exercises with rest-periods. This form of workout promotes muscular endurance development, but is more taxing on the students. Only those students who already exercising regularly and have proven their ability to remain disciplined and follow directions should attempt circuit training.

Proper Technique

Instructors should stress proper exercise technique at all times, especially with beginners to prevent development of bad habits. Whether it is weightlifting, running, or stretching, participants should not force any body part beyond the normal range of motion. Pain is a good indicator of overextension. Living by the phrase, "No pain, no gain", is potentially dangerous. Participants should use slow and controlled movements. In addition, participants must engage in a proper warm-up and cool-down before and after exercise. When lifting weights, lifters should always have a partner. A spotter can help correct the lifter's technique and help lift the weight to safety if the lifter is unable to do so. A partner can also offer encouragement and motivation. Flexibility is an often overlooked, yet important, part of exercise that can play a key role in injury prevention. Participants should perform stretching exercises after each workout session.

PROGRESSIVE RESISTANCE – SAFETY

Possessing the strength and ability to overcome any resistance in one single effort or in repeated efforts over a period of time is muscular strength and endurance. It represents the ability to complete a heavy task in a single effort. Muscular strength and endurance not only helps in keeping body ailments in check, but also in enabling better performance in any sporting event.

Most fitness experts regard calisthenics as the best form of exercises in order to increase muscular development and strength. Although calisthenics are good beginning exercises, later on participants should complement them with progressive resistance training so that there will be an increase in bone mass and connective tissue strength. Such a combination would also help in minimizing any damages or injuries that are apt to occur at the beginning or initial training stages.

Besides calisthenics and progressive resistance training, aerobics can also help in maintaining muscular strength and endurance.

FLEXIBILITY EXERCISES

Flexibility, a form of physical training, encompasses a wide range of activities. With a range of advantages for children, youths, and especially older people (i.e., those with joint problems), flexibility has become an important part of every physical training program.

While starting any exercise program, the best way to begin is by stretching or flexing muscles as a warm up. This will allow the body to adapt to exercise. Flexibility activities are necessary for any physical training or exercising program as they help prevent against injuries.

Activities that can improve flexibility include stretching, bending, doing yoga, dancing, martial arts, and even other muscle work that is gentle and not strenuous at all. The different classifications of stretching and flexibility exercises include proprioceptive neuromuscular facilitation (PNF), static, dynamic, and partner resistance.

Static and dynamic stretching are the two most traditional classifications of flexibility training. Static stretching involves holding a position. In other words, the participant stretches to the farthest point possible and holds for several seconds. Dynamic stretching, on the other hand, involves slow, steady movements through a range of motion. Examples of dynamic stretches include arm and leg swings. Both static and dynamic stretching is suitable to individuals of all developmental levels. Static stretching is effective for improving range of flexibility. A warm up is necessary prior to static stretching to reduce the risk of injury. Dynamic stretching is an excellent warm up in itself because it involves slow, gradual movements.

Proprioceptive neuromuscular facilitation (PNF) is a more advanced form of flexibility training that combines traditional stretching with muscle contraction. Particularly effective for rehabilitation, PNF can also target specific muscle groups and increase muscular strength. PNF is best suited for individuals training at higher levels of fitness. PNF is not suitable for children or any persons whose bones are still growing.

Finally, in partner resistance stretching a partner applies resistance to a specific body part to stretch the targeted muscle actively. This is a more advanced technique that is a key component of PNF. Partner resistance stretching is best suited for more advanced athletes and caution is necessary to avoid injury. Because the partner cannot feel the stretch, he or she must communicate with the participant to prevent overextension.

FLEXIBILITY – SAFETY AND EFFECTIVENESS

Flexibility training is perhaps the most undervalued component of conditioning. Dynamic flexibility is the ability to perform dynamic movements within the full range of motion of the specified joint. Static active flexibility refers to the ability to stretch an antagonist muscle using only the tension in the antagonist muscle. Static-passive flexibility is the ability to hold a stretch using body weight or some other external force.

Dynamic stretching is generally very safe and very effective for warming up muscle groups and moderately improving flexibility. When performing dynamic stretches, participants must be careful to avoid sudden, jerky movements.

Static stretching is also safe, if the participant warms up the muscles prior to stretching. Because cold muscles are less elastic, static stretching without adequate warm up can lead to injury. Static stretching is very effective in increasing muscle flexibility.

Isometric, PNF, and ballistic stretching are more advanced techniques that require extreme caution and supervision. Most physical trainers believe ballistic stretching, bouncing into stretches, is ineffective and dangerous. Most trainers do not recommend ballistic stretching. PNF and isometric stretching are effective in certain situations such as rehabilitation and advanced training, but require close supervision.

SKILL 3.6   Recognize flexibility, strength, and endurance activities appropriate for various developmental levels and purposes.

SEE ALSO Previous Skill

MUSCLE STRENGTH AND ENDURANCE

Muscular strength is the maximum amount of force that one can generate in an isolated movement. Muscular endurance is the ability of the muscles to perform a submaximal task repeatedly or to maintain a submaximal muscle contraction for extended periods of time. Body-support activities (e.g. push-ups and sit-ups) and callisthenic activities (e.g. rope jumping) are good exercises for young students or beginners of all ages. Such exercises use multiple muscle groups and have minimal risk of injury. At more advanced levels of development and for those students interested in developing higher levels of strength and muscle mass, weight lifting is the optimal activity.

To improve muscular strength and endurance a student can:

- Train with free weights
- Perform exercised that use an individual's body weight for resistance (e.g., push-ups, sit-ups, dips, etc.)
- Do strength training exercises two times per week that incorporate all major muscle groups

SKILL 3.7   Identify and analyze techniques for evaluating flexibility and muscular strength and endurance.

EVALUATING FLEXIBILITY

Standard methods of evaluating flexibility include the sit and reach test and having students try to touch their hands behind their backs. Instructors can devise additional flexibility tests to evaluate the range of motion of specific joints. In these cases, the tests should reflect practical function.

EVALUATING MUSCULAR STRENGTH AND ENDURANCE

The standard procedure for evaluating muscular strength and endurance is measurement of repetitions performed and/or amount of weight used for various resistance exercises. For example, the instructor may ask students to perform as many pull-ups as they can or bench press a given weight as many times as they can. Comparing individual results to age- and size-based norms allows instructors to tailor fitness programs to meet the needs of each student.

COMPETENCY 4.0   ***UNDERSTAND PRINCIPLES AND ACTIVITIES FOR DEVELOPING AND MAINTAINING LEVELS OF BODY COMPOSITION THAT PROMOTE GOOD HEALTH***

SKILL 4.1   *Identify and apply principles of nutrition and weight control and ways in which diet and eating habits affect physical development and health.*

NUTRITION AND WEIGHT CONTROL

Identify the components of nutrition

The components of nutrition are **carbohydrates, proteins, fats, vitamins, minerals, and water.**

Carbohydrates – the main source of energy (glucose) in the human diet. The two types of carbohydrates are simple and complex. Complex carbohydrates have greater nutritional value because they take longer to digest, contain dietary fiber, and do not excessively elevate blood sugar levels. Common sources of carbohydrates are fruits, vegetables, grains, dairy products, and legumes.

Proteins – are necessary for growth, development, and cellular function. The body breaks down consumed protein into component amino acids for future use. Major sources of protein are meat, poultry, fish, legumes, eggs, dairy products, grains, and legumes.

Fats – a concentrated energy source and important component of the human body. The different types of fats are saturated, monounsaturated, and polyunsaturated. Polyunsaturated fats are the healthiest because they may lower cholesterol levels, while saturated fats increase cholesterol levels. Common sources of saturated fats include dairy products, meat, coconut oil, and palm oil. Common sources of unsaturated fats include nuts, most vegetable oils, and fish.

Vitamins and minerals – organic substances that the body requires in small quantities for proper functioning. People acquire vitamins and minerals in their diets and in supplements. Important vitamins include A, B, C, D, E, and K. Important minerals include calcium, phosphorus, magnesium, potassium, sodium, chlorine, and sulfur.

Water – makes up 55 – 75% of the human body. Essential for most bodily functions. Attained through foods and liquids.

Determine the adequacy of diets in meeting the nutritional needs of students

Nutritional requirements *vary from person-to-person.* General guidelines for meeting adequate nutritional needs are: *no more than 30% total caloric intake from fats* (preferably 10% from saturated fats, 10% from monounsaturated fats, 10% from polyunsaturated fats), *no more than 15% total caloric intake from protein* (complete), *and* <u>at least</u> *55% of caloric intake from carbohydrates* (mainly complex carbohydrates).

Exercise and diet help maintain proper body weight by equalizing caloric intake and caloric output.

SKILL 4.2   *Analyze the relationship between body type and body composition and apply techniques for evaluating body composition.*

BODY TYPES

Recognizing individual students' physical changes helps with understanding how their physiques affect motor performance. The child's physique has a definite affect on their motor performance. Somatype, another term for body type, deals with how fat, muscular, and linear your body is. The three body types are endomorph, mesomorph, and ectomorph. Everyone is some combination of the three types, with one classification usually prevailing over the others. You cannot change your body type but you can modify it through your eating habits and level of physical exercise, which in turn affects your body-fat percentage. Certain body types are more suited for certain sports, but it doesn't mean you won't be successful if your somatype is different from what's mentioned. Somatype classification is important because it shows how children differ in body physique and how vital it is that instruction accommodates individual differences.

Endomorphs are naturally "large" or "big boned" with a pear-shaped bodies and a slow metabolism. Endomorphs are often very strong, but have little speed. They experience difficulty at most sports, including both aerobic and anaerobic activities. Individual sports such as shot or discus throwing in track, wrestling, and judo are activities well suited for endomorphs.

Mesomorphs are "muscular" with an hourglass figure, broad shoulders, small waist, strong thighs, fast metabolism, and little body fat. Often called "natural athletes," they participate with ease and look forward to physical competition of any sort. These children perform best in team sports that require strength, speed, and agility such as football and baseball, or individual sports such as swimming. Ectomorphs, often called "skinny," are extremely thin, with very little body fat, little or no muscle development, and an ultra fast metabolism. Ectomorphs have difficulty gaining weight or muscle mass. Because they lack power and strength, they are better suited for aerobic endurance activities such as cross-country running, many track and field events such as the high or long jump, sprints, relays, and middle-distance running.

EVALUATING BODY COMPOSITION

Body composition includes the relative amount of fat, bone, and other vital parts of the body. The measurement of body composition allows for the estimation of body tissues, organs, and their distribution in a living person without inflicting harm. It is important to recognize that there is no measurement method that is error-free. Rather, the principle is to make every individual aware of body composition evaluation techniques and the fact that monitoring body composition is an exemplary method for maintaining a maximum level of physical fitness. The different methods of evaluating body composition include skinfold tests, electronic impedance, and body mass index.

Skinfold tests estimate body fat percentage by measuring the thickness of skinfolds at specific sights on the body with calipers. While skinfold tests are not a valid measurement of body fat percentage, they are useful in monitoring progress in body fat reduction.

Electronic impedance is a technique that estimates body fat percentage by measuring the conductive potential of the body. A bioimpedance meter sends a small electrical current through the body and measures conductive potential. Lean tissue (i.e. muscle, bone, ligaments) are more conductive than fat tissue because of the higher water content.

Body mass index (BMI) is a measure of body fat based on height and weight. BMI is a generic measurement that is not specific to the individual. BMI labels individuals as underweight, normal, overweight, or obese. While BMI is a useful tool in estimating body fat and determining a target weight, it can overestimate fatness in muscular or athletic people.

SKILL 4.3   *Demonstrate knowledge of the relationship between physical activity and body composition.*

Exercise and diet maintain proper body weight by equalizing caloric intake to caloric output.

Nutrition and exercise are closely related concepts important to student health. An important responsibility of physical education instructors is to teach students about proper nutrition and exercise and how they relate to each other. The two key components of a healthy lifestyle are consumption of a balanced diet and regular physical activity. Nutrition can affect physical performance. Proper nutrition produces high energy levels and allows for peak performance. Inadequate or improper nutrition can impair physical performance and lead to short-term and long-term health problems (e.g. depressed immune system and heart disease, respectively). Regular exercise improves overall health. Benefits of regular exercise include a stronger immune system, stronger muscles, bones, and joints, reduced risk of premature death, reduced risk of heart disease, improved psychological well-being, and weight management.

SKILL 4.4   *Select appropriate activities and materials for developing and maintaining healthy levels of body composition.*

ACTIVITIES

It is vital to analyze procedures, activities, resources, and benefits involved in developing and maintaining healthy levels of body composition. Maintaining a healthy body composition allows an individual to move freely and to obtain a certain pattern that is necessary for a specific activity. Furthermore, maintaining a healthy body composition is positively related with long-term health and resistance to disease and sickness.

The total weight of an individual is a combination of bones, ligaments, tendons, organs, fluids, muscles and fat. Because muscle weighs three times more than fat per unit of volume, a person who exercises often gains muscle. This could cause an individual to be smaller physically, but weigh more than he/she appears to weigh.

The only proven method for maintaining a healthy body composition is following a healthy diet and engaging in regular exercise. A healthy diet emphasizes fruits, vegetables, whole grains, unsaturated fats, and lean protein, and minimizes saturated fat and sugar consumption. Such a program of nutrition and exercise helps balance caloric intake and output, thus preventing excessive body fat production.

The following is an example of a **body composition** program design:

- **mode:** combining aerobic exercise and weight training and a moderate reduction of caloric intake

- **frequency:** minimum of 3 days/week; however, daily is best

- **intensity:** low intensity, long duration

- **time:** 45 to 60 minutes of aerobic activity; 3 sets with a minimum of 6 reps for weights every other day

- **progression:** periodically increase as individual improves

DIET

A healthy diet is essential for achieving and maintaining optimum mental and physical health. Making the decision to eat well is a powerful investment. Selecting foods that encompass a variety of healthy nutrients will help reduce your risk of developing common medical conditions and will boost your immune system while increasing your energy level.

Experts agree that the key to healthy eating is balance, variety, and moderation. Other tips include:

- Enjoy plenty of whole grains, fruits, and vegetables.
- Maintain a healthy weight.
- Eat moderate portions.
- Eat regular meals.
- Reduce but don't eliminate certain foods.
- Balance your food choices over time.
- Know your diet pitfalls.
- Make changes gradually... Remember, foods are not good or bad.

Select foods based on your total eating patterns, not whether any individual food is "good" or "bad."

SKILL 4.5   Identify and correct misconceptions related to body composition, dieting, nutritional needs, exercise and training.

SEE ALSO Domain 1, Skill 1.6

EATING DISORDER RISK FACTORS

Gender – Females are much more likely to develop an eating disorder than males.

Socioeconomic Standing – Inhabitants of economically developed nations appear to have a higher risk for developing eating disorders.

Age – Eating disorders are most common between the ages of 12 and 25.

Athletics and Certain Professions – Dancers, jockeys, runners, gymnasts, etc. tend to be at higher risk for eating disorders since thinness in these activities is desirable. Models and entertainers also run a high risk of falling victim to eating disorders as many of them experience intense pressure to be thin.

SIGNS AND SYMPTOMS OF EATING DISORDERS

Anorexia

- Dramatic weight loss
- Basing self-worth on body weight and body image
- Frequent skipping of meals
- Eating only a few foods, especially those low in fat and calories
- Frequent weighing of oneself
- Wearing baggy clothes to cover up thinness
- Excessive focus on an exercise plan
- Loss of menstrual cycle
- Dizziness and headaches

Bulimia

- Secrecy surrounding eating
- Eating unusually large amounts of food, with no apparent weight gain
- Complex lifestyle schedules or rituals
- Discolored or callused finger joints or backs of the hands
- Tooth and mouth problems
- Stomach pain and intestinal irregularities

DOMAIN 2.0   MOVEMENT AND SKILL ACQUISITION

COMPETENCY 1.0   UNDERSTAND PRINCIPLES AND CHARACTERISTICS OF MOTOR DEVELOPMENT

SKILL 1.1   *Recognize principles, critical elements, sequences, and characteristics of motor development during infancy, childhood, adolescence, and adulthood.*

SEE ALSO Domain 1, Skill 1.1

Motor-development learning theories that pertain to a general skill, activity, or age level are important and necessary teacher background information for effective lesson planning. Motor-skill learning is unique to each individual but does follow a general sequential skill pattern, starting with general gross motor movements and ending with specific or fine motor skills. Teachers must begin instruction at a level where all children are successful and proceed through the activity to the point where frustration for the majority is hindering performance. Students must learn the fundamentals of a skill, or subsequent learning of more advanced skills becomes extremely difficult. Instructors must spend enough time on beginning skills so they become second nature. Teaching in small groups with enough equipment for everyone is essential. Practice sessions that are too long or too demanding can cause physical and/or mental burnout. Teaching skills over a longer period of time, but with slightly different approaches, helps keep students' attentive and involved as they internalize the skill. The instructor can then teach more difficult skills while continuing to review the basics. If the skill is challenging for most students, allow plenty of practice time so they retain it due to learning in depth before having to use it in a game situation.

Visualizing and breaking the skill down mentally is another way to enhance the learning of motor movements. Instructors can teach students to "picture" the steps involved and see themselves executing the skill. An example is teaching dribbling in basketball. Start teaching the skill with a demonstration of the steps involved in dribbling. Starting with the first skill, introduce key language terms and have students visualize themselves performing the skill. A sample-progression lesson plan to teach dribbling could begin with students practicing while standing still. Next, add movement while dribbling. Finally, introduce how to control dribbling while being guarded by another student.

SKILL 1.2   *Demonstrate knowledge of appropriate developmental progressions and individual variation.*

Physical education helps individuals attain a healthy level of fitness and renders significant experiences in movement. It provides an opportunity to refine and develop motor skills, stamina, strategies and the pure pleasure of physical activity and participation. Children, infants, and the disabled are all entitled to benefit from physical education. Physical activities can be adapted by recognizing the individual's abilities, learning skills, and needs. This requires knowledge about the science of movement, the process of skill development, social and psychological components, physical fitness, assessment of the practices of physical activities, and development and implementation of proper and appropriate activities.

Children are at a developmental stage where their physical, emotional, motor, and social skills are not fully constructed. Children in different age groups have distinct and urgent developmental needs. A developmental need varies from child to child. Instructors should respect each child's developmental needs and pace of learning and deal with all students patiently. Instructors should put each child in an environment that stimulates him and offers challenges that are appropriate to his age, developmental needs, and ability. Instructors should not force a child to take up an activity. Coercion discourages the child and he resists learning. However, incorporating motivation and stimulation into the activity can encourage the child without direct intervention of an adult. Self-motivation is the best tool for learning. Children need to challenge themselves through constant exploration and experimentation. The activity should suit the developmental age of the child so that he/she can perform it with minimal outside assistance. An adult should act as an assistant who provides help only when it is required.

Educators should design the physical education program to suit developmental needs of the students (i.e., constructing their motor skills, concept of movement). Physical activity should be fun, pleasurable and aimed at developing and maintaining health. Motor skills are comprised of locomotor skills, non-locomotor skills and manipulative and coordination skills. Games like Bean Bag, parachute, hoola hoop, gymnastics and ball activities modified and adapted to suit the particular needs of children, are particularly helpful. Physical activity should have the scope to adapt itself to suit an individual child's needs and goals. Instructors can incorporate activities, such as wheelchair races or activities that require use of the hands, to accommodate handicapped students that cannot use their legs. For children in the grades 1 – 3, instructors should incorporate concepts of movement and motor skills, allowing the child to perfect them. Concepts of movements like spatial consciousness regarding location, level or height and direction, body awareness and recognition of how the body can be manipulated to perform an activity, effort required regarding time, flow and force, relationship to the various objects and to others, are developed through various activities.

With greater development of motor skills and concepts about movement, instructors can introduce more energetic and vigorous physical activities like volleyball, gymnastics, football, and hockey. Along with these skills, the curriculum should help develop group participation skills. It is essential to instill the values of physical education and its connection to general well-being and health. Apart from this, physical education for middle grade children should help develop a good body image and enhance their social skills. Instructors can teach activities like advanced volleyball, dance, and gymnastics that will help to develop these areas.

SPECIFIC DEVELOPMENTAL ISSUES

There are several important developmental issues for an educator to consider that affect the different stages of human growth. Play is a fundamental process for learning in young children. It is a method by which they come to grips with their reality and experiment with the world (e.g. playing with toys), experiment with their concept of roles in general, and experiment with their particular roles (e.g. playing "make believe"). Children will also participate in solitary play, parallel play (multiple children playing near each other, but not including each other in their games), and cooperative play (multiple children playing the same game, together). These types of play are ways for children to define their personal comfort levels with the different types of interactions with their peers.

Participation in physical activity in the socialization process is very important, as most human interaction has a physical component to it (though the amount of physical interaction has decreased since the advent of remote communication technology). Physical activity during the socialization process creates an opportunity for children to define personal comfort levels with different types of physical interaction, as well as establish guidelines for what is (and is not) acceptable physical behavior as related to their relationship with other individuals and the scenario in which they find themselves.

Another issue to consider is the preoccupation with physical appearance that surfaces in adolescence (especially earlier adolescence, ages 12-14). This comes from several factors, primarily their burgeoning sexual identities with which they have not yet come to grips that make them care a great deal about the impression they make on members of the opposite sex. Similarly, children at this age are in the process of creating their own identities, separate from the major players in their environments (i.e. their parents). This coupled with their intense concern with their social stature and perceptions in the eyes of their peers, all contribute to the preoccupation with physical appearance (which they will outgrow).

RELATIONSHIP BETWEEN HUMAN GROWTH AND DEVELOPMENT AND APPROPRIATE PHYSICAL ACTIVITY

Understanding the rate of the developmental growth process that occurs during adolescence will help educators understand growth and development norms and identify early or late maturing students. The age when the puberty growth spurt occurs and the speed with which adolescents experience puberty vary greatly within each gender and may affect participation in physical activity and sports. If the instructor pays attention to the varying body sizes and maturity stages, forming teams in co-educational classes can easily accommodate the needs of both genders' changing maturities. Starting in middle school and continuing into high school, it is perfectly acceptable for boys and girls to participate in non-contact physical activities together that rely on lower-body strength and agility (e.g. capture the flag, ultimate Frisbee, running). In more physical activities that require upper body strength, coaches should form teams based on individual skill levels to prevent injury. Matching teams evenly based on skill and maturity is important so that individual skill level deficiencies are not as apparent and the activity remains fun for all participants. Teachers need to monitor and adjust physical activities as needed to ensure a positive, competitive experience. Appropriate activities would include individual or partner badminton or tennis matches and team competitions in flag football.

SKILLS 1.3   Identify principles of perceptual-motor development and components such as visual, auditory, tactile, and kinesthetic discrimination, and evaluate their relationship to motor development and performance.

Perceptual-motor development refers to one's ability to receive, interpret, and respond successfully to sensory signals coming from the environment. Because many of the skills acquired in school rely on the child's knowledge of his body and its relationship to the surroundings, good motor development leads directly to perceptual skill development.

Development of gross motor skills lead to successful development of fine motor skills, which in turn help with learning, reading, and writing. Adolescents with perceptual-motor coordination problems are at risk for poor school performance, low self-esteem, and inadequate physical activity participation. Without a successful intervention, these adolescents are likely to continue avoiding physical activity and experience frustration and teasing from their peers. Children with weak perceptual-motor skills may be easily distracted or have difficulty with tasks requiring coordination. They spend much of their energy trying to control their bodies, exhausting them so much that they physically cannot concentrate on a teacher-led lesson.

Unfortunately, perceptual-motor coordination problems do not just go away and they don't self-repair. Practice and maturity are necessary for children to develop greater coordination and spatial awareness. Physical education lessons should emphasize activities that children enjoy doing, are sequential, and require seeing, hearing, and/or touching. Discussing with students the actual steps involved in performing a fundamental skill is a great benefit. Activities and skills that can be broken down and taught in incremental steps include running, dribbling, catching or hitting a ball, making a basket in basketball, and setting a volleyball. Recommended strategies include introducing the skill, practicing in a variety of settings with an assortment of equipment, implementing lead-up games modified to ensure practice of the necessary skills, and incorporating students into an actual game situation.

COMPETENCY 2.0   UNDERSTAND THE PRINCIPLES OF MOTOR LEARNING AND MOVEMENT SKILLS ACQUISITION

SKILL 2.1   Demonstrate knowledge of principles and stages of motor learning and concepts associated with skill acquisition.

The development of motor skills in children is a sequential process. We can classify motor skill competency into stages of development by observing children practicing physical skills. The sequence of development begins with simple reflexes and progresses to the learning of postural elements, locomotor skills, and, finally, fine motor skills. The stages of development consider both innate and learned behaviors.

STAGES OF MOTOR LEARNING

Stage 1 – Children progress from simple reflexes to basic movements such as sitting, crawling, creeping, standing, and walking.

Stage 2 – Children learn more complex motor patterns including running, climbing, jumping, balancing, catching, and throwing.

Stage 3 – During late childhood, children learn more specific movement skills. In addition, the basic motor patterns learned in stage 2 become more fluid and automatic.

Stage 4 – During adolescence, children continue to develop general and specific motor skills and master specialized movements. At this point, factors including practice, motivation, and talent begin to affect the level of further development.

SKILL 2.2   Apply knowledge of levels of readiness in motor learning.

To accommodate variations in ability, level of development and readiness, and rates of progress, physical education instructors should emphasize non-competitive practice. Instructors should only introduce competitive situations to maintain student interest and challenge more advanced and developed students.

Studies show that physical activity leads to improved motor development in children. Physical activity also enables various other progressions that shape the mind and personality of an individual. Such developments, which are the result of physical activity, include cognitive, psychosocial, and emotional growth.

Very often, we ignore the close relationship shared by motor development and the other aspects of development. Motor development, which starts with the proper nutrition, deeply affects the other aspects of development in an individual. Children acquire a vast range of motor development skills such as grasping, crawling, walking, running, and even speaking during the early stages of their lives. Gradually, such motor skills further develop leading to participation in sport and play activities that promote confidence in children and allow them to develop responsibility, deep emotions, and social etiquette. Through participation in sports, children learn to cooperate and develop competitive skills that will aid them in adulthood.

Studies reveal that the different types of play in childhood link motor development with the other aspects of development. Different kinds of play or physical activity such as cognitive play, social play, physical play, and emotional play, help in the overall development of a child.

Simple motor skills such as repeatedly hitting the ground with a shovel or building sand castles help in developing thinking and cognitive skills. Social play helps children to play with their peers cooperatively, to develop their motor skills, and to develop a sense of social togetherness. Motor activities greatly influence physical development as well. They help in providing the foundation for a normal and healthy physical education program suitable for all children. Research also shows that free play among peers leads to significant cognitive developments (such as improvement of reasoning abilities).

The manner in which children hop, jump, skip, run, climb, and play greatly facilitates their motor and physical development and helps to build other aspects of their personality. Children accomplish this development through their constant interaction with surrounding elements, environments, and persons.

Thus, motor skill development, which encompasses all motor movements by children, is strongly related to the physical, social, and emotional development of children.

CHARACTERISTICS OF PHYSICAL DEVELOPMENT

Physical development – Small children (ages 3-5) have a propensity for engaging in periods of a great deal of physical activity, punctuated by a need for a lot of rest. Children at this stage lack fine motor skills and cannot focus on small objects for very long. Their bones are still developing. At this age, girls tend to be better coordinated, and boys tend to be stronger.

The lag in fine motor skills continues during the early elementary school years (ages 6-8).

Pre-adolescent children (ages 9-11) become stronger, leaner, and taller. Their motor skills improve, and they are able to sit still and focus for longer periods of time. Growth during this period is constant. This is also the time when gender physical predispositions will begin to manifest. Pre-adolescents are at risk of obesity without proper nutritional and adequate activity.

Young adolescents (ages 12-14) experience drastic physical growth (girls earlier than boys do), and are highly preoccupied with their physical appearance.

As children proceed to the later stages of adolescence (ages 15-17), girls will reach their full height, while boys will still have some growth remaining. The increase in hormone levels will cause acne, which coincides with a slight decrease of preoccupation with physical appearance. At this age, children may begin to initiate sexual activity (boys generally more motivated by hormones, and girls more by peer pressure). There is a risk of teen pregnancy and sexually transmitted diseases.

SKILL 2.3   *Identify and apply appropriate instructional cues and prompts for basic motor skills.*

KNOWLEDGE OF ACTIVITIES FOR BODY MANAGEMENT SKILL DEVELOPMENT

Sequential development and activities for locomotor skills acquisition

Sequential Development = crawl, creep, walk, run, jump, hop, gallop, slide, leap, skip, step-hop.

- **Activities to develop walking skills** include walking slower and faster in place; walking forward, backward, and sideways with slower and faster paces in straight, curving, and zigzag pathways with various lengths of steps; pausing between steps; and changing the height of the body.

- **Activities to develop running skills** include having students pretend they are playing basketball, trying to score a touchdown, trying to catch a bus, finishing a lengthy race, or running on a hot surface.

- **Activities to develop jumping skills** include alternating jumping with feet together and feet apart, taking off and landing on the balls of the feet, clicking the heels together while airborne, and landing with a foot forward and a foot backward.

- **Activities to develop galloping skills** include having students play a game of Fox and Hound, with the lead foot representing the fox and the back foot the hound trying to catch the fox (alternate the lead foot).

- **Activities to develop sliding skills** include having students hold hands in a circle and sliding in one direction, then sliding in the other direction.

- **Activities to develop hopping skills** include having students hop all the way around a hoop and hopping in and out of a hoop reversing direction. Students can also place ropes in straight lines and hop side-to-side over the rope from one end to the other and change (reverse) the direction.

- **Activities to develop skipping skills** include having students combine walking and hopping activities leading up to skipping.

- **Activities to develop step-hopping skills** include having students practice stepping and hopping activities while clapping hands to an uneven beat.

Sequential development and activities for nonlocomotor skill acquisition

Sequential Development = stretch, bend, sit, shake, turn, rock and sway, swing, twist, dodge, and fall.

- **Activities to develop stretching** include lying on the back and stomach and stretching as far as possible; stretching as though one is reaching for a star, picking fruit off a tree, climbing a ladder, shooting a basketball, or placing an item on a high self; waking and yawning.

- **Activities to develop bending** include touching knees and toes then straightening the entire body and straightening the body halfway; bending as though picking up a coin, tying shoes, picking flowers/vegetables, and petting animals of different sizes.

- **Activities to develop sitting** include practicing sitting from standing, kneeling, and lying positions without the use of hands.

- **Activities to develop falling skills** include first collapsing in one's own space and then pretending to fall like bowling pins, raindrops, snowflakes, a rag doll, or Humpty Dumpty.

PRACTICE

Frequent, structured practice of motor skills enhances skill development in children. Without practice and instruction, natural ability and talent dictates the extent of motor skill development.

FEEDBACK

Feedback, or input from the tutor or educator, forms an extremely vital part of any learning process. Just as positive feedback works as a motivator enabling an athlete to improve and surge ahead with renewed interest, negative feedback also helps an athlete recognize and correct his or her mistakes.

When performers learn a skill, the skill goes into their short-term memory and receives positive feedback. The skill may eventually go into their long-term memory, creating memory that is more permanent. That is how positive feedback works to encourage the performer and helps in making the performer remember every aspect of the performance.

Negative feedback helps athletes, whether novice or experienced, become conscious of their mistakes. They can use this negative feedback to improve their shortcomings. Without feedback, an athlete is not likely to improve their technique and they will lose motivation.

There are different types of feedback and it is always important for the performer to receive the right type. Some examples of feedback include the following:

Intrinsic feedback – information received by the athlete as a direct result of producing a movement through the kinesthetic senses – e.g. feeling from muscles, joints, and balance.

Extrinsic feedback – information not inherent in the movement itself but which improves intrinsic feedback (this is also known as augmented feedback). There are two main categories: knowledge of performance and information about the technique and performance. The coach can provide extrinsic feedback verbally or visually via video. Extrinsic feedback enables the athlete to establish a kinesthetic reference for the correct movement.

Research also indicates that the stage when an athlete receives feedback is as important as the content of the feedback. Negative feedback might be boring for the beginner. However, if a performer is elite, then knowledge of results is very important. In addition, during the cognitive stage, positive feedback is essential to make sure that the athlete learns a skill successfully. Thus, feedback plays an extremely important role in any learning process, as it facilitates learning to a great extent.

SELF-ASSESSMENT

Self-assessment is a powerful tool in motor skill development. Requiring students to assess their own skills and abilities encourages students to reflect upon their current skill level and take control of the development process.

OBSERVATIONAL LEARNING

Many physical education instructors believe that observational learning is the most effective method of learning motor skills. Visual observation of proper skill performance by an instructor or peer is generally more effective in promoting skill development than verbal instructions.

SKILL 2.4   Identify techniques for detecting errors in and providing corrective feedback for motor performance.

ERRORS IN SKILL PERFORMANCE

Because performing a skill has several components, determining why a participant is performing poorly may be difficult. Instructors may have to assess several components of a skill to determine the root cause of poor performance and appropriately correct errors. **An instructor should have the ability to identify performance errors by observing a student's mechanical principles of motion during the performance of a skill. Process assessment** is a subjective, observational approach to identifying errors in the form, style, or mechanics of a skill.

APPROPRIATE OBJECTIVE MEASUREMENTS OF FUNDAMENTAL SKILLS

Instructors should use **product assessments**, quantitative measures of a movement's end result, to evaluate objectively fundamental skills. How far, how fast, how high, or how many are the quantitative measures of product assessments.

A **criterion-referenced test** (superior to a standardized test) or a **standardized norm-referenced test** can provide valid and reliable data for objectively measuring fundamental skills.

SKILL ASSESSMENT INFORMATION USED TO CORRECT ERRORS IN SKILL PERFORMANCE

Instructors can use criterion-referenced standards to diagnose weaknesses and correct errors in skill performance because such performance standards define appropriate levels of achievement. However, instructors can also use biomechanical instructional objectives. The following list describes the skill assessment criteria in several representative activities:

- Archery - measuring accuracy in shooting a standardized target from a specified place.

- Bowling - calculating the bowling average attained under standardized conditions.

- Golf - the score after several rounds.

- Swimming - counting the number of breaststrokes needed to swim 25 yards.

After assessing student skill performance, the instructor should design drills or tasks that will develop the weakest component of the student's performance. For example, an instructor notices that a group of students attempting to shoot basketball free throw shots cannot get the ball to the basket because they do not use their legs to add power to the shot. The instructor should use this observation to construct drills that encourage leg use and develop strength.

SKILL 2.5   Identify developmentally appropriate instructional and practice experiences to promote acquisition of motor skills.

SEE Domain 2, Skill 2.3

COMPETENCY 3.0   **UNDERSTAND MOVEMENT CONCEPTS AND BIOMECHANICAL PRINCIPLES**

SKILL 3.1   *Identify critical elements of basic movement patterns.*

LOCOMOTOR SKILLS

Locomotor skills move an individual from one point to another.

1. **Crawling** - A form of locomotion where the person moves in a prone position with the body resting on or close to the ground or on the hands and knees.

2. **Creeping** - A slightly more advanced form of locomotion in which the person moves on the hands and knees.

3. **Walking** - with one foot contacting the surface at all times, walking shifts one's weight from one foot to the other while legs swing alternately in front of the body.

4. **Running** - an extension of walking that has a phase where the body is propelled with no base of support (speed is faster, stride is longer, and arms add power).

5. **Jumping** - projectile movements that momentarily suspend the body in midair.

6. **Vaulting** - coordinated movements that allow one to spring over an obstacle.

7. **Leaping** - similar to running, but leaping has greater height, flight, and distance.

8. **Hopping** - using the same foot to take off from a surface and land.

9. **Galloping** - forward or backward advanced elongation of walking combined and coordinated with a leap.

10. **Sliding** - sideward stepping pattern that is uneven, long, or short.

11. **Body Rolling** - moving across a surface by rocking back and forth, by turning over and over, or by shaping the body into a revolving mass.

12. **Climbing** - ascending or descending using the hands and feet with the upper body exerting the most control.

NONLOCOMOTOR SKILLS

Nonlocomotor skills are stability skills where the movement requires little or no movement of one's base of support and does not result in change of position.

1. **Bending** - movement around a joint where two body parts meet.

2. **Dodging** - sharp change of direction from original line of movement such as away from a person or object.

3. **Stretching** - extending/hyper-extending joints to make body parts as straight or as long as possible.

4. **Twisting** - rotating body/body parts around an axis with a stationary base.

5. **Turning** - circular moving the body through space releasing the base of support.

6. **Swinging** - circular/pendular movements of the body/body parts below an axis.

7. **Swaying** - same as swinging but movement is above an axis.

8. **Pushing** - applying force against an object or person to move it away from one's body or to move one's body away from the object or person.

9. **Pulling** - executing force to cause objects/people to move toward one's body.

RHYTHMIC SKILLS

Rhythmic skills include responding and moving the body in time with the beat, tempo, or pitch of music. To develop rhythmic skills, instructors can ask students to clap their hands or stomp their feet to the beat of the music. Dancing and gymnastics requires high levels of rhythmic competency. As with all physical skills, development of rhythmic skills is a sequential process.

MANIPULATIVE SKILLS

Manipulative skills use body parts to propel or receive an object, controlling objects primarily with the hands and feet. Two types of manipulative skills are receptive (catch + trap) and propulsive (throw, strike, kick).

1. **Bouncing/Dribbling** - projecting a ball downwards.

2. **Catching** - stopping momentum of an object (for control) using the hands.

3. **Kicking** - striking an object with the foot.

4. **Rolling** - initiating force to an object to instill contact with a surface.

5. **Striking** - giving impetus to an object with the use of the hands or an object.

6. **Throwing** - using one or both arms to project an object into midair away from the body.

7. **Trapping** - without the use of the hands, receiving and controlling a ball.

SKILL 3.2   *Demonstrate knowledge of basic movement concepts and ways to promote application of movement concepts.*

Research shows that the concepts of space, direction, and speed are interrelated with movement concepts. Such concepts are extremely important for students to understand, as they need to know movement skills with regard to direction in order to move with confidence and avoid collisions.

Movement relates to space, direction, speed, and vision, as a student or player must take all of these elements into consideration in order to perform and understand a sport. A player must decide how to handle their space as well as numerous other factors that arise on the field.

For a player, the concepts are all interconnected. She has to understand how to maintain or change pathways with speed. This refers to the ability to change motion and perform well in space (or the area that the players occupy on the field).

CONCEPT OF BODY AWARENESS APPLIED TO PHYSICAL EDUCATION ACTIVITIES

Body awareness is a person's understanding of his or her own body parts and their capability of movement.

Instructors can assess body awareness by playing and watching a game of "Simon Says" and asking the students to touch different body parts. You can also instruct students to make their bodies into various shapes, from straight to round to twisted, and varying sizes, to fit into different sized spaces.

In addition, you can instruct children to touch one part of their body to another and to use various body parts to stamp their feet, twist their neck, clap their hands, nod their heads, wiggle their noses, snap their fingers, open their mouths, shrug their shoulders, bend their knees, close their eyes, bend their elbows, or wiggle their toes.

CONCEPT OF SPATIAL AWARENESS APPLIED TO PHYSICAL EDUCATION ACTIVITIES

Spatial awareness is the ability to make decisions about an object's positional changes in space (i.e. awareness of three-dimensional space position changes). Developing spatial awareness requires two sequential phases: 1) identifying the location of objects in relation to one's own body in space, and 2) locating more than one object in relation to each object and independent of one's own body. Plan activities using different size balls, boxes, or hoops and have children move towards and away; under and over; in front of and behind; and inside, outside, and beside the objects.

CONCEPT OF EFFORT QUALITIES APPLIED TO PHYSICAL EDUCATION

Effort qualities are the qualities of movement that apply the mechanical principles of balance, time, and force).

Balance - activities for balance include having children move on their hands and feet, lean, move on lines, and balance and hold shapes while moving.

Time - activities using the concept of time can include having children move as fast as they can and as slow as they can in specified, timed movement patterns.

Force - activities using the concept of force can include having students use their bodies to produce enough force to move them through space. They can also paddle balls against walls and jump over objects of various heights.

SKILL 3.3   Recognize biomechanical principles and apply these principles to various movement activities.

CONCEPTS OF EQUILIBRIUM AND CENTER OF GRAVITY APPLIED TO MOVEMENT

When body segments move independently, body mass redistributes, changing the location of the body's center of gravity. Segments also move to change the body's base of support from one moment to the next to cope with imminent loss of balance.

The entire center of gravity of the body shifts in the same direction of movement of the body's segments. As long as the center of gravity remains over the base of support, the body will remain in a state of equilibrium. The more the center of gravity is situated over the base, the greater the stability. A wider base of support and/or a lower center of gravity enhances stability. To be effective, the base of support must widen in the direction of the force produced or opposed by the body. Shifting weight in the direction of the force in conjunction with widening the base of support further enhances stability.

Constant interaction of forces that move the body in the elected direction results in dynamic balance. The smooth transition of the center of gravity changing from one base of support to the next produces speed.

CONCEPT OF FORCE APPLIED TO MOVEMENT

Force is any influence that can change the state of motion of an object; we must consider the objective of movement.

Magnitude of Force – force must overcome the inertia of the object and any other resisting forces for movement to occur.

For linear movement, force applied close to the center of gravity requires a smaller magnitude of force to move the object than does force applied farther from the center of gravity.

For rotational movement, force applied farther from the center of gravity requires a smaller magnitude of force to rotate the object than does force applied closer to the center of gravity.

For objects with a fixed point, force applied anywhere other than through the point of fixation results in object rotation.

Energy – the capacity to do work. (The more energy a body has the greater the force with which it can move something [or change its shape] and/or the farther it can move it).

Movement (mechanical energy) has two types:

1. Potential energy (energy possessed by virtue of position, absolute location in space or change in shape).

> **A. Gravitational potential energy** - potential energy of an object that is in a position where gravity can act on it.

> **B. Elastic (strain) potential energy** - energy potential of an object to do work while recoiling (or reforming) after stretching, compressing, or twisting.

2. Kinetic energy (energy possessed by virtue of motion that increases with speed).

Force Absorption - maintaining equilibrium while receiving a moving object's kinetic energy without sustaining injury or without losing balance while rebounding. The force of impact is dependent on an object's weight and speed. The more abruptly kinetic energy is lost, the more likely injury or rebound occurs. Thus, **absorbing force requires gradually decelerating a moving mass by utilization of smaller forces over a longer period of time**. Stability is greater when the object receives the force closer to the center of gravity.

Striking resistive surfaces - the force of impact per unit area decreases when the moving object's area of surface making contact increases and the surface area that the object strikes increases.

Striking non-resistive surfaces - the force of impact decreases if the moving object's area of surface making contact decreases because it is more likely to penetrate.

The more time and distance that motion stops for a moving object to strike any surface, the more gradually the surface absorbs the force of impact, and the reaction forces acting upon the moving object decrease.

Equilibrium returns easily when the moving body (striking a resistive surface) aligns the center of gravity more vertically over the base of support.

Angular force against a body decreases when the distance between a contacting object and the body decreases and the contact occurs closer to the center of gravity. Also, widening the base of support in the direction of the moving object increases stability.

CONCEPT OF LEVERAGE APPLIED TO MOVEMENT

First-class lever - the axis is between the points of application of the force and the resistance.

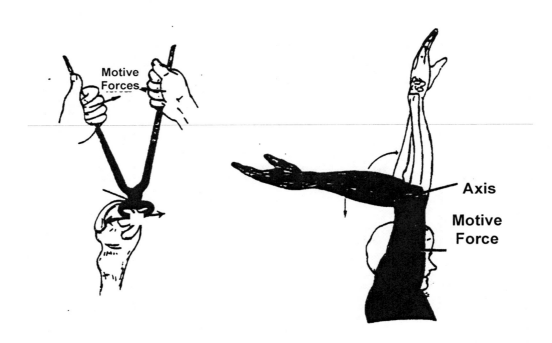

Second-class lever - the force arm is longer than the resistance arm (operator applies resistance between the axis and the point of application of force).

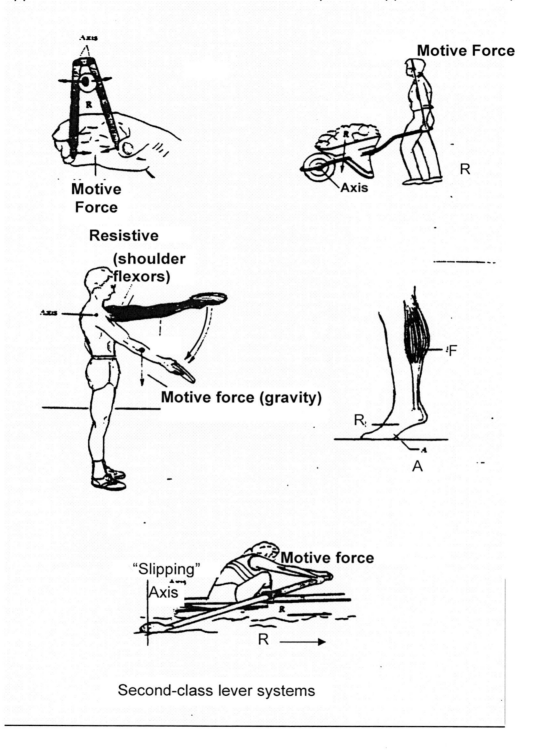

Second-class lever systems

Third-class lever - the force works at a point between the axis and the resistance (resistance arm is always longer than the force arm).

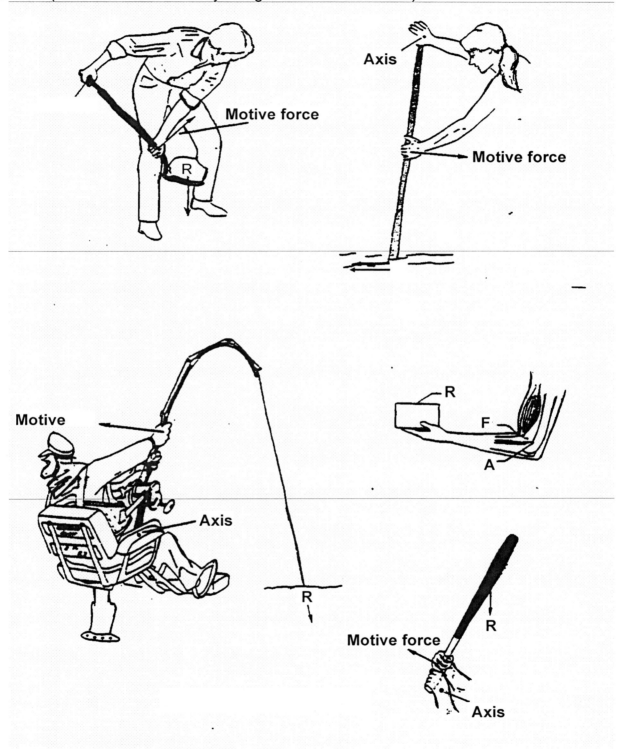

Muscle force is applied where muscles insert on bones.

With a few exceptions, the body consists primarily of third-class levers, with bones functioning as the levers and contracting innervated muscles acting as the fulcrums or by gravity acting on various body masses. As a result, the human body favors speed and range of motion over force.

Because most human body levers are long, their distal ends can move rapidly. Thus, the body is capable of swift, wide movements at the expense of abundant muscle force.

The human body easily performs tasks involving rapid movement with light objects. Very heavy tasks require a device for the body to secure an advantage of force.

Sports instruments increase body levers, thereby increasing the speed of an object's imparting force. However, the use of sports instruments requires more muscle force.

The body's leverage rarely includes one part of the body (a simple, singular lever). Movement of the body is an outcome of a system of levers operating together. However, levers do function in sequence when the force produced by the system of levers is dependent on the speed at the extremity. Many levers function simultaneously for a heavy task (e.g. pushing).

MECHANICAL PRINCIPLES OF MOTION APPLIED TO PHYSICAL EDUCATION ACTIVITIES

1. **Inertia** - tendency of a body or object to remain in its present state of motion; an object will stay in a prescribed straight path and will move at its given speed unless some force acts to change it.

2. **Projecting objects for vertical distance** - the forces of gravity and air resistance prevent vertically projected objects from continuing at their initial velocities. The downward, resistive force of gravity slows a projectile directed upward until it halts (at the peak of vertical path). At this point, the downward force of gravity becomes an incentive force that increases the speed of the object until it confronts another force (the earth or other external object) that slows the object until it stops. When the object stops ascending and begins to descend, gravity alters the object's direction of motion. Air resistance (of still air) always opposes the object's motion. Therefore, an ascending object's air resistance is downward and a descending object's air resistance is upward. An increase in velocity increases air-drag force that decreases the magnitude of the drag as the object moves upward, slowing in velocity. The magnitude of the drag increases as the object moves faster and faster downward. Moreover, the direction and magnitude of the object's acceleration, due to the force of gravity, are constant while direction and magnitude of changes, due to air resistance, are dependent on the object's speed and direction.

An object travels the highest when projected with the greatest velocity, and the object's weight affects neither gravity's upward deceleration nor its downward acceleration. The object's weight, however, is a factor in calculating the net force acting on the object's vertical movement through the air.

- **Projecting the body for vertical distance** - for these activities (e.g. vertical leaping), the height of reach of the hand from the ground is the significant factor. The following three factors determine the body's reach height: 1) the center of gravity's vertical velocity, 2) the center of gravity's height from the ground at takeoff, and 3) the vertical distance of the fingertips relative to the center of gravity at the peak of the jump.

- **Projecting for vertical distance with a horizontal component** - for these activities (e.g. high jumping), a running approach to the point of takeoff produces some horizontal velocity even with a 100% vertical takeoff.

- **Projecting for horizontal distance** - a body will continue to travel horizontally until an external force, usually the ground, halts it. Gravity stops vertical movement while ground friction eventually stops horizontal velocity, preventing any additional horizontal distance. "Air time" increases when the initial upward vertical velocity component is greater. There is a tradeoff between maximum "air time" (determined by vertical velocity) and maximum horizontal distance (determined by horizontal velocity).

- **Horizontal projections where takeoff and landing heights are equal** - maximum horizontal distance occurs when the projection angle is 45-degrees.

- **Horizontal projections where takeoff and landing heights are uneven** – the height of an object's center of gravity depends on a performer's height and his/her location in relation to the ground upon release or impact of the object. The greater the object's travel time forward, the farther the object's distance before landing. Hence, a taller performer has an automatic advantage over a shorter performer who throws with the same projection velocity. In addition, the greater the difference between takeoff and landing heights, the smaller the optimum angle of release - given equal projection velocities.

Projecting objects for accuracy:

- **Vertical plane targets** - accuracy is easiest when using a trajectory that is perpendicular to the target as it coincides with the target face. As projection distance increases, a more curved parabolic path is required.

- **Horizontal plane targets** - the more vertically the projectile arrives at the target (as close to 90 degrees as possible), the greater the likelihood of successfully hitting the target and preventing the object from rolling or sliding away from the target area.

Projecting the body for accuracy - for moving or positioning the body (or its segments) to achieve an ideal/model performance by body maneuvers, the performer projects his body's center of gravity to an imaginary target point in space.

Projecting objects for accuracy when speed may enhance the performance - the performer must increase the angle of projection for slower projection speeds (must consider participant's height).

- **Acceleration** - the movement response (acceleration) of a system depends not only on the net external force applied, but also depends on the resistance to movement change (inertia).

If an object's acceleration is proportional to the applied force, greater force produces greater acceleration. An object's acceleration is inversely proportional to its mass (the greater the mass, the less the acceleration).

- **Angular acceleration** (rate that an object's angular speed or direction changes) - angular acceleration is great when there is a large change in angular velocity in a short amount of time. A rigid body (or segment) encounters angular acceleration or deceleration only when a net external torque is applied. When torque stops, the body reaches and maintains a new velocity until another torque occurs. Acceleration is always in the direction of the acting torque, and the greater the torque, the greater the angular acceleration.

- **Linear acceleration** (time rate of change in velocity) - an object's magnitude of acceleration is significant if there is a large change of velocity in a small amount of time. When the same velocity changes over a longer period of time, acceleration is small. Acceleration occurs only when force is applied. When the force stops, the object/body reaches a new and the object/body continues at the new speed until that a force changes that speed or direction. In addition, the direction of acceleration is the same direction as the applied net force. A large force produces a large acceleration. A small force produces a modest acceleration.

- **Zero/Constant Acceleration** (constant velocity) - there is no change in a system's velocity when the object/body moves at a given velocity and encounters equal, opposing forces. Hence, velocity is constant since no force causes acceleration or deceleration.

- **Acceleration caused by gravity** - a falling object/body continues to accelerate at the rate of 9.8 m/sec. (32 ft/sec.) throughout its fall.

- **Radial acceleration (direction change caused by centripetal force)** - centripetal force is aimed along an illusory line (the circular path) at any instant. Therefore, it is the force responsible for change of direction. The bigger the mass, the greater the centripetal force required. A tighter turn magnifies direction change (radial acceleration), so friction must increase to offset the increased acceleration. Maximum friction (centrifugal force) reduces speed. A combination of the variables mass, radius of curvature, speed of travel, and centripetal force cause radial acceleration.

Action/Reaction - every action has an equal and opposite reaction.

- **Linear motion** - the larger the mass, the more it resists motion change initiated by an outside force.

Body segments exert forces against surfaces they contact. These forces and the reaction of the surfaces result in body movement. For example, a runner propels himself forward by exerting a force on the ground (as long as the surface has sufficient friction and resistance to slipping). The force of the contact of the runner's foot with the ground and the equal and opposite reaction of the ground produces movement. A canoe paddler or swimmer exerts a backward force by pushing the water backwards, causing a specific velocity that is dependent on the stroke's force - as well as the equal and opposite force made by the water pushing forward against the canoe paddle or arm moving the canoe or swimmer forward.

Every torque (angular motion) exerted by one body/object on another has another torque equal in magnitude and opposite direction exerted by the second body/object on the first. Changing angular momentum requires a force that is equal and opposite to the change in momentum.

Performing actions in a standing position requires the counter pressure of the ground against the feet for accurate movement of one or more parts of the body.

SKILL 3.4   *Apply movement concepts and biomechanical principles to the learning and development of new skills.*

SEE Previous Skill

SKILL 3.5   *Analyze various movement patterns for effectiveness.*

In all physical activity or training, there are certain fundamental movement skills that involve patterns necessary for the development of the body. We define them as the foundation movements or precursor patterns to the more specialized complex skills that are useful in all types of sports, dance, and play.

Fundamental movement skills form an indispensable part of all physical activity and physical education. Such basic movement skills are extremely important for children in their early years. These particular skills include running, stopping, changing direction, starting, hopping, skipping, and rolling.

These fundamental movement skills play an important role in the physical well-being of all growing children and are important for adults as well. These skills create the framework of every physical activity and sport.

Physical education instructors should be able to identify mature and immature motor patterns. For example, when observing an overhand throw, there are certain universal characteristics of immature throwing patterns. These include stepping with the foot on the same side of the body as the throwing arm, using only the elbow to propel the object, and facing the target throughout the throwing process. Conversely, characteristics of a mature overhand throwing pattern include leading with the foot opposite the throwing hand, using the entire body and arm to propel the ball, and starting the throwing motion facing perpendicular to the target.

COMPETENCY 4.0   *UNDERSTAND METHODS FOR INTEGRATING LOCOMOTOR, NONLOCOMOTOR, MANIPULATIVE AND RHYTHMIC MOVEMENTS INTO SKILLED COMBINATIONS*

SKILL 4.1   *Demonstrate knowledge of techniques and motor patterns for throwing, catching, dribbling, kicking and striking skills and combinations of manipulative skills in game-like contexts.*

Sequential Development = striking, throwing, kicking, ball rolling, volleying, bouncing, catching, and trapping.

- **Activities to develop striking** begin with the striking of stationary objects by a participant in a stationary position. Next, the person remains still while trying to strike a moving object. Then, both the object and the participant are in motion as the participant attempts to strike the moving object.

- **Activities to develop throwing** include throwing yarn/foam balls against a wall, then at a big target, and finally at targets decreasing in size.

- **Activities to develop kicking** include alternating feet to kick balloons/beach balls, then kicking them under and over ropes. Change the type of ball as proficiency develops.

- **Activities to develop ball rolling** include rolling different size balls to a wall, then to targets decreasing in size.

- **Activities to develop volleying** include using a large balloon and, first, hitting it with both hands, then one hand (alternating hands), and then using different parts of the body. Change the object as students progress (balloon, to beach ball, to foam ball, etc.)

- **Activities to develop bouncing** include starting with large balls and, first, using both hands to bounce and then using one hand (alternate hands).

- **Activities to develop catching** include using various objects (balloons, beanbags, balls, etc.) to catch and, first, catching the object the participant has thrown him/herself, then catching objects someone else threw, and finally increasing the distance between the catcher and the thrower.

- **Activities to develop trapping** include trapping slow and fast rolling balls; trapping balls (or other objects such as beanbags) that are lightly thrown at waist, chest, and stomach levels; trapping different size balls.

ANALYSIS OF BASIC MOVEMENT PATTERNS: OVERHAND THROW, UNDERHAND THROW, KICK

Overhand Throw

The overhand throw consists of a sequence of four movements: a stride, hip rotation, trunk rotation, and forward arm movement. The thrower should align his body sideways to the target (with opposite shoulder pointing towards the target). The overhand throw begins with a step or stride with the opposite foot (i.e. left foot for a right-handed thrower). As the stride foot contacts the ground, the pivot foot braces against the ground and provides stability for the subsequent movements. Hip rotation is the natural turning of the hips toward the target. Trunk rotation follows hip rotation. The hips should rotate before the trunk because the stretching of the torso muscles allows for stronger muscle contraction during trunk rotation. Following trunk rotation, the arm moves forward in two phases. In the first phase the elbow is bent. In the second phase, the elbow joint straightens and the thrower releases the ball.

Development of the overhand throwing motion in children occurs in three stages: elementary, mature, and advanced. In the elementary stage, the child throws mainly with the arm and does not incorporate the other body movements. The signature characteristic of this stage is striding with the foot on the same side of the body as the throwing arm (i.e. placing the right foot in front when throwing with the right hand). In the mature stage, the thrower brings the arm backward in preparation for the throw. Use of body rotation is still limited. Children in the advanced stage incorporate all the elements of the overhand throw. The thrower displays an obvious stride and body rotation.

Underhand Throw

The thrower places the object in the dominant hand. When drawing the arm back the triceps straighten the elbow and, depending on the amount of power behind the throw, the shoulder extends or hyperextends using the posterior deltoid, latissimus dorsi, and the teres major. At the time of drawback, the thrower takes a step forward with the leg opposite of the throwing arm. When coming back down, the thrower moves the shoulder muscles (primarily the anterior deltoid) into flexion. When the object in hand moves in front of the body, the thrower releases the ball. The wrist may be firm or slightly flexed. The thrower releases the object shortly after the planting the foot and the biceps muscle contracts, moving the elbow into flexion during follow through.

Kick

In executing a kick, the object needs to be in front of the body and in front of the dominant leg. The kicker steps and plants with the opposite leg while drawing the kicking leg back. During draw back, the hamstring muscle group flexes the knee. When the kicker plants the opposite foot, the hips swing forward for power and the knee moves into extension using the quadriceps muscle group. The contact point is approximately even with the plant foot and a comfortable follow through completes the action.

COMBINATION OF SKILLS

Locomotor skills are movements that take an individual from one place to another. Walking and running are the simplest examples of locomotor skills. Skipping, jumping, leaping, hopping, and sliding are other locomotor skills that physical educators teach their students.

Trainers adopt various strategies to incorporate the locomotor, nonlocomotor, and object control skills into their workout schedule. These skills are very effective in making students stronger and healthier.

Initially, instructors try to combine those locomotor skills into their training schedule in an easy-to-follow manner. Combining running and sliding or running and jumping will play a huge part in making children understand the fundamentals of locomotor skills.

Once they become familiar with the procedure, physical educators can show students how to balance and transfer weight through the use various locomotor skills. However, the teacher should demonstrate how to control locomotor movements at proper speeds and forces. Shot put, tumbling, and give-and-go are some examples of how to teach students the nuances of locomotor skills.

We can apply the same strategies to nonlocomotor skill instruction. First, the students should learn the basics of every skill from simple nonlocomotive movements such as 360-degree turns and lifting weights, to complex movements like tug-of-war and scissors kicks. It is important for the instructor to maintain a smooth transition. This makes comprehension as unproblematic as possible. Locomotor and nonlocomotor skills make children agile and physically fit. It is the job of a physical educator to make learning and practicing the skills more enjoyable and entertaining.

SKILL 4.2   *Select appropriate activities, materials, and equipment for development of combinations and sequences of locomotor, nonlocomotor, manipulative, and rhythmic movement skills.*

TECHNIQUES TO ENHANCE SKILL PERFORMANCE AND STRATEGY

Playing complex games requires the combination of skills, the use of skills in more complex ways, and relation to others in both offensive and defensive settings. Sequentially progressive activities allow students to acquire the psychomotor, cognitive, and affective skills necessary for participation in complex games. There are four stages of complex skill development.

Stage One concerns **controlling an object.** For striking or throwing objects, students can consistently practice sending objects to a specified location, developing control of the force that accomplishes the objective. For catching or collecting, students can practice control by securing possession of an object from any direction, level, or speed. For carrying and propelling, students can practice maintaining control of an object by moving in different directions and at different paces. Developing control begins with the completion of easily attainable objectives and progresses gradually to more difficult objectives involving movement and different directions, levels, and force.

Stage Two also concerns controlling an object, however, combining skills increases difficulty. Instructors should stress rules to constrain the execution of skills. Drills such as passing and dribbling belong in stage two.

Stage Three focuses on **offense and defense**, utilizing correct skill performance. Students should now be able to control objects; therefore, the focus shifts to obtaining and maintaining possession, as well as offensive and defensive strategies in the midst of opponents. Net activities and keep-away games help develop this stage. In addition, instructors can add more offensive and defensive players, boundaries, scorekeeping, and conduct rules. Students develop by adjusting their responses with each element introduced to the activity.

Stage Four involves **complex activity.** Students execute the complete activity and modified activities that allow participation by all students. Continuous play is important; thus, the instructor may have to modify rules or a part of the activity to keep the flow of the game constant (e.g. eliminating free throws/kicks, substituting volleyball serve with a throw, initiating play out-of-bounds).

SPORTS AND GAMES

All sports require the application of motor skills in complex forms. For example, the motor skills required to play tennis include running, jumping, striking, and volleying. In addition, tennis players must combine these skills. For example, a player often has to strike the ball while running or jumping. To play any sport at a high level, athletes must master many motor skills and develop the ability to combine those skills to master sport-specific movements.

DANCE CONCEPTS AND FORMS

Students of dance acquire many skills during their course of study. The student identifies and demonstrates movement elements in dance performance and uses correct body alignment, strength, flexibility, and stamina (for more demanding performances). Crucial to any form of dance is the concept of coordination in the performance of technical movements. Technical movements must look as though they are easy to perform. The dancer must perform technical dance skills with artistic expression including musicality and rhythm. As the student progresses, he or she will perform more extended movement sequences and rhythmic patterns. The student will then have enough experience to introduce his or her own stylistic nuance into the performance. The student will also be able to use improvisation to solve movement problems and adjust choices based on the movement responses of other dancers in the ensemble. Through continued experience, he or she will become a skillful, seasoned dancer whose technique and ability will transcend any form of dance.

Instructors can create rhythmic activities by putting on music with a strong beat and asking students to dance to the beat. Tell the students to listen to the beat and move accordingly (e.g. stomping their feet or clapping their hands in time with the beat). It's important for children to learn to move to various sounds and use their bodies to mimic the beat. Another idea is to have the students take turns beating on a coffee can while trying to keep movements in sync with the rhythm. In more structured dance forms, technique or skill comes into play. For instance, in ballet, dancers must have good flexibility, body control, and coordination. Ballet dancers must also have a sense of rhythm, an understanding of music, good turnout and alignment, and a sense of balance and counterbalance. These skills take many years to acquire and, once acquired, take many more years to master and maintain. Ballet dancing may express a mood, tell a story, or simply reflect a piece of music and is the most classical of all dance forms. Other types of music may have similar requirements in terms of a sense of musicality and rhythm. For example, tap dance requires a greater degree of footwork and modern is comparable to ballet, but more flowing and less rigid.

GYMNASTIC MOVEMENTS – STUNTS, TUMBLING, APPARATUS WORK, AND FLOOR EXERCISE

Gymnastics is a sport involving the performance of sequences of movements requiring physical strength, flexibility, and kinesthetic awareness (e.g. handsprings, handstands, and forward rolls). Its roots lie in the fitness and beauty practices of ancient Greeks, including skills for mounting and dismounting a horse and circus performance skills. In ancient times the term implied exercise taken by men in a gymnasium, a venue for intellectual and physical education. It is often considered a dangerous sport, as the difficult acrobatic maneuvers often performed on equipment high above the ground puts the athlete at risk of serious injury.

Proper stretching and strength building exercises are necessary for gymnastics. A useful, brief warm-up can consist of push-ups, sit-ups, and flexibility exercises for hamstrings, back, ankles, neck, wrists, and shoulders. An aerial is one example of a stunt (i.e. difficult physical feat) in which the gymnast turns completely over in the air without touching the apparatus with his or her hands. Floor exercise and tumbling can include somersaults, backward and frontward rolls, cartwheels, forward straddle rolls, back tucks, back handsprings, and handstands. Gymnasts perform apparatus work on the vaulting horse, balance beam, and uneven bars. A strong run, dynamism, power, and precision in the rotations are characteristics of an efficient vault. The main characteristics for the beam are a well-developed sense of balance and great power of concentration. The uneven bars demand strength as well as concentration, courage, coordination, precision, and split-second timing.

RHYTHMIC GYMNASTICS AND EDUCATIONAL GYMNASTICS

Rhythmic gymnastics is a sport, which combines dance and gymnastics with the use of balls, hoops, ribbons, ropes, and clubs. Gymnasts perform on a carpet to music either individually or in a group of five. In competition, gymnasts perform leaps, pivots, balances, and other elements to demonstrate flexibility and coordination. The gymnast must completely integrate the apparatus into the routine and perform specific moves with each apparatus. Individual routines last from 1 minute and 15 seconds to 1 minute and 30 seconds, while group routines last from 2 minutes 15 seconds to 2 minutes and 30 seconds. The main difference between rhythmic and artistic gymnastics is that rhythmic gymnasts cannot incorporate acrobatic skill. In fact, judges penalize gymnasts for incorporating acrobatic skill into their routines. However, gymnasts may perform pre-acrobatic elements such as forward and backward shoulder rolls, fish-flops, and tah-dahs. In addition, the new Code of Points permits walkovers and cartwheels. Originality and risk are integral parts of this sport, and no two routines are ever the same.

In educational gymnastics, students learn to use and manage their bodies in safe, efficient and creative ways. Educational gymnastics can utilize certain fixed equipment such as mats, bars, ropes, and boxes and is also know as "body management" because the activities provide opportunities for students to learn to manage their own bodies. Instead of a series of gymnastics stunts, they select, refine and perform the six Basic Movement Patterns of Landings, Locomotions, Statics, Rotations, Swings, and Springs in a variety of contexts and environments. Emphasis is on challenges and problem solving. Instructors use the Movement Variables of Body, Space, Effort, and Relationships to design movement-learning experiences. Students work individually, in pairs, and in groups to create movement sequences and structures.

Elaborate facilities are not required in this approach. In fact, many good educational gymnastics programs take place out-of-doors in natural settings. While large-scale gymnastics equipment is not essential for providing students with quality movement-learning experiences, such equipment is certainly advantageous. Another advantage of educational gymnastics is that it provides for the development of the upper body. It is much easier and more common to develop strength in the lower body than in the upper body. Many everyday events such as walking and running and jumping enhance lower body strength. Most team games and sports emphasize lower body strength and tend to neglect upper body development. Gymnastics also help to build overall muscular strength and flexibility. There is also equal development of both left and right sides of the body because most gymnastics activities involve simultaneous use of both arms (e.g. rolls, hangs, swings, supports) or both legs (e.g. springs, tumbling). In contrast, many game activities that involve the use of an implement (e.g., bat, racquet, stick) or object (e.g., beanbag, ball, Frisbee) tend to favor the development of one side of the body more than the other does.

Finally, if educational gymnastics experiences are to be truly "educational," then we must ask in what ways are they educational? In short, these experiences are educational because they start with the needs of students. The instructor presents the students with movement problems , which the students must solve, asks questions to gain the cognitive involvement of students, offers various solutions in the form of movement sequences, and guides students to reflect upon and synthesize their experiences. Students gain knowledge and understandings of the mechanical principles associated with the Basic Movement Patterns of gymnastics and they increase their ability to apply these principles.

SKILL 4.3   Identify techniques for assessing student performance on combinations and sequences of locomotor, nonlocomotor, manipulative, and rhythmic movement skills.

SKILL ASSESSMENT IN THE EVALUATION OF STUDENT PERFORMANCE

A. General Skills:

1. **Iowa Brace Test** – measures motor educability.

2. **AAHPERD Youth Fitness Test** – measures motor capacity.

3. **AAHPERD Health Related Physical Fitness Test** – measures physical capacity.

4. **McCloy's General Motor Ability and Capacity Test** – measures motor ability and motor efficiency.

5. **Rodgers Strength Test** – measures muscular strength.

6. **Texas PE Test** – measures motor ability.

7. **Skills tests for accuracy** – involve kicking, throwing, or striking an object toward a goal; activities include volleyball serves, basketball free throws, badminton short serves, and basketball passing (e.g. AAHPERD Basketball Passing Test for Accuracy).

8. **Skills test for total bodily movement** – requires performing a test course with movements similar to the sport (e.g. AAHPERD Basketball Control Test).

9. **Wall Volley Test** - measures the number of consecutive successful time/trials to pass, kick, throw, or strike an object at a wall in a given time (e.g. AAHPERD Basketball Passing Test).

10. **Skills Tests for Power or Distance** - involve kicks, throws, or strokes to measure the ability to kick, throw, or strike an object (e.g. Badminton Drive for Distance, Cornish Handball Power Test).

11. **Combination Tests** - composed of previous groupings to assess speed and accuracy.

B. Teacher Ratings: instructors create a numerical scale from one to five and rank performance based on specific, observable movements. An example is evaluating the use of space, use of focus, and variety of movements in a creative movement class.

C. Student Progress: score improvements (e.g. archery, badminton) and charting (e.g. basketball shots missed).

Instructors can administer skills tests for specific sports in one of two ways. First, rate individual performance based on a specified number of trials. Alternatively, evaluate skills using norm-referenced scales for a specific grade level.

Two problems with skill tests are that they take too much time to administer and the reliability is suspect.

COMPETENCY 5.0   **UNDERSTAND TECHNIQUES, SKILLS, STRATEGIES, BASIC RULES, ETIQUETTE AND SAFETY PRACTICES FOR INDIVIDUAL AND GROUP SPORTS**

SKILL 5.1   Demonstrate an understanding of critical elements, skill progressions, strategies, and types and uses of equipment for individual and group sports.

TEAM PASSING SPORTS

Basketball – The fundamental skills of basketball include passing, dribbling, and shooting. As students' skills improve, they may begin to specialize in playing a specific position (point guard, shooting guard, small forward, power forward or center).

Touch/Flag Football – Skills that students will practice include running and passing – tackling is not relevant in touch or flag football situations. As students improve, they may begin to specialize in playing specific positions (e.g. quarterbacks or receivers). They may also become more involved in the study and implementation of strategy.

The main goal of offensive strategy in football is to move closer to the opposing team's end zone, to the point where the ball is close enough to score either a touchdown or a field goal. The aim of defensive strategies is to prevent this same movement towards the end zone by the opposition. Both offensive and defensive strategies make important use of concepts of time management and the possibility of "running out the clock". Formations are central to football strategy, both on offense and on defense, and students should become familiar with simple formations for both.

Lacrosse – Lacrosse players must master the skills of catching and throwing the ball with their sticks and cradling (the motion that allows players to run with the ball in their stick).

Lacrosse strategy has many parallels with other team sports like basketball, soccer, and field hockey. In all of these sports, the team of players has to maneuver to outflank and outsmart their opponents in order to score a goal.

Soccer – Soccer players must master the skills of running, accurate kicking, manipulation of the ball, and footwork that allows the student to maneuver when in motion.

The key to soccer strategy is for students to understand that the goal is to get the ball to the right person's feet – the one who has the most time and space (facing the least pressure) and is in the most advantageous position to score (or make a goal-scoring pass). Broadly, offensive strategy will spread the team out, to allow for coverage of more of the field. Defensive strategy will have the team compress to a compact unit that is able to cover the goal effectively.

Team Handball – Skills that students will learn in a handball class will include catching and accurately throwing the ball, taking steps while bouncing the ball (similar to basketball's dribble), and quick analysis of the playing situation to ascertain who the best target is for a pass.

Strategy in handball centers around staying one step ahead of the opposing team, keeping them guessing, and having multiple contingencies for given situations so that game play doesn't become predictable (and easier to counter). Specific tactics can include types of shots that are harder for the opponent to hit and shots that will put the ball out of play (when it is advantageous to do so).

Ultimate Frisbee – Skills that students must acquire to play ultimate Frisbee proficiently include catching the Frisbee, accurately throwing the Frisbee, and running. Instructors should also emphasize strategic thinking, as there is limited time to select a destination for and execute a throw.

The goal of offensive strategy in ultimate Frisbee is to create open lanes in the field that are free of defenders. Common offensive strategies include the 'vertical stack' and 'horizontal stack' (similar to a spread offense in football). Defensive strategy aims to gain control of the Frisbee and deflect passes made by the opposing team. A basic defensive principle is the 'force', which calls for the defense to cut off the handler's access to half of the field, thereby forcing the offensive player to throw the Frisbee to the other side of the field.

TERMINOLOGY OF VARIOUS TEAM PASSING SPORTS

Basketball Terminology:

- Backcourt players (Guards) – players who set up a team's offensive pattern and bring the ball up the court.

- Backdoor – an offensive maneuver in which a player cuts toward the baseline to the basket, behind the defenders, and receives a ball for a field goal attempt.

- Baseline – the end line of the court.

- Blocking/Boxing out – a term used when a player positions himself under the backboard to prevent an opposing player from achieving a good rebounding position.

- Charging – personal contact by a player with the ball against the body of a defensive opponent.

- Corner players (Forwards) – tall players that make up the sides of the offensive set-up who are responsible for the rebounding and shooting phases of the team's offense.

- Cut – a quick, offensive move by a player attempting to get free for a pass.

- Denial defense – aggressive individual defense to keep an offensive player from receiving a pass.

- Double foul – two opponents committing personal fouls against each other simultaneously.

- Dribble – ball movement by a player in control who throws or taps the ball in the air or onto the floor and then touches it. The dribble ends when the dribbler touches the ball with both hands concurrently, loses control, or permits it to come to rest while in contact with it.

- Drive – an aggressive move by a player with the ball toward the basket.

- Fake (Feint) – using a deceptive move with the ball pulling the defensive player out of position.

- Fast break – quickly moving the ball down court to score before the defense has a chance to set up.

- Field goal – a basket scored from the field.

- Freelance – no structure or set plays in the offense.

- Free throw – the right given a player to score one or two points by unhindered shots for a goal from within the free throw circle and behind the free throw line.

- Give-and-go – a maneuver when the offensive player passes to a teammate and then immediately cuts in toward the basket for a return pass.

- Held ball – occurs when two opponents have one or both hands firmly on the ball and neither can gain possession without undue roughness.

- Inside player (Center, Post, Pivot) – this player is usually the tallest team player who is situated near the basket, around the three-second lane area, and is responsible for rebounding and close-range shooting.

- Jump ball – a method of putting the ball into play by tossing it up between two opponents in the center circle to start the game or any overtime periods.

- Outlet pass – a term used that designates a direct pass from a rebounder to a teammate (the main objective is starting a fast break).

- Overtime period – an additional period of playing time when the score is tied at the end of the regulation game.

- Personal foul – a player foul that involves contact with an opponent while the ball is alive or after the ball is in possession of a player for a throw-in.

- Pick – a special type of screen where a player stands so the defensive player slides to make contact to free an offensive teammate for a shot or drive.

- Pivot – occurs when a player who is holding the ball steps once or more than once in any direction with the same foot while the other foot, called the pivot foot, remains at its point of contact with the floor. Also, another term for the inside player.

- Posting up – a player cutting to the three-second lane area, pausing, and anticipating a pass.

- Rebound – when the ball bounces off the backboard or basket.

- Restraining circles – three circles with a six-foot radius. One is located in the center of the court, and the others are located at each of the free-throw lines.

- Running time – not stopping the clock for fouls or violations.

- Screen – an offensive maneuver positioning a player between the defender and a teammate to free the teammate for an uncontested shot.

- Switching – defensive guards reversing their guarding assignments.

- Technical foul – a non-contact foul by a player, team, or coach for unsportsmanlike behavior or failing to abide by rules regarding submission of lineups, uniform numbering, and substitution procedures.

- Telegraphing a pass – a look or signal to indicate where the ball is going to be passed.

- Throw-in – a method of putting the ball in play from out-of-bounds.

- Traveling – illegal movement, in any direction, of a player in possession of the ball within bounds. Moving with the ball without dribbling.

- Violation – an infraction of the rules resulting in a throw-in from out-of-bounds.

Soccer Terminology:

- Center – passing from the outside of the field near the sideline into the center.

- Charge – illegal or legal body contact between opponents.

- Chip – lofting the ball into the air using the instep kick technique; contacting the ball very low causing it to loft quickly with backspin.

- Clear – attempting to move the ball out of danger by playing the ball a great distance.

- Corner kick – a direct free kick from the corner arc awarded to the attacking player when the defending team last played the ball over their own end line.

- Cross – a pass from the outside of the field near the end line to a position in front of the goal.

- Dead ball situation – the organized restarting of the game after stopping play.

- Direct free kick – a free kick whereby the kicker may score immediately from that initial contact.

- Dribble – the technique of a player self-propelling the ball with the foot in order to maintain control of the ball while moving from one spot to another.

- Drop ball – the method used to restart the game after temporary suspension of play when the ball is still in play.

- Goal area – the rectangular area in front of the goal where the ball is placed for a goal kick.

- Half volley – contacting the ball just as it hits the ground after being airborne.

- Head – playing the ball with the head.

- Indirect free kick – a free kick from which a player, other than the kicker, must contact the ball before a goal can be scored.

- Kickoff – the free kick starting play at the beginning of the game, after each period, or after a score.

- Obstruction – illegally using the body to shield an opponent from reaching the ball.

- One-touch – immediately passing or shooting a received ball without stopping it.

- Penalty area – the large rectangular area in front of the goal where the goalkeeper may use the hands to play the ball.

- Penalty kick – a direct free kick awarded in the penalty area against the defending team for a Direct Free Kick foul.

- Settle – taking a ball out of the air and settling it on the ground so that it is rolling and no longer bouncing.

- Square pass – a pass directed toward the side of a player.

- Tackle – a technique to take the ball away from the opponents.

- Through pass – a pass penetrating between and past the defenders.

- Throw-in – the technique to restart the game when the ball goes out of play over the sideline.

- Touchline – the side line of the field.

- Trap – the technique used for receiving the ball and bringing it under control.

- Two-touch- receiving – trapping and immediately re-passing the ball.

OVERVIEW OF NET/WALL SPORTS

Badminton – Students in a badminton class will have to master the strokes as basic skills and should learn at least some of them by name (e.g. types of serves, net shot, net kills, drive, push, lift). Students should also know which strokes are appropriate from which areas of the court.

Handball – Skills that students will learn in a handball class will include catching and accurately throwing the ball, taking steps while bouncing it (similar to basketball's dribble), and quick analysis of the playing situation to determine who the best target is for a pass.

Strategy in handball centers on staying one step ahead of the opposing team. Keep them guessing and have multiple contingencies for given situations, so that game play doesn't become predictable (and easier to counter). Specific tactics can include types of shots that are harder for the opponent to hit, and shots that will put the ball out of play (when it is advantageous to do so).

Pickleball – Skills that students will learn in pickleball classes include manipulation of the ball with the racket and the variety of strokes.

Pickleball strategy is similar to tennis. Students should learn to vary their strokes to keep their opponents guessing, with the goal of reaching the frontcourt in a net volley position first. This places the students in the best position to win the point.

Table Tennis (Ping Pong) – Skills that students will study when learning table tennis include the variety of grips (e.g. penhold, shakehand, V-grip), and the various types of offensive and defensive strokes. Students will also learn to gauge the force needed to manipulate the ball properly.

Strategies for success in table tennis involve manipulating and minimizing the opponent's ability to return a shot – this includes learning to hit to the opponent's weak side, putting a spin on the ball so as to make its movement less predictable, and setting the opponent up to receive a shot that he cannot return.

Tennis – Skills that students will learn when studying tennis include the proper grips of the racket and stroke techniques, which they should know by name (e.g. flat serve, topspin serve, twist serve, forehand, backhand, volley, overhead).

Volleyball – Students studying volleyball should master six basic skills: the serve, pass, set, attack, block, and dig. Each of these skills comprises a number of specific techniques that are standard volleyball practice.

TERMINOLOGY OF VARIOUS NET/WALL SPORTS

Badminton Terminology:

- Alley – the area on each side of the court used for doubles that is 1.5 feet wide.

- Around the head stroke – an overhead stroke used to hit a forehand-like overhead stroke that is on the backhand side of the body.

- Back alley – the area between the baseline and the doubles long service line.

- Backcourt – the back third of the court.

- Backhand – a stroke made on the non-racket side of the body.

- Baseline – the back boundary line of the court.

- Bird – another name for the shuttlecock/shuttle.

- Block – a soft shot used mainly to defend a smash; intercepting opponent's smash and returning it back over the net.

- Carry/Throw – a call when the shuttle remains on the racket during a stroke. It is legal if the racket follows the intended line of flight.

- Centerline – the mid-line separating the service courts.

- Clear – a high shot that goes over the opponent's head and lands close to the baseline.

- Combination alignment – partners playing both up-and-back and side-by-side during doubles games and/or volleys.

- Crosscourt – a diagonal shot hit into the opposite court.

- Defense – the team or player hitting the shuttle upwards.

- Double hit – an illegal shot where the player contacts the shuttle twice with the racket in one swing.

- Doubles service court – the short, wide area to which the server must serve in doubles play.

- Down the line shot – a straight-ahead shot (usually down the sideline).

- Drive – a hard, driven shot traveling parallel to the floor (clears net but does not have enough height for opponent to smash).

- Drop – a shot just clearing the net and then falling close to it.

- Face – the racket's string area.

- Fault – an infraction of the rules resulting in loss of serve or a point awarded to the server.

- First serve – a term used in doubles play to indicate that the server is the "first server" during an inning.

- Foot fault – Illegal movement/position of the feet by either the server or receiver.

- Forecourt – the front area of the court (between the net and the short service line).

- Forehand – a stroke made on the racket side of the body.

- Game point – the point, if won, that allows the server to win the game.

- Hand in – a term indicating that the server retains the serve.

- Hand out – the term used in doubles to denote that one player has lost the service.

- Home base – a center court position where a player can best play any shot hit by an opponent.

- Inning – the period a player or team holds service.

- Let – stopping the point because of some type of outside interference. Players replay the point.

- Lifting the shuttle – stroking the shuttle underhanded and hitting it upward.

- Long serve – a high, deep serve landing near the long service line in doubles or the back boundary line in singles.

- Love – the term used to indicate a zero score.

- Match – a series of games. Winning two out of three games wins the match.

- Match point – the point, if won by the server, which makes that person the winner of the match.

- Midcourt – the middle-third of the court (between short service line and long service line for doubles).

- Net shot – a shot taken near the net.

- Non-racket side – the opposite side of the hand holding the racket.

- Offense – the team or player that is stroking the shuttle downward.

- Overhead – a motion used to strike the shuttle when it is above the head.

- Racket foot or leg – the foot or leg on the same side as the hand holding the racket.

- Ready position – the position a player assumes to be ready to move in any direction.

- Receiver – the player to whom the shuttle is served.

- Second serve – in doubles, the term indicates that one partner has lost the serve, and the other partner is now serving.

- Server – the player putting the shuttle into play.

- Setting – choosing the amount of additional points to play when certain tie scores are reached.

- Short-serve – a serve barely clearing the net and landing just beyond the short service line.

- Shuttlecock/Shuttle – the feathered, plastic or nylon object that players volley back and forth over the net.

- Side Alley – see alley.

- Smash – an overhead stroke hit downward with great velocity and angle.

- "T" – the intersection of the centerline and the short service line.

- Underhand – an upward stroke to hit the shuttle when it has fallen below shoulder level.

- Unsight – illegal position taken by the server's partner so the receiver cannot see the shuttle.

- Up-and-back – an offensive alignment used in doubles. The "up" player is responsible for the forecourt and the "back" player is responsible for both.

Racquetball/Handball Terminology:

- Ace – a serve that completely eludes the receiver.

- Back-wall shot – a shot made from a rebound off the back wall.

- Box – see service box.

- Ceiling shot – a shot that first strikes the ceiling, then the front wall.

- Crotch – the junction of any two playing surfaces, as between the floor and any wall.

- Crotch shot – a ball that simultaneously strikes the front wall and floor (not good).

- Cut throat – a three-man game in which the server plays against the other two players. Each player keeps an individual score.

- Drive shot – a power shot against the front wall rebounding in a fast, low, and straight line.

- Fault – an illegally served ball.

- Handout – retiring the server who fails to serve legally or when the serving team fails to return a ball that is in play.

- Hinder – interference or obstruction of the flight of the ball during play.

- Kill – a ball rebounded off the front wall so close to the floor that it is impossible to return.

- Passing shot – a shot placed out of an opponent's reach on either side.

- Rally – continuous play of the ball by opponents.

- Receiving line – the broken line parallel to the short line on a racquetball court.

- Run-around shot – a ball striking one sidewall, the rear wall, and the other sidewall.

- Safety zone – a five-foot area bounded by the back edge of the short line and receiving line that is only observed during the serve in racquetball.

- Screen – a hinder due to obstruction of the opponent's vision.

- Server – person in the "hand-in" position and eligible to serve.

- Service box – the service zone bounded by the sidewall and a parallel line 18 inches away; denotes where server's partner must stand in doubles during the serve.

- Service court – the area where the ball must land when it is returned from the front wall on the serve.

- Service line – the line that is parallel to and five feet in front of the short line.

- Service zone – the area to which the server must serve the ball.

- Short line – the line on the floor parallel to front wall and equidistant from front and back wall. The serve must go over this line when returning from the front wall.

- Shoot – attempt kill shots.

- Side out – loss of serve.

- Thong – the strap on the bottom handle of the racquetball racquet that is worn around the player's wrist.

- Volley – returning the ball to the front wall before it bounces on the floor.

- Z-ball – defensive shot that strikes the front wall, a sidewall, and then the opposite sidewall.

Tennis Terminology:

- Ace – serving a ball untouched by the opponent's racket.

- Advantage (Ad) – a scoring term. The next point won after the score is "deuce."

- Alley – the 4.5-foot strip on either side of the singles court used to enlarge the court for doubles.

- Approach shot – a shot hit inside the baseline while approaching the net.

- Backcourt – the area between the service line and the baseline.

- Backhand – strokes hit on the left side of a right-handed player.

- Backspin – spin placed on a ball that causes the ball to bounce back toward the hitter.

- Back swing – the beginning of all groundstrokes and service motion requiring a back swing to gather energy for the forward swing.

- Baseline – the end line of a tennis court.

- Break – winning a game in when the opponent serves.

- Center mark – a short mark bisecting the baseline.

- Center service line – the perpendicular line to the net dividing the two service courts in halves.

- Center strap – the strap at the center of the net anchored to the court to facilitate a constant 3-foot height for the net at its center.

- Center stripe – same as the center service line.

- Chip – a short chopping motion of the racket against the back and bottom side of the ball imparting backspin.

- Chop – placing backspin on the ball with a short, high-to-low forward swing.

- Cross-court – a shot hit diagonally from one corner of the court over the net into the opposite corner of the court.

- Cut off the angle – moving forward quickly against an opponent's cross-court shot, allowing the player to hit the ball near the center of the court rather than near the sidelines.

- Deep (depth) – a shot bouncing near the baseline on groundstrokes and near the service line on serves.

- Default – a player who forfeits his/her position in a tournament by not playing a scheduled match.

- Deuce – a term used when the game score is 40-40.

- Dink – a ball hit very softly and relatively high to ensure its safe landing.

- Double fault – two consecutive out-of-bounds serves on the same point resulting in loss of the point.

- Doubles lines – the outside sidelines on a court used only for doubles.

- Down the line – a shot hit near a sideline traveling close to, and parallel to, the same line from which the shot was initially hit.

- Drive – an offensive shot hit with extra force.

- Drop shot – a groundstroke hit so that it drops just over the net with little or no forward bounce.

- Drop volley – a volley hit in such a manner that it drops just over the net with little or no forward bounce.

- Error – a mistake made by a player during competition.

- Flat shot – a ball hit so there is no rotation or spin when traveling through the air.

- Foot fault – illegal foot movement before service, penalized by losing that particular serve. Common foot faults are stepping on or ahead of the baseline before contacting the ball and running along the baseline before serving.

- Forecourt – the area between the net and the service line.

- Forehand – the stroke hit on the right side of a right-handed player.

- Frame – the rim of the racket head plus the handle of the racket.

- Game – scoring term when a player wins 4 points before an opponent while holding a minimum 2-point lead.

- Grip – the portion of the racket that is grasped in the player's hand.

- Groundstroke – any ball hit after it has bounced.

- Half volley – a ball hit inches away from the court's surface after the ball has bounced.

- Hold serve – winning your own serve. If you lose your own serve, your serve has been "broken."

- Let (ball) – a point replayed because of some kind of interference.

- Let serve – a serve that touches the net tape, falls into the proper square, and is played over.

- Linesman – a match official who calls balls "in" or "out."

- Lob – a ball hit with sufficient height to pass over the out-stretched arm of a net player.

- Lob volley – a shot hit high into the air from a volleying position.

- Love – scoring term that means zero points or games.

- Match – a contest between two or four opponents.

- Match point – the point immediately before the final point of a match.

- Midcourt – the area in front of the baseline or behind the service line of the playing court.

- Netball – a ball that hits the net, falling on the same side as the hitter.

- No man's land – a general area within the baseline and proper net position area. When caught in that area, the player must volley or hit ground strokes near his/her feet.

- Offensive lob – a ball hit just above the racket reach of an opposing net player.

- Open face racket – a racket whose face is moving under the ball. A wide-open racket face is parallel to the court surface.

- Overhead – a shot hit from a position higher than the player's head.

- Over-hitting – hitting shots with too much force; over-hitting usually results in errors.

- Pace – the speed of the ball.

- Passing shot – a shot passing beyond the reach of the net player landing inbounds.

- Poach – to cross over into your partner's territory in doubles in an attempt to intercept the ball.

- Racket face – the racket's hitting surface.

- Racket head – the top portion of the racket frame that includes the strings.

- Rally – opponents hitting balls back and forth across the net.

- Receiver – the player about to return the opponent's serve.

- Server – the player initiating play.

- Service line – the line at the end of the service courts parallel to the net.

- Set – a scoring term meaning the first player to win six games with a minimum two-game lead.

- Set point – the point, if won, which will give the player the set.

- Sidespin – a ball hit rotating on a horizontal plane.

- Signals in doubles – signaling your partner that you are going to poach at the net.

- Singles line – the sideline closest to the center mark that runs the entire length of the court.

- Slice – motion of the racket head going around the side of the ball, producing a horizontal spin on ball.

- Tape – the band of cloth or plastic running across the top of the net.

- Telegraphing the play – indicating the direction of one's intended target before hitting the ball.

- Topspin – forward rotation of the ball.

- Touch – the ability to make delicate, soft shots from several positions on the court.

- Twist – a special rotation applied to the ball during the serve causing the ball to jump to the left (of right-handed server).

- Umpire – the official that calls lines.

- Under spin – a counterclockwise spin placed on the ball (i.e. backspin).

- Volley – hitting the ball in the air before it bounces on the court.

Volleyball Terminology:

- Attack – returning the ball across the net in an attempt to put the opponents at a disadvantage.

- Ball handling – executing any passing fundamental.

- Block – intercepting the ball just before or as it crosses the net.

- Bump – see forearm pass.

- Court coverage – a defensive player's court assignment.

- Dig – an emergency pass usually used to defend a hard-driven attack.

- Dink – a soft shot off the fingertips to lob the ball over a block.

- Double foul – infraction of rules by both teams during the same play.

- Drive – an attacking shot contacted in the center that attempts to hit the ball off the blocker's hands.

- Fault – any infraction of the rules.

- Forearm pass – a pass made off the forearms used to play served balls, hard-driven spikes, or any low ball.

- Free ball – a ball returned by the opponent that is easily handled.

- Frontcourt – the playing area where it is legal to block or attack.

- Held ball – a ball that opponents simultaneously contact and momentarily hold above the net.

- Kill – an attack that the opponents cannot return.

- Lob – a soft attack contacted on the back bottom-quarter of the ball causing an upward trajectory.

- Overhand pass – a pass made by contacting the ball above the head with the fingers.

- Overlap – an illegal foot position when the ball is dead, with an adjacent player putting another out of position.

- Play over – replaying the rally because of a held ball or the official prematurely suspending play. The server re-serves with no point awarded.

- Point – a point is scored when the receiving team fails to return the ball to the opponents' court legally.

- Rotation – clockwise rotation of the players upon gaining the ball from the opponents.

- Serve – putting the ball in play over the net by striking it with the hand.

- Set – placing the ball near the net to facilitate attacking.

- Setter – the player assigned to set the ball.

- Side out – side is out when the serving team fails to win a point or plays the ball illegally.

- Spike – a ball hit with top spin and with a strong downward force into the opponents' court.

- Spiker – the player assigned to attack the ball.

- Spike-roll – an attack that first takes an upward trajectory using the spiking action (with or without jumping).

- Topspin (Overspin) – applying forward spin to the ball during the serve, spike, or spike roll.

OVERVIEW – STRIKING/FIELDING SPORTS

Softball – Skills students in softball classes will acquire include accurate throwing and catching, and the correct way to swing and hit with a softball bat.

Softball is similar in strategy to baseball. Defensive strategy focuses on the pitcher, who is responsible for trying to strike out the team that is at bat. Offensive strategy centers on batting, and attempting to turn batters into runners.

Safety practices in softball are also similar to baseball. Enforcing discipline and maintaining student attentiveness to prevent the chance of injury is of utmost importance. Instructors must also emphasize to the students that they should not swing the bat when other students are in the area.

Equipment required for softball practice includes a softball bat and softball, fielding gloves, appropriate protective gear, and base markers of some sort.

Baseball – Skills that students studying baseball will acquire include accurate throwing and catching, and the correct way to swing and hit with a baseball bat.

Defensive strategy in baseball focuses on the actions of the pitcher, who is responsible for trying to strike out the team that is at bat. Offensive strategy in baseball centers on batting, and attempting to turn batters into runners.

Safety practices in baseball include maintaining discipline among the students, as horseplay and lack of attentiveness can lead to injury (e.g. a ball could hit a student who isn't paying attention). In addition, instructors should remind students the baseball bat is·not a toy, and they should handle it with care and not swing it near other students.

Equipment required for baseball practice includes baseball bats, baseballs, baseball gloves (though for some educational situations, the gloves are not necessary), base markers of some kind, and protective padding for the catcher.

Cricket – Skills that students in cricket class will acquire include accurate throwing and catching, swinging the bat correctly, and the proper form for the execution of an effective pitch.
Unlike baseball and softball, where pitching controls the game, in cricket batting controls the game. Since in cricket the batter can hit in any direction around him, he will focus on weak spots in the opposing team's field deployment, and the defensive strategy of the opposing team will focus on minimizing weak spots for the batter to exploit.

Safety practices in cricket are similar to baseball and softball; enforcing discipline and maximizing attentiveness to prevent the chance of injury, and reminding students that they should not swing the bat when other students are in the vicinity.

Equipment required for cricket practice includes cricket bats, cricket balls, appropriate protective gear, and base markers.

Field hockey – Skills that students of field hockey will acquire include running, tactical thinking on the field, and the ability to manipulate the ball with the stick (including running with the ball and different types of shots).

Offensive strategy in field hockey focuses on maneuvering the ball between team members to prevent the opposing team from intercepting, in order to get close enough to the opposing team's net to score a goal. Defensive strategy will strive to create solid coverage of the advancing team, to enable interception of the ball.

Safety practices include emphasizing mindfulness on the part of the students to prevent accidents, and reinforcing the safety regulations of the game concerning legal use of the hockey stick.

Equipment needed for the practice of field hockey with students includes an appropriate ball, sticks for the students, and appropriate protective gear.

OVERVIEW OF TARGET SPORTS

Golf – The most fundamental skills for students to learn when studying golf include the correct way to execute a golf swing with proper posture and how to judge distance for shot selection correctly. Further, students should learn specific shots and their names (e.g. tee shot, fairway shot, bunker shot, putt).

Strategy in golf centers on properly gauging distances and required force to control the ball to the best extent possible.

Safety practices in golf, especially with students, involve ensuring that the course is clear and there are no students nearby when players are swinging. Instructors should also remind students that golf clubs are not toys, and that misuse can result in injury.

Equipment necessary for a golf class includes a proper set of clubs and golf balls (a golf course or open area for hitting balls is also necessary).

Archery – Skills that students study in archery classes include proper care for their equipment, properly stringing the bow, drawing, and shooting with accuracy (including compensating for distance, angle, and wind).

Safety practices in archery include respectful handling of the equipment (which is potentially dangerous) and ensuring that students only draw bows when pointed at a (non-living) target. Finally, instructors should keep students away from the path between firing students and their targets at all times.

Proper equipment for archery classes include a bow and arrows, which can vary greatly in technical complexity and cost, and a target.

Bowling – Skills that students will learn in bowling classes include learning to select a ball of comfortable weight and appropriate for the shot they need to make, properly controlling the ball so it hits the pins they are aiming for, and learning the dynamics of pin interaction to plan the proper angle of entry for the ball.

Safety practices in bowling include wearing proper footwear, handling the balls cautiously, and preventing horseplay (to avoid situations where a heavy bowling ball may drop inopportunely and cause injury).

Equipment needed for a bowling class include proper footwear, a bowling ball, pins, and a lane.

Frisbee Golf – Skills that students will acquire in a Frisbee golf class include methods of throwing the Frisbee (primarily forehand, side arm, and backhand throws). Students will also gain an intuitive sense for the physics governing the movement of the Frisbee (e.g. stability and speed range).

Frisbee golf strategy focuses on gauging distances and the amount of force and angle of throw required to land the disc in the target.

Frisbee golf safety practices involve ensuring that students don't wander in areas where a disc is in play, as this may result in injury. Instructors should also instruct students to remain alert and not throw the disc if they perceive there is a possibility that they might hit an individual.

Equipment needed for Frisbee golf include a proper disc (though you can substitute a regular Frisbee for school purposes), target nets, and a playing area large enough to accommodate the game without excessive risk of the Frisbee flying irretrievably out of bounds.

Shuffleboard – Depending on whether students are playing deck shuffleboard or table shuffleboard, they will learn to manipulate the discs, either with or without sticks.

Strategy requires students to properly gauge and apply the force needed to propel the disc accurately to a particular spot on the playing area.

Safety practices in shuffleboard include properly instructing and monitoring students to avoid horseplay, which may result in injury caused by the playing equipment.

Equipment needed for a shuffleboard class include a disc with which to play, the equipment to manipulate the disc (this will vary depending on whether the shuffleboard game is played on a deck or on a table), and the appropriate playing area.

Bocce ball – Requires a flat, level playing surface (packed dirt, gravel or grass are ideal). The instructor divides students into two teams of one, two, or four players each. Each team gets four balls, divided equally among the players. A player from the starting team stands behind the foul line (10 feet from the throwing end of the court) and throws the small ball ("pallina") toward the opposite end of the playing surface. The player then throws one of the larger balls ("boccia"), trying to get it as close to the pallina as possible without touching it. Players from the opposing team take turns throwing their balls until one of the balls stops closer to the pallina than the starting player's ball. If they fail to do so, the starting team tries to outdo its first attempt. Teams continue to take turns in this manner until they have thrown all the balls. The team with closest ball gets a point. This game emphasizes throwing skills (coordination, gross and fine motor skills).

DEFINE THE TERMINOLOGY OF VARIOUS TARGET SPORTS

Archery Terminology:

- Addressing the target – standing ready to shoot with a proper shooting stance.

- Anchor point – specific location on the archer's face to which index finger comes while holding and aiming.

- Archery golf (adaptation of golf to archery) – players shoot for holes, scoring according to the number of shots required to hit the target.

- Arm guard – a piece of leather or plastic worn on the inside of the forearm, protecting the arm from the bowstring.

- Arrow plate – a protective piece of hard material set into the bow where the arrow crosses it.

- Arrow rest – a small projection at the top of the bow handle where the arrow rests.

- Back – the side of the bow away from the shooter.

- Bow arm – the arm that holds the bow.

- Bow sight – a device attached to the bow through which the archer sights when aiming.

- Bow weight – designates the amount of effort needed to pull a bowstring a specific distance.

- Cant – shooting while holding the bow slightly turned or tilted.

- Cast – the distance a bow can shoot an arrow.

- Clout shooting – a type of shooting using a target 48 feet in diameter laid on the ground at a distance of 180 yards for men and 120 or 140 yards for women. Participants usually shoot 36 arrows per round.

- Cock/Index feather – the feather that is set at a right angle to the arrow nock; differently colored than the other two feathers.

- Creeping – letting the drawing hand move forward at the release.

- Crest – the archer's identifying marks located just below the fletchings.

- Draw – pulling the bowstring back into the anchor position.

- End – a specific number of arrows shot at one time or from one position before retrieval of arrows.

- Face – the part of the bow facing the shooter.

- Finger tab – a leather flap worn on the drawing hand protecting the fingers and providing a smooth release of the bowstring.

- Fletchings – the feathers of the arrow that give guidance to its flight.

- Flight shooting – shooting an arrow the farthest possible distance.

- Handle – the grip at the midsection of the bow.

- Hen feathers – the two feathers that are not set at right angles to the arrow nock.

- Instinctive shooting – aiming and shooting instinctively rather than using a bow sight or point-of-aim method.

- Limbs – upper and lower parts of the bow divided by the handle.

- Nock – the groove in the arrow's end where the string is placed.

- Nocking point – the point on the string where the arrow is placed.

- Notch – the grooves of the upper and lower tips of the limbs where the bowstring is fitted.

- Over bow – using too strong a bow that is too powerful to pull a bowstring the proper distance.

- Overdraw – drawing the bow so that the pile of the arrow is inside the bow.

- Petticoat – the part of the target face outside the white ring.

- Pile/point – the arrow's pointed, metal tip.

- Plucking – jerking the drawing hand laterally away from the face on the release causing the arrow's flight to veer to the left.

- Point-blank range – the distance from the target where the point of aim is right on the bull's eye.

- Point-of-aim – a method of aiming that aligns the pile of the arrow with the target.

- Quiver – a receptacle for carrying or holding arrows.

- Recurve bow – a bow curved on the ends.

- Release – the act of letting the bowstring slip off the fingertips.

- Round – the term used to indicate shooting a specified number of arrows at a designated distance or distances.

- Roving – an outdoor archery game that uses natural targets (trees, bushes, stumps, etc.) for competition.

- Serving – the thread wrapped around the bowstring at the nocking point.

- Shaft – the long, body part of the arrow.

- Spine – the rigidity and flexibility characteristics of an arrow.

- Tackle – archery equipment referred to in its entirety.

- Target face – the painted front of a target.

- Trajectory – the flight path of the arrow.

- Vane – an arrow's plastic feather.

Bowling Terminology:

- Anchor – the teammate who shoots last.

- Baby split – the 1-7 or 3-10 pin railroads.

- Backup – a reverse hook rotating to the right for a right-handed bowler.

- Bed posts – the 7-10 railroad.

- Blow – an error or missing a spare that is not split.

- Box – a frame.

- Brooklyn – a crossover ball striking the 1-2 pocket.

- Bucket – the 2-4-5-8 or 3-5-6-9 leaves.

- Cherry – chopping off the front pin on a spare.

- Double – two consecutive strikes.

- Double pinochle – the 7-6 and 4-10 split.

- Crossover – same as a Brooklyn.

- Dutch 200 (Dutchman) – a score of 200 made by alternating strikes and spares for the entire game.

- Error – same as a "blow."

- Foul – touching or going beyond the foul line in delivering the ball.

- Frame – the box where scores are entered.

- Gutter ball – a ball that falls into either gutter.

- Handicap – awarding an individual or team a bonus score or score adjustment based on averages.

- Head pin – the number one pin.

- Hook – a ball that breaks to the left for a right-handed bowler and breaks to the right for a left-handed bowler.

- Jersey side – same as a Brooklyn.

- Kegler – synonym for a bowler.

- Lane – a bowling alley.

- Leave – pin or pins left standing after a throw.

- Light hit – hitting the head pin lightly to the right or left side.

- Line – a complete game as recorded on the score sheet.

- Mark – getting a strike or spare.

- Open frame – a frame in which no mark is made, leaving at least one pin standing after rolling both balls in a frame.

- Pocket – space between the head pin and pins on either side.

- Railroad – synonym for a split.

- Sleeper – a pin hidden from view.

- Spare – knocking all pins down with two balls.

- Split – a leave, after throwing the first ball, in which the number one pin plus a second pin are down, and when seven pins remain standing.

- Spot – a bowler's point of aim on the alley.

- Striking out – obtaining three strikes in the last frame.

- Tap – a pin that remains standing after an apparently perfect hit.

- Turkey – three consecutive strikes.

PERSONAL PERFORMANCE AND INDIVIDUAL SPORTS

Track and field – In track and field practice, students will acquire proper running form, the ability to pace their energy expenditure relative to the length of the track, and the ability to manipulate objects in field events.

Track and field strategy focuses on learning to pace energy expenditure relative to the length of the track and analyzing the psychological interaction with other racers and competitors.

Safety practices in track and field include adhering to proper warm up and cool down procedures to prevent injury and handling field equipment (e.g. discus, javelin, shot) with care.

Equipment that is important to track events is minimal, with the only important requirement being appropriate footwear. Field events require specialized equipment. For example, throwing events require a discus, shot, or javelin. Jumping events require a landing area and height or length measuring device.

Fencing – Fencing practice will impart to students proficiency in proper fencing form, techniques (for example parries and strikes), and an awareness of open target areas on their opponents. Students will also acquire efficient movement skills.

Fencing strategy focuses on minimizing the number and size of vulnerable target areas on the body, while maneuvering (with the feet, body, and foil) to maximize the vulnerability of opponent target areas in order to score a point.

Safety practices include proper attention to full protective gear, proper form, and careful monitoring of students in practice. Instructors should remind students frequently that they should not take frustrations out on training partners.

Equipment required for fencing practice includes the full gamut of protective gear (suit and helmet), appropriate footwear, and, of course, the fencing foil or saber. Higher technology suits that record points are also available, but are not required.

Cross-country running – Much like track and field, cross-country running will teach the students proper running form, the ability to pace their energy expenditure relative to the length of the course, and the ability to adapt their running technique to the terrain.

Cross-country running strategy focuses on adapting energy expenditure relative to the length of the course and psychological training to minimize responsiveness to physical exhaustion. Runners should familiarize themselves with a course before running it.

Safety practices, like other running sports, focus on proper attention to warm-ups and cool-downs and remaining attentive to the course, which may be quite rugged. Because cross-country running often takes place in fairly remote, natural settings, it is important to coordinate the availability of first aid.

Equipment required for cross-country running includes proper footwear and water to prevent dehydration on longer runs.

AQUATIC SKILLS

Water safety issues include student familiarity with appropriate medical responses to life-threatening situations. Students should recognize signs that someone needs medical attention (e.g. not moving, not breathing, etc.) and have knowledge of the proper response (e.g. who to contact and where to find them). With older children, the instructor can introduce rudimentary first aid. The instructor must also ensure that students are aware and observant of safety rules (e.g. no running near the water, no chewing gum while swimming, no swimming without a lifeguard, no roughhousing near or in the water, etc.).

Swimming strokes include Butterfly, Breast Stroke, Crawl, Sidestroke, Trudgen, Freestyle, Backstroke, and Dog Paddle. When teaching children how to dive, instructors should emphasize form (arm and body alignment) and safety procedures (e.g. no diving in the shallow end, no pushing students into the water).

Water fitness activities and games should place emphasis on generating a lot of movement in the pool (gross motor activities), and may also incorporate activities that require more coordinated manipulations, like catching a ball (fine motor). Sample games include:

- **Water Tag** – Children can attempt to catch each other in the pool. When someone is caught, he becomes 'it'. Variations include freeze tag (where a caught student isn't allowed to move until someone swims between their legs to free them) and base tag (where some sections of the pool, for example the ladders or the walls, are a safe 'base' – rules must be in place limiting the time that a student can spend on the base). Water tag emphasizes gross motor activities. Safety issue: students may not hold other students or grab other students in the water.

- **Water Dodgeball** – Students divide into two teams, one on either side of the pool. They play dodgeball, throwing a ball from one side to the other. The opposing team captures a student who is hit by the ball, but if the ball is caught, the thrower is captured instead. Safety issue: students may not throw the ball at another student's head at close range.

- **Relay Races** – Students divide into teams and perform relay races (i.e. one student swims the length of the pool and back, when he returns the next one does the same, repeating until the whole team has completed the task). This can incorporate various swimming strokes; either all team members use the same stroke or each team member uses a different stroke.

COMBATIVE ACTIVITIES

Basic knowledge of wrestling includes knowledge of basic techniques (familiarity with pins, reversals, and positioning transitions), drills for practicing technique (e.g. students can drill shooting and sprawling, drill reversals from pinned positions, etc.), and terminology (naming the techniques, e.g. shoot, sprawl, half nelson, full nelson, etc.).

Basic knowledge of self-defense includes familiarity with basic striking techniques (punches and kicks), blocks and evasions, knowledge of major vital points on the body (eyes, nose, ears, jaw, throat, solar plexus, groin, knees, in-step), knowledge of basic escape techniques (from chokes, grabs and bear-hugs) and some situational training (to prevent 'freezing' in a real-life encounter).

Martial arts (e.g. judo, karate) are common forms of self-defense that physical education instructors can teach to students.

In-class focus should be placed on strategies for conflict recognition (based on developing an understanding of threat factors, like individuals in a hostile frame of mind), avoidance (physically avoiding potentially dangerous situations), and diffusion (overview of the psychology of confrontations, evaluation of the motivations behind a hostile encounter, understanding of the way body language and eye contact can impact the situation).

Related safety issues include stressing the potential harm that can result from the techniques being practiced (stressing specific damage potential to musculoskeletal systems), emphasizing students' responsibility for the well-being of their training partners, maintaining discipline throughout the class (ensuring students remain focused on their training activities and alert to the educator's instructions), and ensuring that students are aware and observant of the limits to force that they may apply (no-striking zones, like above the neck and below the belt; limits on striking force, like semi-contact or no-contact sparring; familiarity with the concept of a tap-out indicating submission). Students should perform warm-up, cool-down, and stretching as with any physical training program.

SKILL 5.2   Recognize basic rules, etiquette, and safety practices associated with individual and group sports.

RULES OF PLAY OF VARIOUS GAME AND SPORT SITUATIONS

ARCHERY:

- Arrows that bounce off the target or go through the target count as 7 points.

- Arrows landing on lines between two rings receive the higher score of the two rings.

- Arrows hitting the petticoat receive no score.

BADMINTON:

- Intentionally balking opponent or making preliminary feints results in a fault (side in = loss of serve; side out = point awarded to side in).

- When a shuttlecock falls on a line, it is in play (i.e. a fair play).

- If the striking team hits shuttlecock before it crosses net it is a fault.

- Touching the net when the shuttlecock is in play is a fault.

- The same player hitting the shuttlecock twice is a fault.

- The shuttlecock going through the net is a fault.

BOWLING:

- No score for a pin knocked down by a pinsetter (human or mechanical).

- There is no score for the pins when any part of the foot, hand, or arm extends or crosses over the foul line (even after ball leaves the hand) or if any part of the body contacts division boards, walls, or uprights that are beyond the foul line.

- There is no count for pins displaced or knocked down by a ball leaving the lane before it reaches the pins.

- There is no count when balls rebound from the rear cushion.

RACQUETBALL/HANDBALL:

- A server stepping outside service area when serving faults.

- The server is out (relinquishes serve) if he/she steps outside of serving zone twice in succession while serving.

- Server is out if he/she fails to hit the ball rebounding off the floor during the serve.

- The opponent must have a chance to take a position or the referee must call for play before the server can serve the ball.

- The server re-serves the ball if the receiver is not behind the short line when the ball is served.

- A served ball that hits the front line and does not land back of the short line is "short"; therefore, it is a fault. The ball is also short when it hits the front wall and two sidewalls before it lands on the floor back of the short line.

- A serve is a fault when the ball touches the ceiling from rebounding off the front wall.

- A fault occurs when any part of the foot steps over the outer edges of the service or the short line while serving.

- A hinder (dead ball) occurs when a returned ball hits an opponent on its way to the front wall - even if the ball continues to the front wall.

- A hinder is any intentional or unintentional interference of an opponent's opportunity to return the ball.

TENNIS:

A player loses a point when:

- The ball bounces twice on her side of the net.

- The player returns the ball to any place outside of designated areas.

- The player stops or touches the ball in the air before it lands out-of-bounds.

- The player intentionally strikes the ball twice with the racket.

- The ball strikes any part of a player or racket after initial attempt to hit the ball.

- A player reaches over the net to hit the ball.

- A player throws his racket at the ball.

- The ball strikes any permanent fixture that is out-of-bounds (other than the net).

    o a ball touching the net and landing inside the boundary lines is in play (except on the serve, where a ball contacting the net results in a "let" – replay of the point)

- A player fails, on two consecutive attempts, to serve the ball into the designated area (i.e. double fault).

TRACK AND FIELD:

The following are common track and field events:

- Sprint Races – 100, 200, 400 meter dash; 110, 400 meter hurdles
- Distance Races – one-mile, 5000 and 10000 meter foot races
- Jumping Events – high jump, long jump, broad jump, triple jump, pole vault
- Relay Races – team sprint or distance foot races
- Throwing Events – hammer, discus, javelin, shot put

Rules of track and field events:
- In all sprint races, runners must stay in their lane on the track and the first person to cross the finish line wins.
    o depending on local rules, one or two "false starts" – running before the start signal – results in disqualification

- In all jumping events, participants must take off on or before a designated "foul line" and the person with the longest jump wins.
  - o "foul" jumps do not receive a score
- In all relay races, teams must pass a baton within a designated transition area and the first team to cross the finish line with the baton wins.
  - o failed exchanges result in disqualification
- In all throwing events, participants must release the object within a specified area and the person with the longest throw wins.
  - o releasing the object outside the designated area is a "foul" and foul throws do not receive a measurement

BASKETBALL:

- A player touching the floor on or outside the boundary line is out-of-bounds.

- The ball is out of bounds if it touches anything (a player, the floor, an object, or any person) that is on or outside the boundary line.

- An offensive player remaining in the three-second zone of the free-throw lane for more than three seconds is a violation.

- A ball firmly held by two opposing players results in a jump ball.

- A throw-in is awarded to the opposing team of the last player touching a ball that goes out-of-bounds.

SOCCER:

The following are direct free-kick offenses:

- Hand or arm contact with the ball

- Using hands to hold an opponent

- Pushing an opponent

- Striking/kicking/tripping or attempting to strike/kick/trip an opponent

- Goalie using the ball to strike an opponent

- Jumping at or charging an opponent

- Kneeing an opponent

- Any contact fouls

The following are indirect free-kick offenses:

- Same player playing the ball twice at the kickoff, on a throw-in, on a goal kick, on a free kick, or on a corner kick.

- The goalie delaying the game by holding the ball or carrying the ball more than four steps.

- Failure to notify the referee of substitutions/re-substitutions and that player then handling the ball in the penalty area.

- Any person that is not a player entering playing field without a referee's permission.

- Unsportsmanlike actions or words in reference to a referee's decision.

- Dangerously lowering the head or raising the foot too high to make a play.

- A player resuming play after being ordered off the field.

- Offsides – an offensive player must have two defenders between him and the goal when a teammate passes the ball to him or else he is offsides.

- Attempting to kick the ball when the goalkeeper has possession or interference with the goalkeeper to hinder him/her from releasing the ball.

- Illegal charging.

- Leaving the playing field without referee's permission while the ball is in play.

SOFTBALL:
- Each team plays nine players in the field (sometimes 10 for slow pitch).

- Field positions are one pitcher, one catcher, four infielders, and three outfielders (four outfielders in ten player formats).

- The four bases are 60 feet apart.

- Any ball hit outside of the first or third base line is a foul ball (i.e. runners cannot advance and the pitch counts as a strike against the batter)

- If a batter receives three strikes (i.e. failed attempts at hitting the ball) in a single at bat he/she strikes out.

- The pitcher must start with both feet on the pitcher's rubber and can only take one step forward when delivering the underhand pitch.

- A base runner is out if:

    - A. The opposition tags him with the ball before he reaches a base.
    - B. The ball reaches first base before he does.
    - C. He runs outside of the base path to avoid a tag.
    - D. A batted ball strikes him in fair territory.

- A team must maintain the same batting order throughout the game.

- Runners cannot lead off and base stealing is illegal.

- Runners may overrun first base, but can be tagged out if off any other base.

VOLLEYBALL:

The following infractions by the receiving team result in a point awarded to the serving side and an infraction by serving team results in side-out:

- Illegal serves or serving out of turn.

- Illegal returns or catching or holding the ball.

- Dribbling or a player touching the ball twice in succession.

- Contact with the net (two opposing players making contact with the net at the same time results in a replay of the point).

- Touching the ball after it has been played three times without passing over the net.

- A player's foot completely touching the floor over the centerline.

- Reaching under the net and touching a player or the ball while the ball is in play.

- The players changing positions prior to the serve.

SAMPLE OFFICIATING SITUATIONS

NOTE: Since rules change yearly, acquiring new rulebooks every year is necessary for proper officiating.

Basketball situation: Actions of the spectators interfere with the progression of the game.

Ruling: An official may call a foul on the team whose supporters are interfering with the game.

Basketball situation: A1 is attempting a field goal and B1 fouls him. A1 continues with the field goal attempt and, before releasing the ball, crashes into B2 who has a legal position on the floor. A1 successfully completes the field goal.

Ruling: The ball was immediately dead when A1 fouled B2; therefore, field goal does not count. However, since B1 fouled A1 while A1 attempted the field goal, A1 receives two free throws.

Basketball situation: The official in the frontcourt runs into a pass thrown from the backcourt by A1 and goes out-of-bounds.

Ruling: Throw-in is awarded to B. The official is part of the court.

Basketball Situation: A1 catches the ball in mid-air and lands with the right foot first and then the left foot. A1 pivots on the left foot.

Ruling: A violation has occurred because A1 can only pivot on the foot that first lands on the floor, which was the right foot.

Soccer situation: The ball is alive when a substitute enters the playing field.

Ruling: A non-player foul. Referee can either penalize at location of the next dead ball or at the place of entry (usually when the team offended is at an advantage).

Soccer situation: B1 charges A1's goalie in A1's penalty area.

Ruling: Team A is awarded a direct free kick at the spot of foul. A flagrant charge awards team A a penalty-kick at the other end of the field, and B1 is disqualified.

Soccer situation: The goalie is out of position when a back on team B heads the ball out and falls into the net. A2 gets the ball, passes it to A1, and has only the goalie to beat.

Ruling: A1 is not offside because the B back left the field during legal play.

Volleyball situation: Team A's second volley hits an obstruction directly over the net, returns to A's playing area, and team A plays it again.

Ruling: Fair play and the next play is team A's third play.

Volleyball situation: The serving team has three front line players standing close together in front of the server at the spiking line.

Ruling: Illegal alignment is called for intentional screening.

Volleyball situation: RB and CB on the receiving team are overlapping when the server strikes the serve, and the serve lands out-of-bounds.

Ruling: Serving team is awarded a point because of receiving team's illegal alignment.

Volleyball situation: LB on team B saves a spiked ball and it deflects off his/her shoulder.

Ruling: A legal hit.

APPROPRIATE BEHAVIOR IN PHYSICAL EDUCATION ACTIVITIES

Appropriate Student Etiquette/Behaviors include: following the rules and accepting the consequences of unfair action, good sportsmanship, respecting the rights of other students, reporting own accidents and mishaps, not engaging in inappropriate behavior under peer pressure encouragement, cooperation, paying attention to instructions and demonstrations, moving to assigned places and remaining in own space, complying with directions, practicing as instructed to do so, properly using equipment, and not interfering with the practice of others.

Appropriate Content Etiquette/Behaviors include the teacher describing the performance of tasks and students engaging in the task, the teacher assisting students with task performance, and the teacher modifying and developing tasks.

Appropriate Management Etiquette/Behaviors include the teacher directing the management of equipment, students, and space prior to practicing tasks; students getting equipment and partners; the teacher requesting that students stop "fooling around."

APPLY APPROPRIATE STRATEGIES TO TARGET GAME AND SPORT SITUATIONS

Archery strategies for correcting errors in aiming and releasing:

- Shifting position.

- Relaxing both the arms and shoulders at the moment of release.

- Reaching point of aim before releasing string.

- Pointing aim to the right or left of direct line between the archer and the target's center.

- Aiming with the left eye.

- Sighting with both eyes.

- Using the proper arrow.

Bowling for spares strategies:

- Identifying the key pin and determining where to hit it to pick up remaining pins.

- Using the three basic alignments: center position for center pins, left position for left pins, and right position for right pins.

- Rolling the spare ball in the same manner as rolled for the first ball of frame.

- Concentrating harder for spare ball because of the reduced opportunity for pin action and margin of error.

APPLY APPROPRIATE STRATEGIES TO NET/WALL GAME AND SPORT SITUATIONS

Badminton Strategies:

Strategies for Return of Service

- Returning serves with shots that are straight ahead.

- Returning service so that opponent must move out of his/her starting position.

- Returning long serves with an overhead clear or drop shot to near corner.

- Returning short serves with underhand clear or a net drop to near corner.

Strategies for Serving

- Serving long to the backcourt near centerline.

- Serving short when opponent is standing too deep in his/her receiving court to return the serve, or using a short serve to eliminate a smash return if opponent has a powerful smash from the backcourt.

Handball or Racquetball Strategies:

- Identifying opponent's strengths and weaknesses.

- Making opponent use less dominant hand or backhand shots if they are weaker.

- Frequently alternating fastballs and lobs to change the pace (changing the pace is particularly effective for serving).

- Maintaining position near middle of court (the well) that is close enough to play low balls and corner shots.

- Placing shots that keep opponent's position at a disadvantage to return cross-court and angle shots.

- Using high lob shots that go overhead but do not hit the back wall with enough force to rebound to drive an opponent out of position when he/she persistently plays close to the front wall.

Tennis Strategies:

- Lobbing – using a high, lob shot for defense giving the player more time to get back into position.

- Identifying opponent's weaknesses, attacking them, and recognizing and protecting one's own weaknesses.

- Outrunning and out-thinking an opponent.

- Using change of pace, lobs, spins, approaching the net, and deception at the correct time.

- Hitting cross-court (from corner to corner of the court) for maximum safety and opportunity to regain position.

- Directing the ball where the opponent is not.

SAFETY PRACTICES AND EQUIPMENT – TEAM PASSING SPORTS

Important safety considerations for team passing sports include proper maintenance of facilities and playing fields, use of protective equipment, and proper enforcement of the rules of play. Enforcement of rules is particularly important to prevent participants from injuring other participants either intentionally or unintentionally through reckless play.

The following is a list of sport-specific equipment for team passing sports:

- Basketball – basketballs, goals, appropriate shoes
- Touch or Flag Football – footballs, flags and flag belts, cones to mark boundaries and end zones
- Lacrosse – lacrosse sticks and balls, protective pads, goals (nets)
- Soccer – soccer balls, goals, field markers, protective shin guards
- Team Handball – handballs and goals
- Ultimate Frisbee – Frisbees and an open playing field

SAFETY PRACTICES AND EQUIPMENT – NET/WALL SPORTS

In addition to the general safety procedures discussed in the previous skill, there are several specific safety considerations for net/wall sports. First, because most of these sports involve swinging a racket or paddle and hitting a ball with a great deal of force, monitoring the area of play is very important. Instructors must ensure that students only swing rackets and hit balls at appropriate times. Second, instructors and students must keep the playing area clear of stray balls and other obstacles to prevent injuries. Finally, some of the net/wall sports, such as handball, require use of protective eyewear.

The following is a list of sport-specific equipment for net/wall sports:

- Badminton – rackets, nets, shuttlecocks
- Handball – a wall, handballs, protective eyewear
- Pickleball – wood paddle rackets, plastic balls, nets, a paved surface
- Table Tennis – paddles, balls, table, nets
- Tennis – court, nets, rackets, tennis balls
- Volleyball – nets, volleyballs

SKILL 5.3   Select and apply offensive, defensive, and cooperative strategies in group sports.

Basketball Strategies:

Use a Zone Defense

- To prevent drive-ins for easy lay-up shots.

- When playing area is small.

- When team is in foul trouble.

- To keep an excellent rebounder near opponent's basket.

- When opponents' outside shooting is weak.

- When opponents have an advantage in height.

- When opponents have an exceptional offensive player, or when the best defenders cannot handle one-on-one defense.

Offensive Strategies Against Zone Defense

- Using quick, sharp passing to penetrate zone forcing opposing player out of assigned position.

- Overloading and mismatching.

Offensive Strategies for One-On-One Defense

- Using the "pick-and-roll" and the "give-and-go" to screen defensive players to open up offensive players for shot attempts.

- Teams may use free-lancing (spontaneous one-one-one offense), but more commonly they use "sets" of plays.

Soccer Strategies:

- **Heading** – using the head to pass, to shoot, or to clear the ball.

- **Tackling** – objective is to take possession of the ball from an opponent. Successful play requires knowledgeable utilization of space.

Volleyball Strategies:

Using forearm passes (bumps, digs, or passes) to play balls below the waist, to play hard driven balls, to pass the serve, and to contact balls distant from a player.

SKILL 5.4   Identify and apply developmentally appropriate strategies and instruments to assess learner performance in individual and group sports.

INDIVIDUAL SPORTS

Physical activities that deal with individual sports, recreational activities, and outdoor pursuits are extremely useful for the various developmental levels of children and adults.

Physical activities usually involve the utilization of motor skills in harmony with physical, emotional, psychological, psychomotor, and other types of skill development. Sports activities are a combination of movements and rules that often lead to healthy physical development in a child. In turn, the child is more likely to become stronger and fitter, making various other tasks in life easier. These types of activities lead to other qualities such as sportsmanship, mutual respect, and cooperation. Participants also develop intellectually during the course of play or motor skills development.

Partnership with a teammate or playing individualized sports can help in developing intellectual, social, psychological, emotional, and motor skills. Activities that require physical exertion, which includes different movements of the body, are necessary for the normal development of an individual.

GROUP SPORTS

Team sports form a major part of the physical education curriculum. Designed mainly for promoting physical fitness among students, children, and adults, such sport activities include concepts and strategies, which help students to develop healthy physical, motor, emotional, social, and psychological skills.

These activities have defined steps that help gradually increase the physical development of the students. Apart from this, physical activities associated with team sports also keep diseases and other body ailments at bay. We can effectively deal with body ailments such as obesity, weakness, and heart disease by engaging in the physical activities inherent in sports.

Physical activities usually involve the utilization of motor skills in harmony with physical, emotional, psychological, psychomotor, and mental skills. Sports activities are a combination of movements and rules that often lead to healthy physical development in a child. In turn, the child is more likely to become stronger and fitter, making various other tasks in life easier. These types of activities lead to other qualities such as sportsmanship, mutual respect, and cooperation. Children also develop intellectually during the course of a play or motor skills development. For example, rock climbing and other adventure activities require mental forethought and planning. Participation in such activities promotes the development of critical-thinking, problem solving, and decision making skills.

Further, regard for others and learning to work cooperatively with peers are necessary skills for success in team sports. In addition, participation in sports provides experience in dealing with interpersonal conflict (e.g. between teammates or competitors) and helps develop leadership skills. Children also develop respect for rules, acquire motor skills, and gain the ability to enjoy physical activity early in life, or as soon as they engage in organized or free play.

COMPETENCY 6.0 **UNDERSTAND TECHNIQUES, SKILLS, STRATEGIES, BASIC RULES, ETIQUETTE AND SAFETY PRACTICES ASSOCIATED WITH LIFELONG SPORTS, CREATIVE MOVEMENT, DANCE, NONCOMPETITIVE ACTIVITIES, AND COOPERATIVE ACTIVITIES**

SKILL 6.1 *Demonstrate an understanding of critical elements, skill progressions, strategies, safety practices, types of equipment, and basic rules and etiquette for lifelong sports and activities.*

LIFETIME ACTIVITIES AND RECREATIONAL PURSUITS

Many lifetime activities and recreational pursuits involve physical activity, games, and sports. Some sports, such as tennis and golf, are lifetime activities. Healthy individuals can participate in such lifetime sports well into their 80's and even 90's. Other recreational pursuits, such as hiking, boating, walking, jogging, and bicycling, are important parts of many people's lives. Such pursuits provide recreation, enjoyment, social interaction, and physical fitness to participants. The physical education instructor should introduce students to activities and pursuits that promote lifetime participation and activity.

OUTDOOR EDUCATION

Techniques and skills include:

- **Walking and Hiking** – Instructors can take students on walking/hiking trips through nature reserves and national parks. Such trips can incorporate team-building activities and nature education.

- **Sail Training** – Students taught to sail should display competence in the maintenance and piloting of a boat, including cooperative activities necessary to a successful sailing endeavor (e.g. working together to get the boat into and out of the water, paddling in rhythm, turning the boat, etc.). Prior to the start of sail training, students should understand all safety procedures and acceptable forms of behavior on a boat (e.g. only standing when necessary, no pushing, following instructions, wearing a life jacket, etc.). Students must also demonstrate swimming competence (i.e. ability to tread water, swim a distance continuously, and put on a life jacket while in the water).

Related safety education should emphasize the importance of planning and research. Students should consider in advance what the potential dangers of an activity might be and to prepare plans accordingly (students and instructors should also examine weather forecasts). Of course, educator supervision is required. First-aid equipment and properly trained educators must be present for outdoor education activities. Students should use proper safety gear when appropriate (e.g. helmets, harnesses, etc.). Parental consent is generally required for outdoor education activities.

Bicycling – In bicycling classes, students should learn proper bicycling form and how to gauge which gear is most appropriate for their current speed and level of inclination. Students should also become familiar with the proper way to maintain and care for their bicycles.

Bicycling strategy is similar to track events – learning to gauge the appropriate levels of energy expenditure relative to the length of the track and the fitness of the cyclist.

Safety practices while bicycling include seriousness in practice (no horseplay, which can result in injury) and attentiveness to the track so that students can avoid potentially dangerous bumps or cracks. Instructors should remind students not to race with each other, but rather to focus on their own physical activity.

Equipment required for bicycling with students includes proper gear (which includes clothing without loose appendages that can catch in bicycle gears), water for longer trips, and, of course, the bicycles themselves.

Cross-country skiing – Students in cross-country skiing classes will learn the proper form for cross-country skiing (e.g. herringbone, diagonal stride, double pole) and will greatly improve their fitness (as cross-country skiing is a very taxing activity on a very wide range of muscle groups).
Like most endurance activities, cross-country skiing strategy involves regulating the levels of energy expenditure relative to the length of the course and the fitness level of the athlete. .

Safety practices in cross-country skiing include ensuring the availability of first aid and instructor attentiveness to the students (as it is easier to 'lose track' of a student who is having trouble). Instructors should also instruct students not to wander away from the group – a good solution is the implementation of a buddy system.

Equipment required for cross-country skiing trips includes appropriate dress (make sure students dress warmly), cross-country skis, and poles.

Canoeing – Students in canoeing classes will learn the various forms of paddling strokes, how to manage their weight, and how to work as a team to maneuver a canoe properly.

Strategies for effective canoeing include the clear delineation of members of a rowing team and the role that each individual serves. The 'captain' coordinates the efforts of the rowers on the canoe and should become familiar with the course and destination.

Safety practices for canoeing call for the instructor to ensure that the students are all able to swim and equipped with proper flotation equipment (e.g. lifejackets). First aid should be available and the instructor should see to it that he remains close enough to students in different canoes to be able to hear them and reach them if needed.

Equipment required for canoeing classes includes canoes, canoeing paddles, and proper flotation equipment. Instructors should advise students to have a change of clothes available in the event that they get wet.

Orienteering – Skills that students will acquire during orienteering activities include the ability to read a map, critical thinking stemming from practice identifying locations, navigation ability, and strategic thinking for selection of efficient movement patterns between several points.

Strategies for orienteering include ascertaining early the destination points and mapping an efficient course to pass through all of them.

Safety practices include ensuring the availability and accessibility of first aid, properly instructing the students in emergency procedures (e.g. blow the whistle and remain where you are), and selecting an area small enough so the instructor can hear the whistle from any position.

Equipment required for orienteering with students includes proper outdoor clothing and a whistle for use in emergency situations. Students will also need a map and possibly a compass.

Fishing – Students studying fishing will learn the correct technique for casting a line and will learn to identify spots where fish are most likely to congregate. Fishing also teaches patience to students.

Strategies for effective fishing with groups of students include deploying students in such a way that one will not interfere with another's fishing activities. Students should also learn about the habits of the fish that they are after, to allow them to tailor their approaches accordingly.

Safety practices for fishing call for instructors to remind students that their equipment does not consist of toys and they should not play with it. Students should definitely handle fishing rods and hooks carefully around other students.

Equipment required for fishing includes fishing rods, hooks, bait, gear (e.g. boots), and a bucket or other receptacle for the fish.

Inline skating – Skills that students in inline skating class will acquire include skating techniques (e.g. braking and stopping, skating backwards, skating downhill) and improved balance. Students should also learn to care for their skating equipment.

Strategies in inline skating focus on maintaining proper form during the activity.

Safety practices in inline skating include requiring students to wear appropriate protective gear and ensuring that first aid is available. Instructors should instruct students not to attempt stunts, especially without supervision.
Equipment required for inline skating includes skates and appropriate protective gear (e.g. helmets, kneepads, elbow pads).

SKILL 6.2   Recognize techniques, steps, sequences, activities, etiquette, and safety practices for creative movement and dance activities.

DANCE CONCEPTS, FORMS, AND BASIC VOCABULARY – JAZZ AND BALLET

There are several forms of dance including modern, ballet, jazz, country, ballroom, and hip-hop. Though essentially very different from each other, they all have similarities. A sense of musicality is the one constant required for each of the dance forms. Along with that, we can add timing, coordination, flexibility, and, needless to say, an interest in the concept of dance itself. We all know that we will probably experience greater success when we engage in activities that we are interested in and enjoy. Understanding of most dance forms requires knowledge of basic vocabulary. For example, in jazz, turns or kick ball turns; in tap dance, the shuffle or the flap, etc. Ballet has more specialized vocabulary than any other dance form. For example, plie, to bend; tendu, to stretch; degage, to disengage; fouette, to whip; fondu, to melt; ronde jambe, circle of the leg; pirouette, to turn on one leg; port de bras, movement of the arms; and assemble, to assemble.

Integral to dance and particularly ballet are the concepts of balance and counterbalance, pull-up and turnout, weight distribution and alignment, including shoulders down, hips square, legs turned out, and chest lifted.

In ballet, there are many different dance forms and techniques that a dancer can follow. Three of the larger ones are the Cecchetti, Russian Vaganova, and Royal Academy of Dance, (RAD), programmes. They all have levels for all dancers from beginner to advanced and they all have their advantages and disadvantages. The Cecchetti Society developed the Cecchetti technique from the teachings of the great ballet master Enrico Cecchetti. It is a full syllabus designed to train dancers for professional work. One notable emphasis in the Cecchetti syllabus is that the arms flow and blend from position to position more than any other technique. The Cecchetti technique has formed the core of the program at the National Ballet School of Canada. The Russian Vaganova technique derives and takes its name from the teachings of Agrippina Vaganova, who was the artistic director of the Kirov Ballet for many years. In the Vaganova method, the dancers bring attention to their hands. The hands do not flow invisibly from one position to the, as in the Cecchetti method, rather they are left behind and turn at the last moment. This is where the "flapping" look comes from that many dancers make with their hands. Unlike the RAD method, the Vaganova method does not have formally established exercises for each level. Each teacher choreographs his own class according to specialized guidelines and the students dance that class in their examinations. The Vaganova method forms the core of the program at the Royal Winnipeg Ballet School. The RAD syllabus is very common. It is well suited to dance classes in community dance schools where the students usually do no more than an average of one class per day. If you go to the ballet school in your community, there is a good chance they will use the RAD method. The American School of Ballet teaches the Balanchine method. Created by George Balanchine in the American School of Ballet, the Balanchine method allows dancers to dance Balanchine's choreography much more easily than other dancers can. In the Balanchine method the hands are held differently again from any of the other systems.

DANCE CONCEPTS, FORMS, AND BASIC VOCABULARY – FOLK AND TAP

Folk dance is a term used to describe a large number of dances that originated in Europe and share several common characteristics. Most folk dances practiced today were created before the 20th century, and were practiced by people with little or no training. For this reason, folk dances are usually characterized by a spontaneous style, adaptable movements, and culturally distinctive steps representative of the dance's country of origin. Types of folk dancing include the contra dance, English country-dance, and Maypole dance.

Contra dance is a term used to describe folk dances in which couples dance in two facing lines. A pair of such lines is a set, and these sets generally run the length of a long hall. The head of a set is the end of the line closest to the band and caller. At contra dance events where dancers perform several different folk dances, the caller or dance leader teaches the movements of an individual dance to the dancers during the "walk through," a short period of time before the next type of dance begins. During the walk through, all dancers mark the movements following the caller's instructions. At contra dance events in North America, contra dancers traditionally change partners for every dance, while in the United Kingdom, dancers remain with the same partner for the entire evening.

Square dance refers to a type of folk dance in which four couples begin and end each sequence in a square formation. When four couples align themselves in such a manner, the formation is "sets-in-order," and we call dances that use such formations "quadrilles." Similar to folk dance, American square dance steps are based on traditional European dances. At every square dance event, the dance caller prompts participants through a sequence of steps to the beat throughout the entirety of each dance, but does not usually participate in the dancing. Steps common to many square dances include allemande left and allemande right, where couples face, take hands, and circle around one another; promenade, where partners cross hands and walk to a counter-clockwise position; and circle right and circle left, where all dancers grasp hands and move round in a circle. Traditionally, the caller explains the steps to each individual square dance at the beginning of a session.

Tap is a form of dance born in the United States during the 19th century in which the dancer sounds out the rhythm by clicking taps on the toes and heels of his shoes. This form of percussive music and dance evolved from a fusion of Irish and African Shuffle in New York City during the 1830s. One common characteristic of modern tap dance is "syncopation," where choreographies generally begin on the eighth music beat. Learning to tap dance is a cumulative process in which new information builds on previously learned steps and terms. To teach tap dance successfully, instructors must first teach simple steps that make up the foundation of tap before introducing complex movements. The most basic steps of tap include the walk, step, heel, step-heel, stamp, ball-change, brush, toe tap, shuffle, side shuffle, back shuffle, and cramp roll. Dance instructors can combine these steps to form simple routines for beginners. Once students have mastered these steps, dancers can move on to attempt movements such as the buffalo, Maxi Ford, Cincinnati, pullback, wings, toe clips, and riffs.

DANCE AEROBICS

Dance aerobics is any type of cardiovascular exercise put to music, ranging from country line dancing to hip-hop. Participants can perform aerobic dance on three different levels, high-impact aerobics, in which movements such as jumping cause both feet to lose contact with the ground simultaneously; low-impact aerobics, in which one foot remains in contact with the ground at all times; and step aerobics, in which dancers move on and around a slightly raised platform. A beneficial aerobics session is composed of three stages. During the warm-up, which usually lasts for 5-10 minutes, slow movements such as walking in place and stretching will prepare participants for more vigorous activity. The high-impact stage of dance aerobics follows the warm-up. High impact should last 20-30 minutes, and include anything from a dance routine to a step class. Moves common to many dance aerobic classes include the grapevine combined with kicks and lunges, high kicks, jumping jacks, and forward and back double kicks. Step routines are generally composed of movements on and off a platform, and also include kicks, swats, and lunges. In between movements of the high-impact period, dancers should always maintain constant movement, walking or marching in place to keep up their heart rate and burn more calories. The last 5-10 minutes of a dance aerobics session should be a cool down period, during which participants again stretch all muscles and slowly lower their heart rate.

SKILL 6.3   Identify concepts, strategies, and safety issues in the development of noncompetitive and cooperative activities.

COOPERATIVE AND COMPETITIVE GAMES

Cooperative games are a class of games that promote teamwork and social interaction. The emphasis is on activity, fitness, skill development, and cooperation, rather than competition. There are many cooperative games available to the physical education instructor that help develop various coordination skills and teamwork. Examples of cooperative games include throwing and catching, freeze tag, and parachute.

Competitive games are a class of games that emphasize score, winning, and beating an opponent. Physical education instructors should integrate competitive games into the curriculum to generate student interest and teach concepts of fair play and sportsmanship. Competitive games are most suitable for students that are more mature and possess more developed skills. All of the traditional sporting events are competitive games.

Instructors can organize games by grade levels, homerooms, clubs, societies, physical education classes, study groups, age, height, weight, residential districts, or by arbitrary assignment.

Rope Challenge Courses – A good activity for team-building purposes. Challenges include personal physical challenges (climbing various structures), or group activities (e.g. requiring students to work together to coordinate the crossing of a course). Safety requirements include helmets, harnesses, spotters, trained supervisors, and strict adherence to all safety procedures and educator instructions.

Rock climbing – Students studying rock climbing will gain proficiency in climbing techniques (including body positioning and learning to find proper toeholds and handholds in the rock face) belaying, and managing the climbing and harness equipment.

Strategies in rock climbing require the climber to remain aware not only of the current 'next step' of the climbing process, but to also remain aware of the entire rock face, and to plan on a course that she can follow through to completion (so as to prevent climbing to a dead-end area).

Safety practices include explaining all safety practices so students understand, ensuring that students wear all safety gear (protective gear and harnesses) properly, and that all students have spotters monitoring their activities.

Equipment required for rock climbing activities includes proper attire, suitable footwear, protective equipment, and harnessing equipment.

Alpine skiing (downhill skiing) – The skills that students of alpine skiing will gain center on learning to control the direction and speed of their descent; novices will begin by learning the "snow plough" technique to turn, and will learn to point their skis inward to stop. More advanced technique will center on "carving", which allows the skis to turn without skidding or slowing down.

Alpine skiing strategy calls for awareness of the practitioner's current level of skill and avoiding over-reaching (i.e. attempting courses that are too advanced and thus dangerous). Instructors should teach students to be aware of the course ahead of them, allowing them to better plan their movements.

Safety practices in alpine skiing include proper inspection of the equipment to ensure that everything is in order and instructing the students in appropriate safety procedures. Most importantly, instructors should not allow students to attempt courses that are beyond their current skill levels.

Equipment required for alpine skiing includes appropriate dress that is adequately warm (hats, gloves, and goggles), skis, and poles.

Camping – Camping imparts a wide range of skills, from tent pitching to fire building to outdoor cooking.

Successful camping strategy focuses on planning and preparing the students (mentally, physically, and in terms of their equipment) for the camping experience.

Safety practices for camping include packing a first aid kit and emergency supplies (e.g. a map, compass, whistle), checking the weather before departure, avoiding areas of natural hazards, and putting out fires appropriately. Instructors should teach students to identify and avoid poisonous plants.

Camping equipment includes a tent, lean-to, or other shelter device, a sleeping bag and sleeping pad (or air mattress), a portable stove (where campfires are impractical or not allowed), a lantern or flashlight, a hatchet, axe or saw, ropes, and tarps.

SKILL 6.4   *Identify and apply developmentally appropriate strategies and instruments to assess learner performance.*

SEE ALSO Domain 2, Skill 4.3

INDIVIDUAL/DUAL SPORT ACTIVITIES APPROPRIATE FOR VARIOUS DEVELOPMENTAL LEVELS AND PURPOSES

Team sports form a major part of the physical education curriculum. Designed mainly for promoting physical fitness among students, children, and adults, such sport activities include concepts and strategies, which help students to develop healthy physical, motor, emotional, social, and psychological skills.

These activities have defined steps that help gradually increase the physical development of the students. Apart from this, physical activities associated with team sports also keep diseases and other body ailments at bay. Physical activity inherent in spots can help remedy and prevent potential body ailments such as obesity, weakness, and heart disease.

Physical activities usually involve the utilization of motor skills in harmony with physical, emotional, psychological, psychomotor, and mental skills. Sports activities are a combination of movements and rules that often lead to healthy physical development in a child. In turn, the child is more likely to become stronger and fitter, making various other tasks in life easier. These types of activities lead to other qualities such as sportsmanship, mutual respect, and cooperation. Children also develop intellectually during the course of a play or motor skills development. For example, rock climbing and other adventure activities require mental forethought and planning. Participation in such activities promotes the development of critical-thinking, problem solving, and decision making skills.

Further, regard for others and learning to work cooperatively with peers are necessary skills for success in team sports. In addition, participation in sports provides experience in dealing with interpersonal conflict (e.g. between teammates or competitors) and helps develop leadership skills. Children also develop respect for rules, acquire motor skills, and gain the ability to enjoy physical activity early in life, or as soon as they engage in organized or free play.

DOMAIN 3.0   **THE ROLE OF PHYSICAL EDUCATION IN PROMOTINGDEVELOPMENT**

COMPETENCY 1.0   *UNDERSTAND THE ROLE PHYSICAL EDUCATION IN THE DEVELOPMENT OF POSITIVE PERSONAL BEHAVIORS*

SKILL 1.1   *Identify developmental progressions in the cognitive and affective domains.*

Cognitive development – Language development is the most important aspect of cognitive development in small children (ages 3-5). Allowing successes, rewarding mature behavior, and allowing the child to explore can improve confidence and self-esteem at this age.

Early elementary school children (Ages 6-8) are eager to learn and love to talk. Children at this age have a very literal understanding of rules and verbal instructions and must develop strong listening skills.

Pre-adolescent children (ages 9-11) display increased logical thought, but their knowledge or beliefs may be unusual or surprising. Differences in cognitive styles develop at this age (e.g. field dependant or independent preferences).
In early adolescence (ages 12-14), boys tend to score higher on mechanical/spatial reasoning, and girls on spelling, language, and clerical tasks. Boys are better with mental imagery, and girls have better access and retrieval of information from memory. Self-efficacy (the ability to self-evaluate) becomes very important at this stage.

In later adolescence (ages 15-17), children are capable of formal thought, but don't always apply it. Conflicts between teens' and parents' opinions and worldviews will arise. Children at this age may become interested in advanced political thinking.

Social development – Small children (ages 3-5) are socially flexible. Different children will prefer solitary play, parallel play, or cooperative play. Frequent minor quarrels will occur between children, and boys will tend to be more aggressive (children at these ages are already aware of gender roles).

Early elementary school children (ages 6-8) are increasingly selective of friends (usually of the same sex). Children at this age enjoy playing games, but are excessively preoccupied by the rules. Verbal aggression becomes more common than physical aggression, and adults should encourage children of this age to solve their own conflicts.

Pre-adolescent children (ages 9-11) place great importance on the (perceived) opinions of their peers and of their social stature, and will go to great lengths to 'fit in'. Friendships at this age are very selective, and usually of the same sex.

Young adolescents (ages 12-14) develop greater understanding of the emotions of others, which results in increased emotional sensitivity and impacts peer relationships. Children at this age develop an increased need to perform.

In the later stages of adolescence (ages 15-17), peers are still the primary influence on day-to-day decisions, but parents will have increasing influence on long-term goals. Girls' friendships tend to be close and intimate, whereas boys' friendships are based on competition and similar interests. Many children this age will work part-time, and educators should be alert to signs of potential school dropouts.

Emotional development – Small children (ages 3-5) express emotion freely and have a limited ability to learn how emotions influence behavior. Jealousy at this age is common.

Early elementary school children (ages 6-8) have easily bruised feelings and are just beginning to recognize the feelings of others. Children this age will want to please teachers and other adults.

Pre-adolescent children (ages 9-11) develop a global and stable self-image (self-concept and self-esteem). Comparisons to their peers and the opinions of their peers are important. An unstable home environment at this age contributes to an increased risk of delinquency.

Young adolescence (ages 12-14) can be a stormy and stressful time for children, but, in reality, this is only the case for roughly 20% of teens. Boys will have trouble controlling their anger and will display impulsive behavior. Girls may suffer depression. Young adolescents are very egocentric and concerned with appearance, and will feel very strongly that "adults don't understand."

In later stages of adolescence (ages 15-17), educators should be alert to signs of surfacing mental healthy problems (e.g. eating disorders, substance abuse, schizophrenia, depression, and suicide).

FACTORS INFLUENCING AFFECTIVE DEVELOPMENT

Factors that influence cognitive growth and development include exposure to sufficient stimuli to prompt the development of cognitive systems and skills and proper nutrition, which is vital. Excessively high stress levels (for example, caused by an abusive home environment) will negatively affect the cognitive development of the child.

Factors that influence social growth and development include the opportunity to create positive social bonds with peers and stable and supportive relationships with the child's caregivers.

Factors that influence emotional growth and development in children are found mostly in the home and school environments. One important factor is the personal experiences of success or failure (and the reactions of parents and peers to those successes and failures). In this way, children develop their self-concept, self-image, and self-esteem based on the perceptions and opinions of others.

SKILL 1.2 *Recognize the relationship between physical activity and the development of personal identity and psychological well-being.*

There is an important relationship to consider between physical activity and the development of personal identity and emotional and mental well-being, most notably the impact of positive body image and self-concept. Instructors can help children develop positive body image and self-concept by creating opportunities for the children to experience successes in physical activities and to develop a comfort level with their bodies. This is an important contributor to their personal and physical confidence. The following are lists of the signs of stress and the psychological benefits of physical activity:

Emotional signs of stress include: depression, lethargy, aggressiveness, irritability, anxiety, edginess, fearfulness, impulsiveness, chronic fatigue hyper excitability, inability to concentrate, frequent feelings of boredom, feeling overwhelmed, apathy, impatience, pessimism, sarcasm, humorlessness, confusion, helplessness, melancholy, alienation, isolation, numbness, purposelessness, isolation, numbness, self-consciousness; inability to maintain an intimate relationship.

Behavioral signs of stress include: elevated use of substances (alcohol, drugs; tobacco), crying, yelling, insomnia or excessive sleep, excessive TV watching, school/job burnout, panic attacks, poor problems solving capability, avoidance of people, aberrant behavior, procrastination, accident proneness, restlessness, loss of memory, indecisiveness, aggressiveness, inflexibility, phobic responses, tardiness, disorganization; sexual problems.

Physical signs of stress: pounding heart, stuttering, trembling/nervous tics, excessive perspiration, teeth grinding, gastrointestinal problems (constipation, indigestion, diarrhea, queasy stomach), dry mouth, aching lower back, migraine/tension headaches, stiff neck, asthma attacks, allergy attacks, skin problems, frequent colds or low grade fevers, muscle tension, hyperventilation, high blood pressure, amenorrhea, nightmares; cold intolerance.

Psychological benefits of physical activity include the following: relieves stress, improved mental health via better physical health, reduces mental tension (relieves depression, improves sleeping patterns; fewer stress symptoms), better resistance to fatigue, better quality of life, more enjoyment of leisure, better capability to handle some stressors, opportunity of successful experiences, better Self-Concept, better ability to recognize and accept limitations, improved appearance and sense of well-being, better ability to meet challenges, and better sense of accomplishments.

COOPERATION AND COMPETITION

Cooperation refers to the practice of students working together with agreed-upon goals and possibly methods, instead of working separately in competition. Hence, cooperation is the opposite of competition. Competition is the act of striving against another force for the purpose of achieving dominance or attaining a reward or goal. The need or desire to compete with others is a very common impetus that motivates individuals to organize into a group and cooperate with each other in order to form a stronger competitive force. Therefore, in a game of football, we would encourage cooperation and a team spirit and perhaps in track we would encourage competition to be the fastest person.

TRUST BUILDING

Trust building activities can break down barriers and build deep feelings of trust and reliance between individuals and within small groups of students. However, the power of these activities is a double-edged sword and instructors must use caution in selecting and conducting trust-based activities. If instructors introduce trust activities too early or too fast, emotional and/or physical harm can occur, with trust broken rather than built. For example, a common trust building activity involves blindfolding a person and having another member of the group guide. It is vital to demonstrate and actively encourage a high level of care and responsibility towards people in these exercises who take the risk of trusting. It is not ok to have a blindfolded and trusting person walk into a wall or low bench. For example, we could use the circle of trust game where a group of students forms a circle around a blindfolded student or a student with her eyes closed. The blindfolded student keeps her entire body stiff and leans/falls forward or backward. The other students, keeping hands raised the entire time, keep her from falling. This is an exercise requiring both diligence and vigilance in keeping the blindfolded student safe, but the trust building rewards are worth it.

RISK TAKING

Healthy risk taking is a positive tool in an adolescent's life for discovering, developing, and consolidating his or her identity. It is important to remember that learning how to assess risks is a process that we work on throughout our lives. Children and adolescents need support, tools, and practice in order to do this. Teachers can help support students by encouraging a student to participate in something that may stretch his abilities, but not to the point where his limitations place him in a dangerous situation. For example, participation in an unfamiliar sport where the other students welcoming and supportive provides a degree of satisfaction for the student. A bad example would be putting a student on a team of large football players when he is either small-framed, inexperienced, or both.

You can observe the styles of risk taking by the way a student handles a new social situation. Although there are many styles, we can observe certain patterns, such as the cautious risk taker, the middle-of-the-roader, the adventurer or high-end risk taker, and the social risk taker whose boldness increases when he or she is with friends. It is also important to note that some children may be risk takers in one area – social, physical, intellectual, artistic – and not in others.

ENJOYMENT AND PERSONAL EXPRESSION

In addition to the previously discussed achievement benefits of physical activity, physical activity also provides many people with pure enjoyment and the opportunity for personal expression. Exercise promotes a sense of well-being and usually improves a person's mood. Sports also provide a venue for social interaction and enjoyment of nature. Finally, many sports and activities, especially freestyle activities like skateboarding, figure skating, dance, and surfing, allow for a high level of personal expression.

SKILL 1.3   *Evaluate the role of physical activity in fostering awareness and enjoyment of aesthetic and creative aspects of skilled performance.*

We can divide the benefits of lifelong participation in dance and aesthetic activities, personal performance activities, and outdoor and adventure activities into physical and psychological dimensions (which, of course, have a reciprocal relationship).

On a physical level, personal performance activities contribute to the health and physical fitness of the participating individual. Physical benefits include increased cardiorespiratory fitness, improved circulation, and an increase in muscle tone.

On a psychological level, these activities contribute to the individual's sense of accomplishment and ability to deal with adversity (which is a part of any personal performance activity). When participants become more involved in their personal performance activity of choice, it can contribute to their sense of positive personal identity.

Strategies for promoting enjoyment and participation in personal performance activities throughout life are centered on matching the right activity to the interests, lifestyle, availability, and physical capabilities of the individual. Individuals must enjoy personal performance activities to devote their time on a regular basis, and the time required has to fit into the lifestyle and schedule of the person in question. It is also important to consider the physical condition of the individual. The activity in question must be compatible with their capabilities and they should work their way into the activity gradually.

- **Human Growth and Development** – Movement activities promote personal growth and development physically, by way of stimulating muscular development, and emotionally, by raising personal confidence levels among children and by allowing them to explore concepts of inter-group equity that may at first seem threatening. To the insecure child, the concept that another group may be equal to his own may seem to 'demote' his group and the child by extension.

- **Psychology** – Observation and interaction with the behavior of children from diverse backgrounds in a training environment (where the training activities tend to focus more on 'doing', which feels more genuine to children than the classroom setting of raising hands and answering questions) allows the child to see in others the same sorts of behavioral reasoning processes that he sees in himself. This humanizes others from diverse backgrounds, and promotes concepts of equity among diverse groups.

- **Aesthetics** – Human movement activities create an opportunity for individual participation in activities with intrinsic aesthetic qualities. A gymnastic technique or a perfectly executed swing of a baseball bat relies on both physical training and a level of intuitive action. This is an artistic form of expression that is readily accessible to children. Recognizing beauty in the activities and performances of others (in some cases from groups different from that of the viewing student) is a humanizing experience.

SKILL 1.4   *Demonstrate an understanding of the ways in which physical activities can promote positive behaviors.*

For most people, the development of social roles and appropriate social behaviors occurs during childhood. Physical play between parents and children, as well as between siblings and peers, serves as a strong regulator in the developmental process. Chasing games, roughhousing, wrestling, or practicing sport skills such as jumping, throwing, catching, and striking, are some examples of childhood play. These activities may be competitive or non-competitive and are important for promoting social and moral development of both boys and girls. Unfortunately, fathers will often engage in this sort of activity more with their sons than their daughters. Regardless of the sex of the child, both boys and girls enjoy these types of activities.

Physical play during infancy and early childhood is central to the development of social and emotional competence. Research shows that children who engage in play that is more physical with their parents, particularly with parents who are sensitive and responsive to the child, exhibited greater enjoyment during the play sessions and were more popular with their peers. Likewise, these early interactions with parents, siblings, and peers are important in helping children become more aware of their emotions and to learn to monitor and regulate their own emotional responses. Children learn quickly through watching the responses of their parents which behaviors make their parents smile and laugh and which behaviors cause their parents to frown and disengage from the activity.

If children want the fun to continue, they engage in the behaviors that please others. As children near adolescence, they learn through rough-and-tumble play that there are limits to how far they can go before hurting someone (physically or emotionally), which results in termination of the activity or later rejection of the child by peers. These early interactions with parents and siblings are important in helping children learn appropriate behavior in the social situations of sport and physical activity.

Children learn to assess their social competence (i.e., ability to get along with and acceptance by peers, family members, teachers and coaches) in sport through the feedback received from parents and coaches. Initially, authority figures teach children, "You can't do that because I said so." As children approach school age, parents begin the process of explaining why a behavior is right or wrong because children continuously ask, "why?"

Similarly, when children engage in sports, they learn about taking turns with their teammates, sharing playing time, and valuing rules. They understand that rules are important for everyone and without these regulations, the game would become unfair. The learning of social competence is continuous as we expand our social arena and learn about different cultures. A constant in the learning process is the role of feedback as we assess the responses of others to our behaviors and comments.

In addition to the development of social competence, sport participation can help youth develop other forms of self-competence. Most important among these self-competencies is self-esteem. Self-esteem is how we judge our worth and indicates the extent to which an individual believes he is capable, significant, successful and worthy. Educators have suggested that one of the biggest barriers to success in the classroom today is low self-esteem.

Children develop self-esteem by evaluating abilities and by evaluating the responses of others. Children actively observe parents' and coaches' responses to their performances, looking for signs of approval or disapproval of their behavior. Children often interpret feedback and criticism as either a negative or a positive response to the behavior. In sports, research shows that the coach is a critical source of information that influences the self-esteem of children.

Little League baseball players whose coaches use a "positive approach" to coaching (e.g. more frequent encouragement, positive reinforcement for effort and corrective, instructional feedback), had significantly higher self-esteem ratings over the course of a season than children whose coaches used these techniques less frequently. The most compelling evidence supporting the importance of coaches' feedback was found for those children who started the season with the lowest self-esteem ratings and increased considerably their self-assessment and self-worth. In addition to evaluating themselves more positively, low self-esteem children evaluated their coaches more positively than did children with higher self-esteem who played for coaches who used the "positive approach." Moreover, studies show that 95 percent of children who played for coaches trained to use the positive approach signed up to play baseball the next year, compared with 75 percent of the youth who played for untrained adult coaches.

We cannot overlook the importance of enhanced self-esteem on future participation. A major part of the development of high self-esteem is the pride and joy that children experience as their physical skills improve. Children will feel good about themselves as long as their skills are improving. If children feel that their performance during a game or practice is not as good as that of others, or as good as they think mom and dad would want, they often experience shame and disappointment.

Some children will view mistakes made during a game as a failure and will look for ways to avoid participating in the task if they receive no encouragement to continue. At this point, it is critical that adults (e.g., parents and coaches) intervene to help children to interpret the mistake or "failure." We must teach children that a mistake is not synonymous with failure. Rather, a mistake shows us that we need a new strategy, more practice, and/or greater effort to succeed at the task.

POSITIVE SOCIAL BEHAVIORS

Physical education activities can promote positive social behaviors and traits in a number of different ways. Instructors can foster improved relations with adults and peers by making students active partners in the learning process and delegating responsibilities within the class environment to students. Giving students leadership positions (e.g. team captain) can give them a heightened understanding of the responsibilities and challenges facing educators.

Team-based physical activities like team sports promote collaboration and cooperation. In such activities, students learn to work together, both pooling their talents and minimizing the weaknesses of different team members, in order to achieve a common goal. The experience of functioning as a team can be very productive for development of loyalty between children, and seeing their peers in stressful situations that they can relate to can promote a more compassionate and considerate attitude among students. Similarly, the need to maximize the strengths of each student on a team (who can complement each other and compensate for weaknesses) is a powerful lesson about valuing and respecting diversity and individual differences. Varying students between leading and following positions in a team hierarchy are good ways to help students gain a comfort level being both followers and leaders.

Fairness is another trait that physical activities, especially rules-based sports, can foster and strengthen. Children are by nature very rules-oriented, and have a keen sense of what they believe is and isn't fair. Fair play, teamwork, and sportsmanship are all values that stem from proper practice of the spirit of physical education classes. Of course, a pleasurable physical education experience goes a long way towards promoting an understanding of the innate value of physical activity throughout the life cycle.

SOCIOLOGICAL BENEFITS of physical activity include the opportunity to spend time with family and friend, making new friends, the opportunity to be part of a team, the opportunity to participate in competitive experiences; the opportunity to experience the thrill of victories.

SKILL 1.5   *Analyze the influence of performance expectations related to gender, physical appearance, and skill level on the development of self-image.*

BIOLOGICAL AND ENVIRONMENTAL INFLUENCES ON GENDER DIFFERENCES IN MOTOR PERFORMANCES

The differences between males and females in motor performance result from certain biological and environmental influences. Generally, people perceive the males as stronger, faster, and more active than females. This higher activity level can stem from childhood behaviors influenced by certain environmental factors and superior motor performance results largely from the biological make up of males versus females.

In most cases, the male body contains less fat mass and more muscle mass than the female body. In addition, the type of muscle differs between males and females. Males have more fast-twitch muscle fibers allowing for more short duration, high intensity movements such as jumping and sprinting. In addition, males generally, but not always, display better coordination. Females have proved their superiority at certain activities, such as skipping, and tend to display better fine movements, such as neater handwriting.

Certain environmental factors also contribute to the gender differences in motor performance. As children, boys tend to be more physically active. Society expects boys to participate in sports and play games that involve running around, such as tag and foot races. On the other hand, society expects girls to be more social and less active. They participate in activities such as playing with dolls. In addition, parents rarely ask girls to perform tasks involving manual labor.

While these sedentary tasks have value, it is important for both males and females to participate in an adequate amount of physical activity each day. If children develop this type of active lifestyle early in life, they are more likely to maintain it throughout adulthood.

BODY IMAGE

Expectations relating to body image influence the development of self-concept by creating a benchmark of assumed correlations between body image and other traits. For example, a slight and skinny (ectomorphic) student may see himself as unathletic, even though students with ectomorphic body types often excel at endurance sports. Students are also likely to generalize from body image to perceived ability to master new physical skills (for example, an athletic child might expect to be better at a new sport than less athletic children, even if the sport is new to both of them).

PHYSICAL APPEARANCE

Expectations relating to physical appearance influence the development of self-concept by virtue of assumptions correlating physical appearance with likeability. In fact, the relationship is reciprocal, and stronger in the opposite direction (students that are popular will tend to develop a more positive self-concept about their physical appearance).

SKILL LEVEL

Expectations relating to skill level influence the development of self-concept by setting the baseline for the performance that students will expect to deliver, both when attempting tasks that they are familiar with and new tasks (students with a high skill level will expect to do well, and students who are good at several things will expect to be good at other, new things).

MEDIA

Media-based expectations influence the development of self-concept by setting media-based role models as the benchmarks against which students will measure their traits. Self-concept is a set of statements describing the child's own cognitive, physical, emotional, and social self-assessment. These statements will usually tend to be fairly objective ("good at baseball" or "has red hair"), media-based expectations can change the statements to be measurements against role models ("athletic like this actor" or "tall like that pop star").

CULTURE

Cultural expectations influence the development of self-concept by suggesting to the child traits they should include in their personal self-assessment. For example, students from a very warm and energetic cultural background, where there is a strong emphasis on family life, may develop self-concepts that incorporate those traits into their personal self-description. Cultural gender roles may also express themselves in this way.

COMPETENCY 2.0 *UNDERSTAND THE ROLE PHYSICAL EDUCATION IN THE DEVELOPMENT OF POSITIVE SOCIAL BEHAVIORS AND ATTITUDES*

SKILL 2.1 *Demonstrate an understanding of socialization processes that occur through physical activity.*

Physical fitness activities incorporate group processes, group dynamics, and a wide range of cooperation and competition. Ranging from team sports (which are both competitive and cooperative in nature) to individual competitive sports (like racing), to cooperative team activities without a winner and loser (like a gymnastics team working together to create a human pyramid), there is a great deal of room for the development of mutual respect and support among the students, safe cooperative participation, and analytical, problem solving, teamwork, and leadership skills.

Teamwork situations are beneficial to students because they create opportunities for them to see classmates with whom they might not generally socialize, and with whom they may not even get along, in a new light. It also creates opportunities for students to develop reliance on each other and practice interdependence. Cooperation and competition can also offer opportunities for children to practice group work. These situations provide good opportunities to practice analytical thinking and problem solving in a practical setting.

The social skills and values gained from participation in physical activities are as follows:

- The ability to make adjustments to both self and others by an integration of the individual to society and the environment.

- The ability to make judgments in a group situation.

- Learning to communicate with others and be cooperative.

- The development of the social phases of personality, attitudes, and values in order to become a functioning member of society such as being considerate.

- The development of a sense of belonging and acceptance by society.

- The development of positive personality traits.

- Learning for constructive use of leisure time.

- A development of attitude that reflects good moral character.

- Respect of school rules and property.

ACTIVITIES THAT ENHANCE SOCIALIZATION

At the junior high level, students indicate a desire to play on a team. They also emphasize that they want to learn activities that would prove useful in their leisure hours.

The senior high level students desire to play harmoniously with others and to participate in team play. Students view activities such as dance and sports as a place to learn respect for their fellow students. The change of pace that physical education classes from academic offerings provides opportunities for enhanced socialization.

Basketball, baseball, football, soccer, and volleyball are social, team activities. Tennis and golf are social activities that are useful in leisure hours.

SKILL 2.2   *Recognize the ways in which physical activities can promote positive social attitudes and behaviors.*

SEE Previous Skill and Domain 3, Skill 1.4

SKILL 2.3   *Demonstrate knowledge of the socio-cultural benefits of participation in a variety of individual and group physical activities.*

SEE Domain 3, Skills 1.4 and 2.1

COMPETENCY 3.0   *UNDERSTAND THE ROLE OF PHYSICAL EDUCATION IN THE DEVELOPMENT OF CRITICAL THINKING, PROBLEM-SOLVING, AND DECISION-MAKING SKILLS*

SKILL 3.1   *Analyze techniques, strategies, and activities for developing higher-order thinking skills in the context of physical education activities.*

Physical education instructors can foster critical-thinking and evaluative skills in the context of physical education and health-related activities by making children active partners in the entire learning and training process. If instructors provide students with an understanding of the mechanisms (e.g. cardiorespiratory, muscular, circulatory) underlying their training (in addition to the knowledge they are given about specific training exercises), students can get more involved and think more critically about their training routines and how they could adapt them to better suit their needs.

Instructors should encourage students to employ self-assessment and self-monitoring techniques and skills. For example, they could keep a journal tracking their personal achievements – cardiorespiratory (measured in resting heart rate, active heart rate, intensity, and duration of exercise), muscular development (measured by their ability to perform callisthenic exercises).

Instructors should also encourage students to explore and increase their understanding (with educator assistance) of the way that the underlying bodily systems work in relation to other disciplines. For example, students can learn about the chemistry involved in the gas and energy exchanges happening between the cardiorespiratory and circulatory system, they can learn about the biology of the digestive system and the effects of different types of nutrition on the body, and they can learn about the physics involved in energy expenditure by the muscular system.

Teaching methods that facilitate cognitive learning include:

1. **Problem Solving** - The instructor presents the initial task and students come to an acceptable solution in unique and divergent ways,

2. **Conceptual Theory** - The instructor's focus is on acquisition of knowledge,

3. **Guided Inquiry** - careful stages of instructions strategically guide students through a sequence of experiences, helping them reach their goals.

Initially, performing skills will be variable, inconsistent, error prone, "off-time," and awkward. Students' focus will be on remembering what to do. Instructors should direct corrections of errors in gross movement at the significant elements of the skill, and they should emphasize the skill's biomechanics. So students will not be overburdened with too much information, one or two elements at a time should be performed. Motivation occurs with supportive and encouraging comments.

Techniques to facilitate cognitive learning include:

1. **Transfer of learning** - identifying similar movements of a previous learned skill and the new skill,

2. **Planning for slightly longer instructions and demonstrations** as students memorize cues and skills,

3. **Using appropriate language** for the level of the students,

4. **Conceptual Thinking** - giving those students' more responsibility for their learning who are capable of doing so.

Aids to facilitate cognitive learning include:

1. Assessing students' performance frequently,

2. Moving activities incorporating principles of biomechanics,

3. Using laser discs; computers and software,

4. Videotaping students' performance

SKILL 3.2   *Recognize the role of physical activity, sports, and games in the development of conflict-resolution skills.*

SEE ALSO Domain 2, Skill 5.4

Interpersonal conflict is a major source of stress and worry. Teaching students to successfully manage conflict will help them reduce stress levels throughout their lives, thereby limiting the adverse health effects of stress. Physical activity, sports, and games provides a forum for practicing and developing conflict-resolution skills. The following is a list of conflict resolution principles and techniques.

1. Think before reacting – In a conflict situation, it is important to resist the temptation to react immediately. You should step back, consider the situation, and plan an appropriate response. In addition, do not react to petty situations with anger.

2. Listen – Be sure to listen carefully to the opposing party. Try to understand the other person's point of view.

3. Find common ground – Try to find some common ground as soon as possible. Early compromise can help ease the tension.

4. Accept responsibility – In every conflict there is plenty of blame to go around. Admitting when you are wrong shows you are committed to resolving the conflict.

5. Attack the problem, not the person – Personal attacks are never beneficial and usually lead to greater conflict and hard feelings.

6. Focus on the future – Instead of trying to assign blame for past events, focus on what we need to do differently to avoid future conflict.

SKILL 3.3   Identify key elements and steps in self-assessment, goal-setting, problem-solving, and decision-making processes in relation to physical activity.

SEE ALSO Domain 1, Skill 1.5

PROBLEM SOLVING

Problem solving is a higher-order cognitive process that requires the modulation and control of more routine or fundamental skills. It is the ability to solve a problem. We would have the students call upon their problem-solving skills during a game of chess. Alternatively, they could strategize during a timeout in the last few seconds of a basketball game where their team is down by two points. Development of adequate problem solving skills also provides the student with self-confidence and a sense of accomplishment.

ASSESSMENT

The trend in physical education assessment is to move increasingly away from norm- and criterion-referenced evaluations (i.e. measuring a student's achievements against the achievements of a normative group or against criteria that are arbitrarily set by either the educator or the governing educational body), and towards performance-based, or "authentic" evaluations. This creates difficulty for physical educators because it eliminates preset reference points.

The advantage of performance-based evaluations is they are equally fair to individuals with diverse backgrounds, special needs, and disabilities. In all cases, the instructor evaluates students based on their personal performance.

.

Portfolio construction is one way of assessing the performance of a student. The student chooses the achievements to add to the portfolio. This creates a tool that assesses current abilities and serves as a benchmark against which the instructor can measure future performance (thus evaluating progress over time, and not just a localized achievement).

Student self-assessment is often an important part of portfolios. The instructor should ask children questions like, "Where am I now? Where am I trying to go? What am I trying to achieve? How can I get from here to there?" This type of questioning involves the child more deeply in the learning process.

DOMAIN 4.0   THE PHYSICAL EDUCATION PROGRAM

COMPETENCY 1.0   UNDERSTAND THE DEVELOPMENT AND
                      EVALUATION OF PHYSICAL EDUCATION
                      PROGRAMS

SKILL 1.1   Analyze and evaluate historical, philosophical, social, political, and
             economic issues that influence the physical education profession
             and their impact on instructional programs at the local, state,
             national and global levels.

KNOWLEDGE OF THE HISTORY OF PHYSICAL EDUCATION AS A
PROFESSION

Leading men and women in physical education

Physical education (P.E.) is a course of study in the curriculum of most
educational systems designed to utilize both mental and physical capacities. The
goal of this course of study is to instill in students the knowledge, skills, and
enthusiasm required to maintain a healthy lifestyle into adulthood. Physical
education is not necessarily dependent on an individual's physical capabilities.
Physical education is a class that provides students with an understanding of
rules, concepts, strategies, and teamwork that will benefit students throughout
their lives.

The term physical education derives from the Latin word "physica," meaning
physics, and "education," meaning the training of the bodily organs and powers
to promote health and strength. We can trace the history of physical education
back to the Greeks who held the first Olympic Games in 776 BC, which equated
honor and fame with physical strength and skill. In 1420, an Italian physician
named Vittorini da Feltre recognized the importance of the simultaneous
development of mind and body and initiated physical education classes for
children in Italy. Physical education classes did not begin in the United States
until Charles Beck initiated them in 1825.

Jean-Jacques Rousseau was an Enlightenment philosopher of the 18th century
who made great contributions to the field of educational theory. Rousseau
argued that humankind was subject to a system of justice derived from nature
rather than society. He called this set of rules "natural law," and was a strong
advocate of equal education for children of all social classes and physical
abilities. Rousseau promoted the training of the body as well as the mind in
schools and other educational systems because of the close and interconnected
relationship of mental and physical processes, believing that if the body
exercised, so did the mind.

Horace Mann was another figure involved in the promotion of education of the entire body in United States school systems. Mann served in both the Massachusetts House of Representatives and Senate in the 1830s, but generated the most educational reform as secretary of the Board of Education of Massachusetts in 1837. Mann's primary goal for education was to create a more equal playing field for the masses, believing that an education would provide the means to better one's lot in life. Mann argued that acquiring knowledge was the same as acquiring power, and placed equal importance on the teaching of academic subjects such as spelling and arithmetic, and the teaching of non-academia such as music and physical education that promoted healthy living habits.

Contributions of early societies to the profession

Games often had a practical, educational aim like playing house. In addition, games such as gladiatorial games had political aims. Economic games included fishing and hunting. Families played board games. There were ceremonial reasons for games found in dances. Finally, ball games provided an opportunity for socialization.

Early society - The common activities performed in early societies included war-like games, chariot racing, boating and fishing, equestrian, hunting, music and dancing, boxing and wrestling, bow and arrow activities, dice, and knucklebones.

Egyptian - The common activities performed in Egypt were acrobatics, gymnastics, tug of war, hoop and kick games, ball and stick games, juggling, knife-throwing games of chance, board games, and guessing games (e.g. how many fingers are concealed).

Bronze Age - The activities performed during the Bronze Age (3000 to 1000 BC) were bullfights, dancing, boxing, hunting, archery, running, and board games.

Greek Age - The Greeks are best known for the Olympic Games, but their other contributions were the pentathlon, which included the jump, the discus, and the javelin. The Pankration was a combination of boxing and wrestling. The Greeks also played on seesaws, enjoyed swinging, hand guessing games, blind man's bluff, dice games (losers had to carry their partner's pick-a-back), and hoop and board games. There also were funeral games in The Iliad.

Romans - The Romans kept slaves and were advocates of "blood sports." Their philosophy was to die well. There were unemployment games. Roman baths were popular, as were ball games, stuffed feathers, pila trigonalis, follis, and balloon or bladder ball. The Capitoline games were held in 86 AD. These union guild athletes were paid for their activities, which included artificial fly-fishing. The games that were popular during this period were top spinning, odds and evens, riding a long stick, knucklebones, and hide and seek.

Chinese - The Chinese contributed the following: jujitsu, fighting cocks, dog racing, and football. In Korea, Japan, and China, children played with toys and lanterns. Common activities included building snowmen, playing with dolls, making/playing with shadows, flying kites, and fighting kites. Children enjoyed ropewalker toys, windmills, turnip lanterns, ring puzzles, and playing horse. Noblemen engaged in hopping, jumping, leapfrog, jump rope, seesaw, and drawing.

Major events in the history of physical education and the historical relationship of physical education to health and fitness

Egypt - Sport dancing among the nobility, physical skills among the masses, and physical training for wars.

Cretans - learned to swim.

Spartan and Greeks - emphasized severe physical training and NOT competitive sport.

Athenians - believed in the harmonious development of the body, mind and spirit.

Romans – The Romans established the **worth of physical education**. During the dark ages, children learned fitness and horsemanship. The squires learned how to become knights by boxing and fencing. Swimming was also popular. During the Renaissance, people developed the body for health reasons. The Romans **combined the physical and mental** aspects of exercise in their daily routines.

1349-1428 - Physical education was necessary for a person's total education and also a means of recreation.

In **1546,** Martin Luther saw PE as a substitute for vice and evil.

Sweden - Ling in 1839 strove to make PE a **science.**

Colonial period - religions denounced play. Pleasures were either banned or frowned upon.

The **National Period** began in 1823. Games and sports were available as after school activities. There was an introduction of **gymnastics and calisthenics.**

Civil War (1860) - Gymnastics and non-military use of PE. Physical Education became **organized**. PE became part of the school curriculum and held a respectable status among other subjects. **YMCA's** were founded. Gulick was the Director of PE at NYC and Dudley Allen Sargent was teaching physical education at Harvard.

Great Depression of the 1930s - **Physical fitness movement.** Bowling was the number one activity. Dance, gymnastics and sports were popular. The Heisman Trophy was awarded in 1935. After WWII, outdoor pools were common for the average American.

Major trends since WWII influencing physical education

WWII - Selective Service examinations revealed the poor physical fitness condition of the country's youth. Thus, **physical education classes focused on physical conditioning.**

1942 - President Roosevelt established the **Division of Physical Fitness** run by John B. Kelly (who alerted Roosevelt about the poor fitness levels of youths). This division was dissolved and **placed under the Federal Security Agency** [FSA] with numerous organizations **promoting fitness**. Under the FSA, Frank Lloyd was Chief of the Physical Fitness Division, William Hughs was Chief Consultant, and Dorothy LaSalle was head of the work for women and children. **After WWII ended, the eagerness for fitness waned.**

1953 - **Kraus-Webber tests** - Of the 4,264 USA participants, 57% failed a general muscular fitness test. Only 8.7% of Europeans failed. Again, John Kelly alerted the President (Eisenhower) of the **need for a fitness movement.** Eisenhower ordered a **special conference** that was held in **June 1956.**

1956 - AAHPERD Fitness Conference established the President's Council on Youth Fitness and a President's Citizens Advisory Committee on the Fitness of American Youth.

Modern dance gave way to contemporary. Gymnastics had new equipment, including a higher balance beam, trampolines, and uneven parallel bars. The Swedish gymnastics boom was over, and ropes and ladders, wands, dumbbells, and Indian clubs were no longer fashionable. Core sports for boys were football, baseball, basketball, and track and field. Core sports for women were basketball and volleyball.

John Fitzgerald Kennedy changed the name of the President's Citizens Advisory Committee of Fitness of American Youth to the **President's Council on Physical Fitness.**

Lyndon Baines Johnson changed the name to **President's Council on Physical Fitness and Sports.**

1972 - **passage of Title IX** of the Educational Amendments Act to ensure girls and women receive the same rights as boys and men for educational programs - including physical education and athletics

1970 to Present Trends - Preventative medicine, wellness, physical fitness, and education that is more scholarly, more specialized, and more applicable to all segments of population such as the elderly, handicapped persons, and those out of organizations (Non-School sports): AAU - mid 20th century controlled amateur sports; Little League; North American Baseball Association.

International Amateur Sports: Olympic Governing Committee.

Intercollegiate: National Collegiate Athletic Association (NCAA scholarship in 1954); National Association of Intercollegiate Athletics (NAIA); National Junior College Athletic Association (NJCAA).

Interscholastic Sports: National Federation of State High School Athletic Associations.

Organizations for Girls' and Women's Sports: Athletic and Recreation Federation of College Women (ARFCW); the Women's Board of the U.S. Olympic Committee; National Section of Women's Athletics (NSWA - promoted intercollegiate sports such as US Field Hockey and Women's International Bowling and established special committees). The Women's Division of NAAF merged its interests in the NSWA of AAHPERD changing its name to National Section for Girls and Women's Sports (NSGWS). **Mel Lockes, chairperson of NSGWS in 1956, was against intercollegiate athletics for women.** In 1957, NSGWS changed its name to Division of Girls and Women's Sports (DGWS), still a division of AAHPER. A lack of funds hurt DGWS.

TRENDS

Physical education instructors can use national and state documents, standards, benchmarks, trends and philosophies to design and develop effective curricula.

First, governmental organizations (e.g. U.S. Department of Education, individual state departments of education) regularly release documents outlining standards for physical education. Common physical education standards require that students learn skills necessary to participate in a variety of physical activities, become physically fit, participate regularly in physical activity, understand the benefits and implications of physical fitness, and value physical activity as part of a healthy lifestyle. Instructors must mold their curricula to ensure that their students meet these standards.

In addition, governmental organizations often determine benchmarks that define physical development and fitness in school-age children. For example, standards may indicate what motor skills students should possess at certain ages and the specific performance criteria that define physical fitness. Instructors can use the benchmarks and tests to evaluate student development and fitness and plan curricula for student improvement.

Finally, national trends and philosophies greatly affect physical education curricula. National trends toward greater longevity, increased obesity, and sedentary lifestyles increase the need for a renewed emphasis on fitness and activity to prevent and reduce fitness related health problems. The philosophies of life-long learning and fitness are also an important aspect of physical education. Instructors should design curricula that encourage and motivate students to become active and take a life-long interest in the physical health of their bodies.

NASPE FEDERAL CONTENT STANDARDS

The goal of physical education is to impart the knowledge, skills, and confidence necessary for students to enjoy a life of healthful physical activity. The National Association for Sport and Physical Education identifies six content standards for physical education:

- **Standard 1:** Demonstrates competency in motor skills and movement patterns needed to perform a variety of physical activities.

- **Standard 2:** Demonstrates understanding of movement concepts, principles, strategies, and tactics as they apply to the learning and performance of physical activities.

- **Standard 3:** Participates regularly in physical activity.

- **Standard 4:** Achieves and maintains a health-enhancing level of physical fitness.

- **Standard 5:** Exhibits responsible personal and social behavior that respects self and others in physical activity settings.

- **Standard 6:** Values physical activity for health, enjoyment, challenge, self-expression, and/or social interaction.

(Source: National Association for Sport & Physical Education)

A comprehensive physical education curriculum emphasizes the importance of physical activity and nutrition to lifelong wellness. In addition, physical education should introduce students to various activities that promote healthy living. Finally, physical education should provide students with strategies to maintain proper nutrition and activity and design personal fitness programs.

"A REPORT OF THE SURGEON GENERAL"

In 1996, the Surgeon General released a report that evaluated the status of physical fitness in America. Some of the important conclusions of the report were that physical activity had many health benefits, a majority of Americans was not physically active, and there was a significant decrease in physical education programs. The report emphasizes the benefits of physical activity and cites physical education as an important tool in promoting greater levels of physical activity.

LOSS OF PHYSICAL EDUCATION FACILITIES

With increasingly tight public school budgets and increased emphasis on academic standards and testing, many schools are experiencing a loss of physical education facilities. In many school districts, physical education operates on a shoestring budget. The loss of facilities such as gymnasiums, playing fields, swimming pools, and related equipment limits the scope of physical education programs. Inadequate facilities prevent instructors from utilizing many types of activities. Thus, instructors must use the available facilities in the best way possible to maximize the physical education experience for all students.

INCLUSION AND MAINSTREAMING

A major goal of contemporary physical education is inclusion and mainstreaming of all types of students. Instructors must modify activities to include students with disabilities and students of all ability levels. In addition, the physical education program should embrace the cultural, linguistic, and familial differences of all students. Inclusion and mainstreaming shifts the focus of physical education from competitive, athletic activities to cooperative, skill-building activities that benefit all children and promote inclusion. Thus, the primary goal and focus of physical education is promotion of physical activity, motor-skill development, and socialization.

SKILL 1.2   *Identify and apply principles and procedures for organizing and administering a comprehensive physical education programs for all student populations.*

The first few weeks of the school year is the most effective time for teaching class management structure (behavioral rules, terms for compliance and violation of rules, and classroom routines).

Instructors must manage all essential procedures and routines (roll call, excuses, tardiness, changing, and showering) to productively use available class time. Good class management also insures the safety of the group through procedures and routines, provides a controlled classroom atmosphere to make instruction easier, promotes individual self-discipline and self-motivation, develops a sense of responsibility towards others, develops rapport between teacher and students that promotes learning, creates a group camaraderie where each student feels good about him/herself and feels at ease within the group, uses the instructor's time and energy productively, and organizes and coordinates classes for the most effective instruction and learning.

Long-term planning for the semester and year, as well as daily, weekly, and seasonal planning, is necessary. Instructors must effectively plan activities so that they proceed with precision, minimize "standing-around time", and allow for maximum activity time for each student. Instructors should arrange activities in advance and prepare any necessary line markings.

To determine student progress and effectiveness of teaching, instructors must plan appropriate measurement and evaluation opportunities. Instructors also must wear suitable clothing, have good knowledge of the subject, and promote desirable attitudes toward and understandings of fitness, skill learning, sportsmanship, and other physical education objectives.

The main goals and purpose of physical education is to introduce students to fitness, activity, and nutrition concepts and allow students to be physically active during the school day. Proper structure and organization allows the realization of these goals.

SKILL 1.3   Recognize the value orientations, goals, and models pf physical education curriculum design and analyze factors affecting curriculum design.

RECOGNIZE THE INFLUENCE OF PAST AND PRESENT EDUCATION PHILOSOPHIES

The various philosophies of education greatly influence the goals and values of physical education. Important educational philosophies related to physical education are Idealism, Realism, Pragmatism, Naturalism, Existentialism, Humanism, and Eclecticism.

Idealism – The **mind**, developed through the acquisition of knowledge, is of highest importance. Values exist independently of individuals. Fitness and strength activities contribute to the development of one's personality. Horace Mann, Wadsworth, Kant, Plato, and Descartes were Idealists.

Realism – The physical world is **real.** A realist believes in the laws of nature, the scientific method, and mind and body harmony. Religion and philosophy co-exist. Physical fitness results in greater productivity, physical drills are important to the learning process, athletic programs lead to desired social behavior, and play and recreation help life adjustment. Aristotle was a realist.

Pragmatism – **Experience** is key to life. Dynamic experience shapes individuals' truth. Education is child-centered. Varied activities present experiences that are more meaningful. Activities are socializing. Problem solving accomplishes learning. John Dewy and Charles Pierce were pragmatists.

Naturalism – This philosophy is materialistic. Things that actually exist are found only within the physical realm of nature. Nature is valuable. The individual is more important than society. Self-activities accomplish learning and activities are more than physical in nature. Naturalists promote play and discourage high levels of competition. Physical education takes a holistic approach.

Existentialism – The chief concern is **individualism.** Existentialists do not want the individual to conform to society. They promote freedom of choice and a variety of interests. Individuals need to have their own system of values. Playing develops creativity and the discovery of the "inner self." Sartre, Soren, and Kierkegaard were Existentialists.

Humanism and **Eclecticism** – The modern philosophies of physical education that most schools follow today. The basis of the Humanistic philosophy is the development of individual talents and total fulfillment that encourages total involvement and participation in one's environment. Humanists encourage self-actualization and self-fulfillment. Curriculums based on the Humanistic approach are more student-centered. The Eclectic approach combines beliefs from different philosophies and does not resemble any single philosophy. When blended skillfully, the Eclectic approach affords a sound philosophy for an individual.

PHILOSOPHIES OF EDUCATION APPLIED TO PHYSICAL EDUCATION GOALS

Physical/Organic Development Goal (Realism philosophy) – activities build physical power by strengthening the body's systems, resulting in the ability to sustain adaptive effort, shorten recovery time, and develop resistance to fatigue. The core values are individual health, greater activity, and better performance by an adequately developed and properly functioning body.

Motor/Neuromuscular Development Goal (Realism philosophy) – develops body awareness producing movement that is proficient, graceful, and aesthetic and uses as little energy as possible. Students develop as many skills as possible so their interests are wide and varied to allow more enjoyment and better adjustment to group situations. Varied motor development skills affect health by influencing how leisure time is spent. Values include reducing energy expenditure, building confidence, bringing recognition, enhancing physical and mental health, making participation safer, and contributing to aesthetic sense.

Cognitive Development Goal (Idealism philosophy) – deals with acquiring knowledge and ability to think and interpret knowledge. Scientific principles explain time, space, and flow of movement. Learning physical activities requires thinking and coordination of movement and mastering and adapting to one's environment. Individuals also should acquire knowledge of rules, techniques, and strategies of activities. Cognitive values include healthy attitudes and habits such as body awareness, personal hygiene, disease prevention, exercise, proper nutrition, and knowledge of health service providers.

Social/Emotional/Affective Development Goal (Existentialism philosophy) – deals with helping individuals make adjustments – personal, group, and societal – by positively influencing human behavior. Performance defines success, and success develops self-confidence. Wholesome attitudes throughout the various growth stages promote the development of an appropriate Self-Concept, which is very important. Values include meeting basic social needs (sense of belonging, recognition, self-respect, and love) that produce a socially, well-adjusted individual.

CHARACTERISTICS OF VARIOUS CURRICULUM MODELS

With a history that spans centuries and roots traceable to the ancient Greeks, physical education is a technique that helps in promoting the physical fitness and well-being of a body.

The primary aim of physical education, otherwise known as physical training, is to equip students with the knowledge, skills, capabilities, values, and enthusiasm necessary to the maintenance of a healthy lifestyle into adulthood, regardless of physical ability. Activities included in the program promote physical fitness, develop motor skills, instill knowledge and understanding of rules, concepts, and strategies, and teach students to work as part of a team or as individuals in a wide variety of play-based and competitive activities.

Physical education has come to occupy a very important role in most school programs. There are various curriculum models for physical education courses. Such curricula stress the meaning of human movement, physiology of exercise, sport sociology, aesthetic appreciation of movement, and the acquisition of skills. Modern curricula include all of these competencies.

The modern physical education curriculum provides students a basic experience in the following activities: aquatics, conditioning activities, gymnastics, individual/dual sports, team sports, and rhythm and dance. All states in the United States offer physical education to students in grades K through 12, and many states require the self-contained classroom teacher to implement a physical education program.

All curriculum models have the following characteristics: physical activity, by which students will become competent in a variety of, and proficient in a few, physical activities; human movement, in which students will understand and apply principles of human movement to the learning and development of motor skills; fitness; responsible behavior, wherein students will exhibit responsible personal and social behavior in physical activity settings; respect for differences; and benefits of physical activity, by which students will identify and understand how physical activity provides personal enjoyment, challenge, self-expression, and social interaction.

SKILL 1.4   Establish appropriate criteria and select tools for the evaluation of a physical education program.

TYPES OF EVALUATION

Summative evaluation strategies involve assigning the student a letter or number grade, which can reflect both the student's performance and progress. Examples include:

- Performance evaluations – the instructor assigns a letter or number grade based on the student's performance on a task or set of tasks (e.g. push-ups and sit-ups, time to run one mile, etc.).

- Progress evaluations – the instructor assigns a letter or number grade based on the student's improvement in the ability to perform a task or set of tasks.

- Effort evaluations – the instructor assigns a letter or number grade based on the student's effort in working towards training goals.

- Behavior evaluations – the instructor assigns a letter or number grade based on the student's behavior in and attitude towards training and the training environment.

Formative evaluation strategies do not provide a letter or number grade to the student, but rather focus on a textual analysis of the student's performance and progress. Examples include a written analysis of the student's performance, progress, effort, attitude, and behavior.

BASIC STATISTICAL APPLICATIONS

Statistical applications for physical education assessment purposes allow us to evaluate where the score of a given assessment stands in comparison to other assessments and compare different assessments of the same student's abilities (in other fields – tracking intra-individual differences, or in the same field over time – tracking the student's progress).

Central tendency and variability determine where a range of scores cluster on the assessment scale and whether they are all highly localized around one point on the scale, or spread out over a range.

Standard scores and norms allow us to evaluate where assessment results stand in relation to the 'normal' expected achievement level.

Correlations allow us to evaluate the frequency at which two assessment trends appear in conjunction. Note that correlation does not imply causation.

STUDENT AND PROGRAM EVALUATIONS IN PHYSICAL EDUCATION

The **Cheffers Adaptation of the Flanders Interaction Analysis System** (CAFAIS) and the **Academic Learning Time in Physical Education** (ALT-PE) are *Systematic Analyses* that detect continuous and discrete behaviors, actions and interactions, and teaching characteristics. Relating the goals of a systematic analysis to the data obtained during the instructional process can indicate which of the following instructional strategies need changing:

- The ability of the teacher to question and the time engaged in questioning

- The cognitive response of students

- The time spent on task instruction (rate per minute)

- The number of times task instruction takes place (rate of occurrence)

Instructors can use the following **Systematic Observational Evaluations** to identify necessary changes in events, in duration, in groups, and in self-recording:

- **Event Recording** (rate-per-minute, rate of occurrence) – counts the number of attempts students have to try a skill and the number of positive teacher-student interactions.

- **Duration Recording** – measures amount of time teacher spends on instructions, time spent on managing student activities, and time spent managing the participation of students.

- **Group Time Sampling/Playcheck Recording** – counts the number of students participating in the activity.

- **Self-Recording** – students sign in their arrival time to class and how many completed tasks they accomplish.

Student assessments that can facilitate changes in instructional strategies include:

- **Formal assessments** such as win/loss records, written tests, skills tests, performance records, and reviewing videotaped performances.

- **Informal assessments** such as rating scales, observational performance descriptions, completion of skills checklist, and observational time utilization.

ASSESSMENT IN THE AFFECTIVE DOMAIN

The affective domain includes interests, appreciations, attitudes, values, and adjustments inherent in the acquisition of physical activities. To measure in the affective domain, the teacher can observe the student and keep a record of those observations. Alternatively, the instructor can use opinion polls or surveys. To measure the social progress of an individual, use a sociogram. It plots the associations an individual student has with his peers.

The following is a list of appropriate tools for the assessment of affective development.

SOCIAL MEASURES (behavior, leadership, acceptance, and personality/character):

- **Harrocks Prosocial Behavior Inventory** (HPBBI) – measures prosocial play behavior of 5th and 6th graders in recreational play.

- **Adams Prosocial Inventory** – measures high school students' prosocial behaviors in physical education classes.

- **Nelson Leadership Questionnaire** – determines leaders as perceived by instructors, coaches, classmates, and teammates.

- **Cowell Personal Distance Scale** – measures congruity of a student within a group and his/her yearly development.

- **Blanchard Behavior Rating Scale** – measures student personality and character.

ATTITUDE MEASURES (predisposition to certain actions):

- **McKethan Student Attitude Inventory-Instructional Processes in Secondary Physical Education** (SAI-IPSPE) – measures attitudes of students toward instructional processes (e.g. teacher's verbal behavior, nature of activities, patterns of class organization, and regulations and policies in conceptual physical education environment).

- **Toulmin Elementary Physical Education Attitude Scale** (TEPEAS) – measures attitudes of the physical education program of elementary school students.

- **Feelings About Physical Activity** – measures commitment to activity.

- **Children's Attitudes Toward Physical Activity -Revised** (CATPA) – measures significance students place on physical activity.

- **Willis Sports Attitudes Inventory - Form C** - measures motives of competition in sports (achievement, power, success, avoiding failure).

- **Sport Orientation Questionnaire - Form B** - measures behaviors of achievement and competition during exercising and sports.

- **McMahan Sportsmanship Questionnaire** – measures high school students' attitudes toward sportsmanship.

- **Physical Estimation and Attraction Scale** – measures motivation and interest.

SELF-CONCEPT MEASURES (self-perception):

- **Cratly Adaptation of Piers-Harris Self-Concept and Scale** – measures/estimates students' own feelings about their appearance and skill performance abilities.

- **Merkley Measure of Actual Physical Self** – measures perception of physical self relating to exercise and activity.

- **Nelson-Allen Movement Satisfaction** – measures satisfaction of movement.

- **Tanner Movement Satisfaction Scale** – measures students' own level of satisfaction/dissatisfaction with their own movement.

STRESS AND ANXIETY:

- **Stress Inventory** (Miller and Allen) – measures level of stress according to stress indicators.

- **Sport Competition Anxiety Tests** – measures anxiety toward competition via one's perception of the competition as threatening or non-threatening.

ASSESSMENT IN THE COGNITIVE DOMAIN

1. **Standardized Tests** – scientifically constructed test with established validity and reliability.

2. **Teacher-made Tests** – developed personally by the teacher.

3. **Essay Tests/Written Assignments** – tests the ability to organize information presented logically in written paragraphs.

4. **Objective Tests** – true/false, multiple choice, matching, diagrams, completion, or short written response.

5. **Norm-Referenced Tests** – compares individual's score to the scores of others.

6. **Criterion-Referenced Tests** – Interpreting a score by comparing it to a predetermined standard.

SKILL 1.5   *Revise a given physical education program based on a needs assessment or other appropriate evaluation.*

Adapting and modifying physical education programs is analogous to modifying individual fitness plans. Modification and adaptation involves identifying areas of strength and weakness from the assessment results and adjusting goals and activities to address the weaknesses. For example, if the students in a particular physical education program score poorly on cardiovascular fitness tests, the instructor should integrate more aerobic activities into the curriculum.

INDIVIDUAL FITNESS PLAN ADAPTATION

After assessing an individual's fitness level, a personal fitness trainer or instructor can prescribe a training program. Prescription of a fitness program begins with:

1. Identifying the components of fitness that need changing (via assessment)

2. Establishing short-term goals

3. Developing a plan to meet the established goals

4. Keeping records to record progress

5. Evaluating progress of goals and making changes based on success or failure

For successful programs, the instructor and student should formulate new goals and change the personal fitness program to accomplish the new goals.
For unsuccessful programs, changing the goals, particularly if the goals were too unrealistic, is an appropriate response. Adjusting goals allows individuals to make progress and succeed. In addition, analyzing positive and negative results may identify barriers preventing an individual's success in her personal fitness program. Incorporating periodic, positive rewards for advancing can provide positive reinforcement and encouragement.

SKILL 1.6   *Demonstrate an understanding of factors that affect the preparation of a budget to support the physical education program.*

Factors that affect the preparation of a budget to support the physical education program include resources (pre-existing funds and fundraising), prioritization (allocation of resources), and justification of the priorities selected to the "powers that be".

In terms of resources, we need to consider the resources already available to us as physical educators, and the general availability of funds in the institution and community (i.e. "if we don't already have enough money at our disposal, how much more will we realistically be able to get?"). Once we have a sense of the funds that we can raise in the school and community, we need to consider the fundraising activities that would best communicate with the appropriate parties (i.e. "what's the best way for us to convince the people who have the money to give it to us, so that we can use it for our physical education program?"). This ties in closely to prioritization and justification issues that we will examine below.

Prioritization is a matter of appraising how to best use the resources at our disposal to benefit our students. This isn't only a matter of avoiding the allocation of 90% of available funds to one big project, leaving nothing for anything else (e.g. spending the entire budget on the construction of an indoor skating rink) – it's also a matter of assessing what resources the most students can use to the greatest benefit.

Finally, there comes the matter of justifying the priorities that we've chosen to the administrative bodies – the people who need to approve our budgets. For this phase of the budget preparation process, it is important to explain why each funding request is necessary for the students, and how the students will benefit.

COMPETENCY 2.0   **UNDERSTAND PRINCIPLES AND PROCEDURES OF SAFETY, EMERGENCY FIRST AID AND EQUIPMENT MAINTENANCE**

SKILL 2.1   *Recognize and apply managerial and instructional routines that create safe environments.*

The management of facilities, supplies, and other resources is an important part of the physical educator's job. Instructors must plan the availability, use, and safety of facilities. In addition, instructors must develop procedures for transporting, distributing, and collecting equipment. Finally, instructors must develop lesson plans that maximize the use of time and keep students active.

Facility management is the first task physical educators must consider. Instructors must ensure, through communication with other school personnel, that the required facilities are available when needed. In addition, instructors must inspect facilities prior to use to ensure the safety of the students. Instructors should carefully note uneven surfaces, holes, obstructions, and obstacles. Instructors may also have to modify rules or game procedures as the facility dimensions dictate.

Equipment management is another important responsibility of physical educators. Instructors must develop procedures for transporting equipment to and from the playing field or gymnasium. One way to simplify equipment transportation is to use a shopping cart, which many grocery stores will donate, to carry equipment. Instructors can also designate students as equipment managers to help carry and distribute equipment. Equipment distribution and collection is another important concern for physical educators. Spreading equipment throughout the playing area can speed the distribution process. Instructors should also establish a protocol for equipment return and set up areas for collection. Finally, instructors should develop signals, either verbal or visual, that direct students to stop the activity and either hold or put down the equipment.

One final concern of physical educators is the management of class time. One effective strategy for maximizing participation and the use of class time and equipment is to use stations. Stations allow students to rotate through a series of different activities in small groups. Instructors should use stations only for activities that the students are familiar with and are able to complete without constant supervision.

STRATEGIES FOR INJURY PREVENTION

Participant screenings – evaluate injury history, anticipate and prevent potential injuries, watch for hidden injuries and reoccurrence of an injury, and maintain communication.

Standards and discipline – ensure that athletes obey rules of sportsmanship, supervision, and biomechanics.

Education and knowledge – stay current in knowledge of first aid, sports medicine, sport technique, and injury prevention through clinics, workshops, and communication with staff and trainers.

Conditioning – programs should be yearlong and participants should have access to conditioning facilities in and out of season to produce more fit and knowledgeable athletes that are less prone to injury.

Equipment – perform regular inspections; ensure proper fit and proper use.

Facilities – maintain standards and use safe equipment.

Field care – establish emergency procedures for serious injury.

Rehabilitation – use objective measures such as power output on an isokinetic dynamometer.

PREVENTION OF COMMON ATHLETIC INJURIES

Foot – start with good footwear, foot exercises.

Ankle – use high top shoes and tape support; strengthen plantar (calf), dorsiflexor (shin), and ankle eversion (ankle outward).

Shin splints – strengthen ankle dorsiflexors.

Achilles tendon – stretch dorsiflexion and strengthen plantar flexion (heel raises).

Knee – increase strength and flexibility of calf and thigh muscles.

Back – use proper body mechanics.

Tennis elbow – lateral epicondylitis caused by bent elbow, hitting late, not stepping into the ball, heavy rackets, and rackets with strings that are too tight.

Head and neck injuries – avoid dangerous techniques (i.e. grabbing facemask) and carefully supervise dangerous activities like the trampoline.

School officials and instructors should base **equipment selection** on quality and safety; goals of physical education and athletics; participants interests, age, sex, skills, and limitations; and trends in athletic equipment and uniforms. Knowledgeable personnel should select equipment; keeping in mind continuous service and replacement considerations (i.e. what's best in year of selection may not be best the following year). One final consideration is the possibility of reconditioning versus the purchase new equipment.

ACTIONS THAT PROMOTE SAFETY AND INJURY PREVENTION

The following is a list of practices that promote safety in all types of physical education and athletic activities.

1. Having an instructor who is properly trained and qualified.

2. Organizing the class by size, activity, and conditions of the class.

3. Inspecting buildings and other facilities regularly and immediately giving notice of any hazards.

4. Avoiding overcrowding.

5. Using adequate lighting.

6. Ensuring that students dress in appropriate clothing and shoes.

7. Presenting organized activities.

8. Inspecting all equipment regularly.

9. Adhering to building codes and fire regulations.

10. Using protective equipment.

11. Using spotters.

12. Eliminating hazards.

13. Teaching students correct ways of performing skills and activities.

14. Teaching students how to use the equipment properly and safely.

SKILL 2.2   *Identify procedures and issues related to the use, maintenance, and storage of equipment, technology, and other physical education resources.*

School officials and instructors should base **equipment selection** on quality and safety; goals of physical education and athletics; participants interests, age, sex, skills, and limitations; and trends in athletic equipment and uniforms. Knowledgeable personnel should select equipment; keeping in mind continuous service and replacement considerations (i.e. what's best in year of selection may not be best the following year). One final consideration is the possibility of reconditioning versus the purchase new equipment.

Additional Guidelines for Selection of Equipment

- follow purchasing policies

- relate purchasing to program, budget, and finances

- consider maintenance

- abide by legal regulations

- recognize administrative considerations (good working relationships at all personnel levels)

- determine best value for money spent

- ensure that participants have own equipment and supplies when necessary

- purchase from reputable manufacturers and distributors

- follow competitive purchasing regulations

- use school forms with clearly identified brand, trademark, and catalog specifications

Equipment Maintenance Procedures

- inspect supplies and equipment upon arrival

- label supplies and equipment with organization's identification

- have policies for issuing and returning supplies and equipment

- keep equipment in perfect operating condition

- store properly

- properly clean and care for equipment (including garments).

Facility Selection Considerations

- bond issues for construction

- availability to girls, women, minorities, and the handicapped

- energy costs and conservation

- community involvement

- convertibility (movable walls/partitions)

- environment must be safe, attractive, clean, comfortable, practical, and adaptable to individual needs

- compliance with public health codes

- effective disease control.

Facility Maintenance Procedures

- custodial staff, participants, and the physical education and athletic staffs must work together to properly maintain facility

- for pool's, water temperature, hydrogen ion concentration, and chlorine need daily monitoring

- gymnasium play areas must be free from dust and dirt

- showers and drying areas need daily cleaning and disinfecting

- participants' clothing should meet health standards to prevent odor and bacterial growth

- outdoor playing fields must be clear of rocks and free of holes and uneven surfaces

- disinfect and clean drinking fountains, sinks, urinals, and toilets daily

- air out and sanitize lockers frequently.

TECHNOLOGY

The best sources of current technological resources for accessing information on physical activity and health are the Internet and computers.

Internet resources form an important part of current technology, which helps in accessing information on physical activity and health. There are internet sources, which also enable educators, students, performers, parents, and athletes to stay aware of up-to-date information and programs about physical activity and health.

Numerous websites also exist that allow educators as well as performers to know about the developments in the physical education training systems. Use of technological resources also helps students to grasp more knowledge about physical activity and health-related issues.

Some organizations such as the NASPE also provide information on physical fitness and health. For example, NASPE invites school districts nationwide to post their school wellness policy on the NASPE Forum.

Research also shows there are different types of devices that athletes can use to monitor physical activity and health. Such devices include virtual bicycles, rowing machines, and tread mills. Such technology helps plan and implement workouts and view workout results.

Technology is the application of science to commercial, educational, health-related, military, or industrial objectives. Technology includes the use of computers, calculators, communication devices (telephone, videoconference devices), or other entities and methodologies to achieve those objectives.

Successful physical education instructors integrate technology into the instructional process. Technology is not simply a practice tool or device without purpose. The use of a particular technological device or product of technology should be appropriate to the lesson content.

Instructors can be use technology in a variety of ways to help students and athletes improve or learn. Some ways in which instructors can use technology include:

1. Actual use of technology – the teacher and the students use the technology in a "hands-on" setting. For example, students use a video or digital camera in physical education to analyze their skills.

2. Use of products of technology – the use of products of technology in instruction and learning. May include gathering information or resources from the Internet, imaging results for analyzing a motor skill, etc. In such a situation, the teacher can use the technology, or the products of technology, to present information, to provide examples and illustrations, and as the medium or object of intrusion.

Some of the offered examples currently available in technology-mediated instruction include audio technologies such as radio, telephone, voice mail, and audiocassettes; video technologies such as television, teleconferencing, compressed video, and prerecorded videocassettes; and information technologies such as stand-alone workstations, CD ROM prepackaged multimedia, e-mail, chat rooms, bulletin boards, and the World Wide Web.

SKILL 2.3   *Identify potential safety issues related to physical education activities and demonstrate an understanding of principles and techniques of injury prevention.*

SEE ALSO Domain 4, Skill 2.1

HARMFUL EXERCISE TECHNIQUES AND ENVIRONMENTAL CONDITIONS

Instructors and participants should make safety and injury prevention top priority in exercise activities. There are a number of potential risks associated with physical activity, and instructors must be familiar with all the risks to prevent an emergency situation.

Equipment

Exercise equipment in poor condition has the potential for malfunction. Instructors should perform weekly checks to ensure all equipment is in proper working order. If it is not, the instructor or maintenance staff must repair the equipment before students use it. Placement of exercise equipment is also important. There should be adequate space between machines and benches to ensure a safe environment.

Technique

Instructors should stress proper exercise technique at all times, especially with beginners to prevent development of bad habits. Whether it's weightlifting, running, or stretching, participants should not force any body part beyond the normal range of motion. Pain is a good indicator of overextension. Living by the phrase, "No pain, no gain", is potentially dangerous. Participants should use slow and controlled movements. In addition, participants must engage in a proper warm-up and cool-down before and after exercise. When lifting weights, lifters should always have a partner. A spotter can help correct the lifter's technique and help lift the weight to safety if the lifter is unable to do so. A partner can also offer encouragement and motivation. Flexibility is an often overlooked, yet important, part of exercise that can play a key role in injury prevention. Participants should perform stretching exercises after each workout session.

Environment

Environmental conditions can be very dangerous and potentially life threatening. Be cautious when exercising in extremely hot, cold, and/or humid conditions. High humidity can slow the body's release of heat from the body, increasing the chances of heat related illnesses. Hydration in hot environments is very important. Drink two cups of water two hours before exercise and hydrate regularly during exercise at the same rate of the amount of sweat that is lost. In exercise lasting a long period of time, it is possible to drink too much water, resulting in a condition known as hyponutremia, or low sodium content in the body. Water cannot replace the sodium and other electrolytes lost through sweat. Drinking sports drinks can solve this problem. Cold environments can also be a problem when exercising. The human body works more efficiently at its normal temperature. Wear many layers of clothing to prevent cold-related illnesses such as frostbite and hypothermia. In populations suffering from asthma, wearing a cloth over the mouth during exercise increases the moisture of the air breathed in and can help prevent an attack.

EMERGENCY ACTION PLANS

The first step in establishing a safe physical education environment is creating an Emergency Action Plan (EAP). The formation of a well-planned EAP can make a significant difference in the outcome of an injury situation.

Components of an Emergency Action Plan
To ensure the safety of students during physical activity, an EAP should be easily comprehensible yet detailed enough to facilitate prompt, thorough action.

Communication
Instructors should communicate rules and expectations clearly to students. This information should include pre-participation guidelines, emergency procedures, and proper game etiquette. Instructors should collect emergency information sheets from students at the start of each school year. First-aid kits, facility maps, and incident report forms should also be readily available. Open communication between students and teachers is essential. Creating a positive environment within the classroom allows students to feel comfortable enough to approach an adult/teacher if she feels she has sustained a potential injury.

Teacher Education
At the start of each school year, every student should undergo a pre-participation physical examination. This allows a teacher to recognize the "high-risk" students before activity commences. The teacher should also take note of any student that requires any form of medication or special care. When a teacher is aware of his/her students' conditions, the learning environment is a lot safer.

Facilities and Equipment

It is the responsibility of the teacher and school district to provide a safe environment, playing area, and equipment for students. Instructors and maintenance staff should regularly inspect school facilities to confirm that the equipment and location is adequate and safe for student use.

First Aid Equipment

It is essential to have a properly stocked first aid kit in an easily reachable location. Instructors may need to include asthma inhalers and special care items to meet the specific needs of certain students. Instructors should clearly mark these special care items to avoid a potentially harmful mix-up.

Implementing the Emergency Plan

The main thing to keep in mind when implementing an EAP is to remain calm. Maintaining a sufficient level of control and activating appropriate medical assistance will facilitate the process and will leave less room for error.

SKILL 2.4   *Evaluate physical and environmental factors and potential safety hazards associated with games, sports, and recreational and outdoor activities.*

SEE ALSO Domain 4, Skill 2.1

Unsound equipment and poorly maintained facilities are the two most potentially hazardous elements of the physical education environment. Instructors must carefully inspect all equipment and facilities to ensure safety. In addition, improper student clothing and footwear is a significant hazard. Instructors should ensure that students wear rubber soled, closed-back shoes that fasten securely to the child's foot. Backless shoes (e.g. sandals, flip-flops) are inappropriate because they can easily slip off of the child's foot. The type of activity dictates the type of clothing that is appropriate. For example, baggy pants or long dresses are inappropriate for bicycle riding because such clothing can get caught in the bicycle and cause injury.

SKILL 2.5   Demonstrate knowledge of first-aid principles and procedures for a variety of emergency situations.

INJURY TREATMENT AND FIRST AID

Immediate treatment tips

When a student endures a physical injury, the first priority is to avoid further damage. Following an injury the teacher should look for the obvious cause of the accident (i.e., ill-fitting equipment, improper sliding technique, a missed step while running). The next step is to reduce swelling. The primary means of accomplishing this is a sequence of treatments (rest, ice, compression, elevation) known as **R.I.C.E.** It is vital to implement this procedure following an injury since swelling causes pain and a loss of motion.

Steps for the immediate treatment of an injury

1. Stop the activity immediately
2. Wrap the injured part in a compression bandage (i.e., an ACE bandage).
3. Apply ice to the injured part (crushed ice or frozen vegetables are ideal) for no more than 15 minutes at a time. You should allow the area to warm periodically.
4. Elevate the injured part.
5. For a proper diagnosis, send the injured student to the school's nurse or, for more serious injuries, to a physician.

Treating specific illnesses

Diabetes
Most children with diabetes suffer from Type 1 (insulin-dependent or juvenile) diabetes. Type 1 diabetes limits the pancreas' ability to produce insulin, a hormone vital to life. Without insulin, the body cannot use the sugar found in blood. In order to stay alive, an individual suffering from Type 1 diabetes must take one or more injections of insulin daily.

Diabetics control their disease by keeping the level of sugar (glucose) in the blood as close to normal as possible. The means to achieve diabetes control include proper nutrition, exercise, and insulin. Most children with diabetes self-monitor blood glucose levels to track their condition and respond to changes.

Some rules of thumb to keep in mind when dealing with a diabetic child are:

- Food makes the glucose level rise
- Exercise and insulin make the glucose level fall
- Hypoglycemia occurs when the blood sugar level is low
- Hyperglycemia occurs when the blood sugar level is high

Low Blood Sugar (Hypoglycemia)

This is the diabetic emergency most likely to occur. Low blood sugar may result from eating too little, engaging in too much physical activity without eating, or by injecting too much insulin.

Symptoms:
- Headache
- Sweating
- Shakiness
- Pale, moist skin
- Fatigue/Weakness
- Loss of coordination

Treatment:

Provide sugar immediately. You may give the student ½ cup of fruit juice, non-diet soda, or two to four glucose tablets. The child should feel better within the next 10 minutes. If so, the child should eat some additional food (e.g. half a peanut butter, meat, or cheese sandwich). If the child's status does not improve, treat the reaction again.

High Blood Sugar (Hyperglycemia)

Hyperglycemia can result from eating too much, engaging in too little physical activity, not injecting enough insulin, or illness. You can confirm high blood sugar levels by testing with a glucose meter.

Symptoms:
- Increased thirst
- Weakness/Fatigue
- Blurred vision
- Frequent urination
- Loss of appetite

Treatment:

If hyperglycemia occurs, the instructor should contact the student's parent or guardian immediately.

Dehydration

Dehydration occurs when a person loses more fluids than he/she takes in. The amount of water present in the body subsequently drops below the level needed for normal body functions. The two main causes of dehydration are gastrointestinal illness (vomiting, diarrhea) and sports. It is essential to replace fluids lost by sweating to prevent dehydration, especially on a hot day.

Symptoms:
- Thirst
- Dizziness
- Dry mouth
- Producing less/darker urine

Prevention/Treatment:
- Drink lots of fluids. Water is usually the best choice.
- Dress appropriately (i.e., loose-fitting clothes and a hat).
- If you begin to feel thirsty/dizzy, take a break and sit in the shade.
- Drink fluids prior to physical activity and then in 20-minute intervals after activity commences.
- Play sports or train in the early morning or late afternoon. You will avoid the hottest part of the day.

CPR BASICS

Cardiopulmonary resuscitation (CPR) is a first-aid technique used to keep victims of cardiac arrest alive. It is also prevents brain damage while the individual is unconscious and more advanced medical help is on the way. CPR keeps blood flowing through the body and in and out of the lungs.

CPR Steps
- Step 1 – Call 911
- Step 2 – Tilt head, lift chin, check breathing
- Step 3 – Give two breaths
- Step 4 – Position hands in the center of chest
- Step 5 – Firmly push down two inches on the chest 15 times

Continue with two breaths and 15 pumps until help arrives. The American Heart Association and the American Red Cross both offer classes to train individuals in CPR.

COMPETENCY 3.0   *UNDERSTAND LEGAL AND ETHICAL ISSUES THAT INFLUENCE PHYSICAL EDUCATION PROGRAMS*

SKILL 3.1   *Demonstrate an understanding of legal responsibilities and issues associated with teaching physical education.*

There are many issues related to the legal responsibilities of the professional physical educator. Failing to foresee potential hazardous conditions and to take practical steps to avoid these situations can result in litigation. In general, teachers must follow the standard of care expected of any physical education practitioner with a similar level of education and training. Liability refers to a legal responsibility. Often in litigious situations, the term liability refers to negligence, or breach of duty. Negligence refers to actions that do not meet the minimum standard of care. In successful litigation, the defense proves the existence of the following: duty, breach of duty, injury, and proximate cause. When determining liability, courts will determine whether the injury was foreseeable.

To avoid legal action, professional physical educators must meet their legal responsibilities in several areas: equipment and facilities, instruction, supervision, and general safety. Regular inspection of the instructional area identifies potential hazards. When physical educators find hazards, they should submit written notification to the principal immediately. Students should also receive proper instruction of equipment use prior to the first use. In an instructional setting, the physical educator protects students from unreasonable harm. Students receive appropriate training before and during activity. Supervision of all activities in a school setting is mandatory. An unsupervised student in the school at any time or on the school grounds during the school day is unacceptable. The approach to overall safety should be proactive.

Physical educators participate in safety in-service programs each year. The teacher or another school medical professional reviews student medical records prior to allowing participation in physical education. Physical education practitioners teach the safety rules for each activity at the beginning of each unit. When a student sustains an injury in physical education class, the school nurse or other medical professional evaluates the student. The physical educator completes and files an accident report the same day that the accident occurred.

An Emergency Action Plan (EAP) should be in place for the physical education department at each school. The EAP identifies the following: emergency care procedures and the individual responsible for rendering care, the individual responsible for parental notification, the individual responsible for activating the emergency medical system (EMS), the policy for transportation of injured students, and a copy of a blank student accident report. To reduce the financial consequences of litigation, each teacher should purchase and maintain personal professional liability insurance. Teachers should not rely on school district legal liability insurance for personal financial protection.

In addition to legal responsibilities, the physical educator also has ethical responsibilities. Teachers are responsible for helping each student to realize his or her abilities. Physical educators are accountable for the welfare of each student entrusted to their care. Teachers should maintain a professional relationship with their students. Teachers should maintain confidentiality. Physical educators should follow national, state, and district or school curricular standards. Teachers should establish and maintain a classroom routine that promotes student achievement. Finally, the physical education teacher is responsible for promoting healthful living within the school community.

LIABILITY CONCERNS IN PHYSICAL EDUCATION

Historically, common-law rules stated that individuals could not sue government agencies without consent of the agencies. However, federal and state courts have begun to allow individuals to sue both federal and state governments. Thus, public schools and school districts are now subject to liability lawsuits.

Compulsory elements of the school curriculum, such as physical education, prompt courts to decide based on what is in the best interests of the public.

Although school districts still have immunity in many states, teachers do not have such immunity. Whether employed by private person or a municipal corporation every employee owes a duty not to injure another by a negligent act of commission.

The following is a list of common legal terms and conditions applicable to physical education.

1. Tort – a legal wrong resulting in a direct or indirect injury; includes omissions and acts intended or unintended to cause harm.

2. Negligence – failing to fulfill a legal duty according to common reasoning; includes instruction and facility maintenance; instructors must consider sex, size, and skill of participants when planning activities and grouping students.

3. In Loco Parentis – acting in the place of the parent in relation to a child.

4. Sports Product Liability – liability of the manufacturer to the person using the manufacturer's product who sustains injury/damage from using the product.

5. Violence and legal liability (intentional injury in sports contests) – harmful, illegal contact of one person by another (referred to as battery).

6. Physical education classes held off campus and legal liability – primary concern is providing due care, which is the responsibility of management and staff members of sponsoring organization; failing to observe "due care" can result in findings of negligence.

7. Attractive Nuisance – an object that results in physical injury that the responsible party should have foreseen.

ACTIONS THAT CAN AVOID LAWSUITS

1. Knowing the health status of each person in the program.

2. Considering the ability and skill level of participants when planning new activities.

3. Grouping students to equalize competitive levels.

4. Using safe equipment and facilities.

5. Properly organizing and supervising classes.

6. Never leaving a class.

7. Knowing first aid (Do not diagnose or prescribe).

8. Keeping accident records.

9. Giving instruction prior to dangerous activities.

10. Being sure that injured students get medical attention and examination.

11. Getting exculpatory agreements (parental consent forms).

12. Having a planned, written disposition for students who suffer injuries or become ill.

13. Providing a detailed accident report if one occurs.

SKILL 3.2   *Recognize state and federal laws and guidelines regarding gender equity, special education, religious issues, privacy and other aspects of student's rights.*

ESTABLISHMENT OF CURRICULUM FRAMEWORKS AND STUDENT PERFORMANCE STANDARDS

A curriculum framework is a set of broad guidelines that aids educational personnel in producing specific instructional plans for a given subject or study area. The legislative intent was to promote a degree of **uniformity and instructional consistency** in curriculum offerings.

Student achievement standards relate to the intended outcomes of the selected curriculum frameworks. The legislature developed student performance standards for 40 physical education courses and 15 dance courses.

STATE LEGISLATION

State governments (Department of Education) are primarily responsible for education. Departments of education establish policies for course curriculum, number of class days and class time, and amount of credits required for graduation.

IMPACT OF EDUCATION REFORMS AND FEDERAL LEGISLATION

Enrollment went up and there was renewed administrative, parental, and student support. Additional impacts include: coeducational classes, separate teams for boys and girls and men and women (otherwise the school must create a coeducational team), equal opportunities for both sexes (for facilities, equipment and supplies, practice and games, medical and training services, academic tutoring and coaching, travel and per diem allowances, and dining and housing facilities), and equitable expenditure of funds for both sexes.

The Department of Health and Human Services recommended legislative changes - including those for education. **Title IX** prohibits sex discrimination in educational programs and **PL 94-142** requires schools to provide educational services for handicapped students. In 1990, Congress passed the **Individuals with Disabilities Education Act** (IDEA) that amended earlier laws. IDEA specifies physical education as a required educational service. In addition, IDEA defines physical education as the development of physical fitness, motor skills, and skills in-group and individual games and dance, aquatics, and lifetime sports.

Title IX takes precedence over all conflicting state and local laws and conference regulations. Federal aid (even aid not related to physical education or athletics) must comply with Title IX. Finally, Title IX prohibits discrimination in personnel standards and scholarships selection.

Finally, Congress enacted the Physical Education for Progress (PEP) Act in 2000. The PEP program provides funds that the Department of Education uses to award grants to help initiate, expand, and develop physical education programs for Kindergarten through 12th grade students.

ADAPTED PHYSICAL EDUCATION NATIONAL STANDARDS

Physical education standards adapted for disabled students include:

STANDARD 1 HUMAN DEVELOPMENT: Sets the foundation of proposed goals and activities for individuals with disabilities. Grounded in a basic understanding of human development and its applications to those with various needs.

STANDARD 2 MOTOR BEHAVIOR: Sets the standard on teaching individuals with disabilities, which requires knowledge of typical physical and motor development as well as understanding the influence of developmental delays on these processes.

STANDARD 3 EXERCISE SCIENCE: The focus of this standard is on the principles that address the physiological and biomechanical applications encountered when working with diverse populations.

STANDARD 4 MEASUREMENT AND EVALUATION: Sets the standards on the measurements in gauging motor performance that is, to a large extent, based on a good grasp of motor development and the acquisition of motor skills covered in other standards.

STANDARD 5 HISTORY AND PHILOSOPHY: This standard sets the basic knowledge base of educators on legal and philosophical factors involved in current day practices in adapted physical education (APE). This standard also covers a review of history and philosophy related to special and general education.

STANDARD 6 UNIQUE ATTRIBUTES OF LEARNERS: This standard refers to information based on the disability areas found in the Individuals with Disabilities Education Act (IDEA).

STANDARD 7 CURRICULUM THEORY AND DEVELOPMENT: Sets the standards on knowledge of certain curriculum theory and development concepts, such as selecting goals based on relevant and appropriate assessment.

STANDARD 8 ASSESSMENT: This seeks to establish the parameters and conduct of assessment, which goes beyond data gathering to include measurements for the purpose of making decisions about special services and program components for individuals with disabilities.

STANDARD 9 INSTRUCTIONAL DESIGN AND PLANNING: Administration must develop standards on instructional design and planning before an APE teacher can provide services to meet legal mandates, educational goals, and, most importantly, the unique needs of individuals with disabilities.

STANDARD 10 TEACHING: This standard integrates many of the principles addressed earlier in covering areas such as human development, motor behavior, and exercise science. This will ensure that schools meet other standards to effectively provide quality physical education to individuals with disabilities.

STANDARD 11 CONSULTATION AND STAFF DEVELOPMENT: This standard sets the key competencies that an adapted physical educator should know in relation to consultation and staff development.

STANDARD 12 STUDENT AND PROGRAM EVALUATION: Sets the standards on how to conduct program evaluation, integrating the entire range of educational services.

STANDARD 13 CONTINUING EDUCATION: This standard sets the parameters on ways teachers of APE can remain current in their field.

STANDARD 14 ETHICS: This standard ensures that teachers of APE not only understand the importance of sound ethical practices, but also adhere to and advance such practices.

STANDARD 15 COMMUNICATION: This standard includes setting the quality of information on how to communicate with families and other professionals effectively. The standard encourages a team approach to enhance service delivery to individuals with disabilities.

SKILL 3.3   Demonstrate an understanding of the boundaries of professional responsibilities when working with students, colleagues, families, and community members.

As educators invested in the growth and development of our students, it is easy for the boundaries of professional responsibilities to blur, especially those between us and our students, colleagues, families, and community members. This applies even more so for physical educators, who don't only deal with their students on an academic level, but often on a more personal level (in the role of "coach").

To observe professional responsibilities without crossing boundaries, which may be both immoral and illegal depending on the circumstances, we need to maintain a clear idea of what we are not. We are not our students' primary care-givers, nor are we their legal guardians. As such, it is not our place to decide how they should be raised, nor is it our place to step in if we feel that our students' parents or guardians are not making the decisions that we believe are best for them.

This is not to say that we should not get involved or advise our students. That is part of our jobs as educators. The final decisions about our students' lives, however, are in the hands of their parents or guardians (note that this does not refer to situations of abuse, in which case there is a legal obligation to report any suspected abusive behavior).

SKILL 3.4   Apply ethical, professional, and legal guidelines in making decisions in various physical education settings and situations.

There are many issues related to the ethical and legal responsibilities of the professional physical educator.

Physical educators at all levels should regularly inspect the instructional area for potential hazards. At the elementary and middle school level, the instructional areas might include the gymnasium and any outdoor areas utilized for instruction. At the high school level, the instructional area might not only include the gymnasium and outdoor field area, but might also include a weight training facility and/ or a swimming pool and surrounding deck area.

The physical education practitioner will also inspect equipment prior to student use. At the elementary and middle school level, inspected equipment might include such items as racquets, game standards, archery bows and arrows, scooters, gymnastics equipment, protection gear for high velocity sports, and golf equipment. At the high school level, inspected equipment would also include any weights and machines utilized in the weight training facility. Naturally, the physical educator provides proper instruction of equipment use prior to the first use at every grade level.

Strict enforcement of safety rules is essential. Elementary students allowed to swing a hockey stick to shoulder height might seriously injure a classmate. Supervision of all activities in a school setting is mandatory. This is especially true of the gymnasium and any other area where unsupervised students might misuse equipment. The approach to overall safety at each grade level should be proactive.

As students mature in middle school and high school, it is important to partner students for safe participation by size and ability. At the middle school level, it is especially important for teachers to be aware of potential bullying situations. Teachers should maintain a professional relationship with their students. It is particularly crucial at the middle school and high school levels for teachers to maintain a professional distance from their students. A teacher who considers students as "friends" is at risk for accusations of improper conduct. Additionally, teachers should avoid being alone with a student in a secluded or enclosed classroom at any time.

Teachers should also maintain confidentiality. At all levels, teachers should be conscious of the fact that others may overhear conversations. Sharing unnecessary student information may not only be harmful to the student's reputation, but other students or parents may overhear the unprofessional conversation. Physical educators should follow national, state, and district or school curricular standards. Teachers should establish and maintain a classroom routine that promotes student achievement. Clear definition and enforcement of classroom expectations helps to maintain an environment that promotes student achievement.

Finally, the physical education teacher is responsible for promoting healthful living within the school community. The promotion of healthful living might include such things as helping middle school and high school students make wise nutritional choices at lunch, starting a walking club for teachers and students, initiating and managing a weight loss program for faculty members, or supervising an outdoor adventure club at the high school level.

COMPETENCY 4.0   UNDERSTAND PRINCIPLES AND PROCEDURES FOR EFFECTIVE ADVOCACY, COMMUNICATION AND COLLABORATION

SKILL 4.1   *Recognize how to use community resources to enhance physical activity opportunities, and demonstrate an understanding of how to advocate effectively to promote physical activity opportunities within the community.*

An important task for physical educators is to convince other educators, parents, and political decision makers of the importance of physical education. This responsibility is unique to teachers of subjects outside of the traditional academic core. Few people will question the importance of math or reading, while many will question the importance of physical education, arts, and music. One effective strategy for promoting physical education is to relate physical education to the academic curriculum. In addition, physical educators should point out the many physical, psychological, and social benefits of physical education.

An effective physical education instructor always projects a positive message about physical activity. Methods of projecting a positive message include creating an organized program with a structured schedule and delivering lessons enthusiastically. Instructors should never diminish the importance of physical education in comparison to academic subjects. Sticking to a structured schedule creates a positive environment and shows students that the instructor takes his subject seriously. The instructor's enthusiasm can inspire students to engage in physical activity outside of school.

Finally, physical education instructors should give students homework just as academic teachers do. For example, when teaching the overhand throw, the instructor may ask his students to practice throwing with a friend during recess or a parent at home. Instructors should also be familiar with local sports leagues and other opportunities for physical activity in the community. The instructor can inform students of such opportunities and promote participation in physical activities throughout the year.

COMMUNITY RESOURCES

There are many community resources that are available to physical education professionals and that students can make use of during out-of-school hours. Private and public organizations and clubs, such as sporting teams, gyms, and community and recreation centers are all places that offer resources for physical activities. Similarly, public and private pools and skating rinks are valuable resources (participants must observe the safety regulations of the location as well as any unspecified, common-sense safety guidelines). Public parks are available for outdoor physical activities.

There are major socio-cultural benefits of participating in physical activity with others. It serves as a very important part of the socialization process. Physical activity during the socialization process creates an opportunity for children to define personal comfort levels with different types of physical interaction, as well as to establish guidelines for what is (and is not) acceptable physical behavior as related to their relationship with other individuals.

Participating in physical activity with others is also a step away from the trend of "playground to PlayStation", where students are less and less physically active, and spend less and less time engaging in outdoor physical activity. Physical activity on a socio-cultural level is an important aspect of the struggle against rising obesity levels in the United States, as well as related problems (like heart disease).

In order to maintain and improve personal and community resources in relation to physical activity and fitness, educators must enhance the levels of commitment to physical activities and related resources (on both an individual and community level). Educators must also stress the value and importance of physical activity (for fitness, health and wellness, and community-building purposes).

Educators can promote this commitment by emphasizing the need to make time for family and community activities, which often have physical activity components (or can be entirely based on physical activity, like a family hiking trip). Educators can take this a step further, by instituting activities (on a family or community level) to actually maintain or improve the state of physical activity resources. For example, the educator can organize a sponsored walk or run to fund-raise for the maintenance of school exercise equipment, or a family might come together to construct a jungle-gym in their back yard for the children to play on.

Another important step in strengthening the commitment of individuals and the community to physical activities and related resources is to educate about the role of physical activity as a resource for everyone, regardless of age and ability. It is important that there are concrete examples of services and activities available that serve as opportunities for all age groups and ability/skill levels to participate in and benefit from physical activity (if physical activity is truly available to everyone, it is easier to make the case that it is a community resource that the community should be maintain and improve).

SKILL 4.2   Demonstrate an understanding of strategies and mechanisms for communicating with a variety of constituencies.

An effective strategy for promoting the physical education curriculum is to relate physical education to the purposes and goals of the entire educational process. By providing satisfying, successful, and enriching experiences that are properly taught, physical educators shape a physically, mentally, and socially fit society.

Advocates should relate physical education to the total educational process through the cognitive, affective, and psychomotor domains.

The following is a list of talking points for physical education advocates. These points emphasize how physical education positively affects student development.

Benefits of physical education in the Cognitive Domain

- contributes to academic achievement

- promotes higher thought processes via motor activity

- contributes to knowledge of exercise, health and disease

- contributes to an understanding of the human body

- contributes to an understanding of the role of physical activity and sport in American culture

- contributes to the knowledgeable consumption of goods and services

Benefits of physical education in the Affective Domain

- contributes to self-actualization, self-esteem, and a healthy response to physical activity

- contributes to an appreciation of beauty

- contributes to directing one's life toward worthy goals

- emphasizes humanism

- affords individuals the chance to enjoy rich social experiences through play

- promotes cooperative play with others

- teaches courtesy, fair play, and good sportsmanship

- contributes to humanitarianism

Benefits of physical education in the Psychomotor Domain

- develops movement skills for participation in sports and other physical activities

- develops skills to utilize leisure hours in mental and cultural pursuits develops skills necessary to the preservation of the natural environment

COMMUNICATION OF ASSESSMENT RESULTS

Instructors should compare assessment data to grade equivalency norms to determine where each child is relative to where he should be. However, the instructor should place the most emphasis on evaluating the child relative to past performance. Progress is more important than current achievement. A learning-disabled child might display below average levels of achievement despite having made a great deal of progress, while a gifted child might be above grade equivalency norms despite stagnation.

Instructors should communicate assessment data should differently to students, parents, and school board members.

- **Assessment data communicated to students** should be encouraging, and should be limited to a textual analysis of the child's progress and effort (it is not helpful or encouraging to remind a child that he is below grade level norms, especially if he has worked hard and made progress). The ultimate purpose of assessment data communicated to a child is to encourage further hard work.

- **Assessment data communicated to parents** should also be encouraging and should focus on the child's progress and effort. That said, it is also important that a parent receive an accurate picture of the child's status relative to grade level norms, especially if the child is in need of remedial assistance.

- **Assessment data communicated to school board members** is generally more summative in nature (a letter or number grade). Since school board members will generally see evaluations of entire classes at a time without knowing the individual children, it is not important for them to receive an encouraging picture of an individual child's progress. It is more important for them to see both current achievement levels and rates of progress to properly assess curriculum design, lesson planning, and program evaluation.

SKILL 4.3   *Identify strategies for communication, consulting, and collaborating with teachers, counselors, special education personnel, administrators, and other colleagues.*

SEE Domain 4, Skills 4.1 and 4.2 (Previous Skills)

SKILL 4.4   Recognize the roles of state and national professional organizations for physical educators.

Schools and instructors can promote physical fitness programs through cooperation and partnership between parents, health organizations, health providers and the government, on topics such as physical activity, sporting organizations, and the media's influence.

PHYSICAL EDUCATION PROFESSIONAL ORGANIZATIONS AND ACTIVITIES THAT PROMOTE PROFESSIONAL DEVELOPMENT

1. Amateur Athletic Union (AAU) – protects amateur sports from becoming corrupted. Conducts pre-Olympic trials.

2. American Alliance for Health, Physical Education, Recreation, and Dance (AAHPERD) – works with legislatures concerning education and research, works with president's council on physical fitness and sport, and influences public opinion. Various associations make up the alliance.

3. American College of Sports Medicine – promotes scientific studies of sports and conducts research and post-graduate work.

4. National Association for Sport and Physical Education (NASPE) – a non-profit, professional membership organization that is the preeminent national authority on physical education. **Developed national standards for physical education.**

5. National Intramural Association

6. National Junior College Athletic Association

7. Phi Epsilon Kappa – fraternity for people pursuing careers in health, physical education, recreation, or safety.

CURRENT PROFESSIONAL LITERATURE, RESEARCH, AND OTHER SOURCES OF INFORMATION THAT ENHANCE PROFESSIONAL GROWTH

1. AAU Publication Amateur Athlete Yearbook, AAU News (monthly)

2. American Academy of PE – position papers, studies for and by the academy.

3. Journal of PE, Recreation, and Dance

4. Research Quarterly

5. School Health Review

6. The Foil - the official publication of Delta Psi Kappa, newsletter The Psi Kappa Shield.

7. NEA - Today's Education

8. National Jr. College Athletic Association

9. Journal of PE – published bi-monthly.

10. YMCA Magazine – public affairs news.

SKILL 4.5   *Demonstrate familiarity with professional development opportunities associated with physical education, sports, and fitness, as well as related qualifications, educational requirements, and job responsibilities.*

Many occupations today require a college-educated individual who can write, speak well, solve problems, learn new information quickly, and work well with others or on a team. This means that college graduates use their education in a wide variety of fields. An individual's future career may relate more to his/her personal career interests, work values, and transferable skills than to any specific academic major.

Individuals interested in the field of physical education often become teachers, participate in health studies, instruct students in safety practices associated with different environments including swimming pools, gymnasiums, and playing fields, or undertake compulsory health education programs. In addition, other careers associated with physical activity include athletic coaching, recreational and sport management, fitness training, nutrition, and professional athletics. Most of these careers, with the possible exception of coaching and professional athletics, require at least college degrees in an appropriate field.

MOVEMENT SCIENCE AND KINESIOLOGY

The systematic study of human movement applied to the field of physical injury. It is concerned with the understanding of how and why we move and the factors that limit and enhance our capacity to move. This particular field also relates to studies about exercising for health or the regaining of function of an injured body.

Human Movement is based on a solid liberal arts and science education designed to foster development of human values and effective interpersonal skills. A scientific foundation is necessary for the study of the ability to function both didactically and clinically.

The aim of the study of human movement is to further the understanding of the mechanisms and processes underlying skilled movements and the means by which they are influenced by physiological, biomechanical, psychological and social factors.

Finally, kinesiology encompasses human anatomy, physiology, neuroscience, biochemistry, biomechanics, exercise psychology, and sociology of sport. Kinesiologists also study the relationship between the quality of movement and overall human health. Kinesiology is an important part of physical therapy, occupational therapy, chiropractics, osteopathy, exercise physiology, kinesiotherapy, massage therapy, ergonomics, physical education, and athletic coaching. The purpose of these applications may be therapeutic, preventive, or high-performance. The application of kinesiology can also incorporate knowledge from other academic disciplines such as psychology, sociology, cultural studies, ecology, evolutionary biology, and anthropology. The study of kinesiology is often part of the physical education curriculum and illustrates the truly interdisciplinary nature of physical education.

SPORTS MANAGEMENT

Sports management is a broad career field that encompasses many areas of sports, leisure, and recreation. Sports management professionals work with the financial, social, and business aspects of sport and recreation. Many universities have specialized master's degree programs in sports management. In addition, traditional business and business management degree programs prepare students for careers in sports management. Graduates of business programs looking to enter the sports market can find jobs in intercollegiate athletics, professional athletics, event and facility management, sports law, corporate and international sport, and marketing.

RECREATION

Many people interested in sports and athletics find jobs in the recreation industry. Such jobs may or may not require a college education. Many universities offer degrees in recreational services and management. Interested persons can find recreation jobs at country clubs, health centers, fitness clubs, public parks, national parks, swimming pools, beaches, and local athletic leagues.

COACHING

There are many levels of athletic coaching, from youth leagues to professional. All sports require coaches. While there is no specific training required for coaching, many amateur coaches have college degrees and teach at public or private elementary and secondary schools. The types of institutions that employ coaches include colleges and universities, high schools, middle schools, country clubs (e.g. golf and tennis), public parks and recreational facilities, and local athletic leagues.

SPORTS MEDICINE

Sports medicine is an interdisciplinary specialty aimed at treating and preventing sports related injuries that includes physicians and surgeons, athletic trainers, coaches, and physical therapists. Different members of the sports medicine team have different qualifications and responsibilities. Physicians and surgeons have medical degrees, provide specialized medical care, and prescribe treatment for athletic injuries. Athletic trainers, which usually complete a university program and achieve certification, work with athletes to develop training and nutritional programs and provide routine treatment and preventative care to athletes. Physical therapists help athletes recover from injuries by designing and implementing rehabilitation programs. Sports medicine specialists can find employment with professional and collegiate athletic teams, professional and amateur sports organizations, and health clubs. In addition, many sports medicine doctors and surgeons have individual practices.

SPORTS PSYCHOLOGY

Sports psychology is a specialty of psychology that analyzes and attempts to understand the factors that affect athletic performance, physical activity, and exercise. Sports psychologists may work with competitive athletes to help them improve their performance through reduction of pressure and stress. In addition, sports psychologists may work with everyday people looking to overcome obstacles preventing them from achieving their exercise or fitness goals. Sports psychologists can operate individual practices or may seek employment with professional or collegiate sports teams or organizations.

ANNOTATED LIST OF RESOURCES FOR PHYSICAL EDUCATION

This list identifies some resources that may help candidates prepare to take the Physical Education examination. While not a substitute for coursework or other types of teacher preparation, these resources may enhance a candidate's knowledge of the content covered on the examination. The references listed do not represent a comprehensive listing of all potential resources. Candidates need not read all of the materials listed below, and passage of the examination will not require familiarity with these specific resources. When available, we have provided a brief summary for the reference cited. We have organized the resources alphabetically and by content domain in subtest order.

GROWTH, MOTOR DEVELOPMENT, AND MOTOR LEARNING

Colvin, A. Vonnie; Nancy J.; and Walker, Pamela. (2000). *Teaching the Nutes and Bolts of Physical Education: Building Basic Movement Skills.* Champaign, IL: Human Kinetics.

> Provides foundational content knowledge in locomotor and manipulative skills. Topics include rolling, throwing, catching, passing, dribbling, striking, kicking, and punting.

Fronske, H. (2001). *Teaching Cues for Sports Skills* (2nd edition). San Francisco, CA: Pearson/Cummings.

> Designed to provide verbal and alternate teaching cues and point out common errors in a variety of sports.

Graham, George. (1992). *Teaching Children Physical Education: Becoming a Master Teacher.* Champaign, IL: Human Kinetics.

> Includes the skills and techniques that successful teachers use to make their classes more interesting and developmentally appropriate. A reference for K-5 teachers and physical education department chairs and administrators.

Lawson, H.A. (1984). *Invitation to Physical Education.* Champaign IL: Human Kinetics.

> Shows students and practitioners how to apply basic business management principles to a variety of health promotion programs.

Pangrazi, Robert. (2004). *Dynamic Physical Education for Elementary School Children* (14th edition). San Francisco, CA: Pearson/Cummings.

> Provides step-by-step techniques for teaching physical education while navigating through today's challenging educational terrain.

Powers, S.K., and Howley, E.T. (2003). *Exercise Physiology* (5th edition). New York, NY: McGraw Hill.

> Explains theory of exercise science and physical education with application and performance models to increase understanding of classroom learning.

Schmidt, R.A., and Lee, T.D. (1999). *Motor Control Learning: A Behavioral Emphasis* (3rd Edition). Champaign: IL: Human Kinetics.

> Addresses many factors that affect the quality of movement behaviors and the ease with which students can learn them.

Sherrill, C. (1998). *Adapted Physical Activity, Recreation and Sport: Cross-disciplinary and Lifespan* (5th edition). Dubuque, IA: WCB McGraw Hill.
> Emphasizes attitude change, inclusion, and psychosocial perspectives for understanding individual differences.

Siedentop, D. (1994). *Sport Education.* Champaign, IL: Human Kinetics.
> Shows how sport can help students learn fair play, leadership skills, and self-responsibility, in addition to becoming competent players. Also shows physical educators how to implement effective sport education programs to achieve these goals.

Summers, J.J. (1992). *Approaches to the Study of Motor Control and Learning.* Amsterdam: Elsevier Science.
> Provides analysis of research with particular emphasis on the methods and paradigms employed and the future direction of their work.

Thomas, Katherine, et al. (2003). *Physical Education Methods for Elementary Teachers.* Champaign, IL: Human Kinetics.
> Takes a research approach and offers a user-friendly technique to applicable teaching modalities for physical education for grades K-12.

Winnick, J.P. (2000). *Adapted Physical Education and Sport* (3rd edition). Champaign, IL: Human Kinetics.
> Provides a thorough introduction for students preparing to work with individuals with disabilities in a variety of settings.

THE SCIENCE OF HUMAN MOVEMENT

Birrell, S., and Cole, C.L. (1994). *Women, Sport, and Culture.* Champaign, IL: Human Kinetics.
> A collection of essays that examine the relationship between sport and gender.

Grantham, W.C.; Patton, R.W.; Winick, M.L.; and York, T.D. (1998). *Health Fitness Management.* Champaign, IL: Human Kinetics.
> Brings conventional business management principles and operational guidelines to the unconventional business of health and fitness.

Hall, S. (2003). *Basic Biomechanics.* Boston, MA: McGraw-Hill.

Hamill, J., and Knutzen, K. (1995). *Biomechanical Basis of Human Movement.* Hagerstown, MD: Lippincott, Williams & Wilkins.
> Integrates aspects of functional anatomy, physics, calculus, and physiology into a comprehensive discussion of human movement.

Hopper, Chris; Fisher, Bruce; and Muniz, Kathy. (1997). *Health-Related Fitness: Grades 1-2, 3-4, 5-6.* Champaign, IL: Human Kinetics.
> These three books provide a wealth of health and fitness information and are an excellent resource for classroom teachers with limited backgrounds in physical education.

Lawson, H.A. (1984). *Invitation to Physical Education.* Champaign, IL: Human Kinetics.
> Shows students and practitioners how to apply basic business management principles to a variety of health promotion programs.

Sample Test

1. **The Greek's best-known early contribution to the physical education profession was:**

    A. The Pentathlon

    B. The Olympics

    C. The Pankration

    D. Acrobatics

2. **A major event in the history of physical education occurred among the Romans. Which of the following did the Romans identify?**

    A. Severe physical training

    B. Harmonious development of the body, mind, and spirit

    C. The worth of physical education

    D. Physical training only for warriors

3. **President Eisenhower was alerted to the poor fitness levels of American youths. How was the poor physical conditioning of youths discovered in the Eisenhower Administration?**

    A. By WWII Selective Service Examination

    B. By organizations promoting physical fitness

    C. By the Federal Security Agency

    D. By the Kraus-Webber Tests

4. **In 1956, the AAHPER Fitness Conferences established:**

    A. The President's Council on Youth Fitness

    B. The President's Citizens' Advisory Committee

    C. The President's Council on Physical Fitness

    D. A and B

5. The physical education philosophy based on experience is:

A. Naturalism

B. Pragmatism

C. Idealism

D. Existentialism

6. The modern physical education philosophy that combines beliefs from different philosophies is:

A. Eclectic

B. Humanistic

C. Individualism

D. Realism

7. A physical education teacher emphasizes healthy attitudes and habits. She conducts her classes so that students acquire and interpret knowledge and learn to think/analyze, which is necessary for physical activities. The goals and values utilized and the philosophy applied by this instructor is:

A. Physical Development Goals and Realism Philosophy

B. Affective Development Goals and Existentialism

C. Motor Development Goals and Realism Philosophy

D. Cognitive Development Goals and Idealism Philosophy

8. Social skills and values developed by activity include all of the following except:

A. Winning at all costs

B. Making judgments in groups

C. Communicating and cooperating

D. Respecting rules and property

9. **Activities that enhance team socialization include all of the following except:**

    A. Basketball

    B. Soccer

    C. Golf

    D. Volleyball

10. **Through physical activities, John has developed self-discipline, fairness, respect for others, and new friends. John has experienced which of the following?**

    A. Positive cooperation psycho-social influences

    B. Positive group psycho-social influences

    C. Positive individual psycho-social influences

    D. Positive accomplishment psycho-social influences

11. **Which of the following psycho-social influences is not negative?**

    A. Avoidance of problems

    B. Adherence to exercise

    C. Ego-centeredness

    D. Role conflict

12. **Which professional organization protects amateur sports from corruption?**

    A. AIWA

    B. AAHPERD

    C. NCAA

    D. AAU

13. **Which professional organization works with legislatures?**

    A. AIWA

    B. AAHPERD

    C. ACSM

    D. AAU

14. **Research in physical education is published in all of the following periodicals except the:**

    A. School PE Update

    B. Research Quarterly

    C. Journal of Physical Education

    D. YMCA Magazine

15. **The most effective way to promote the physical education curriculum is to:**

    A. Relate physical education to higher thought processes

    B. Relate physical education to humanitarianism

    C. Relate physical education to the total educational process

    D. Relate physical education to skills necessary to preserve the natural environment

16. **The affective domain of physical education contributes to all of the following except:**

    A. Knowledge of exercise, health, and disease

    B. Self-actualization

    C. An appreciation of beauty

    D. Good sportsmanship

17. **A physical education instructor anticipates and prevents potential injuries, watches for hidden injuries, and takes an injury evaluation of the entire class. Which of the following strategies to prevent injuries is the teacher demonstrating?**

    A. Maintaining hiring standards

    B. Proper use of equipment

    C. Proper procedures for emergencies

    D. Participant screening

18. **Which of the following is not a consideration for the selection of a facility?**

    A. Community involvement

    B. Custodial staff

    C. Availability to women, minorities, and the handicapped

    D. Bond issues

19. **Which of the following is not a class-management technique?**

    A. Explaining procedures for roll call, excuses, and tardiness

    B. Explaining routines for changing and showering

    C. Explaining conditioning

    D. Promoting individual self-discipline

20. Long-term planning is essential for effective class management. Identify the management techniques not essential to long-term planning.

A. Parental observation

B. Progress evaluation

C. Precise activity planning

D. Arrangements for line markings

21. Although Mary is a paraplegic, she wants to participate in some capacity in the physical education class. What federal legislative act entitles her to do so?

A. PE 94-142

B. Title IX

C. PL 94-142

D. Title XI

22. A legal wrong resulting in a direct or an indirect injury is:

A. Negligence

B. A Tort

C. In loco parentis

D. Legal liability

23. All of the following actions help avoid lawsuits except:

A. Ensuring equipment and facilities are safe

B. Getting exculpatory agreements

C. Knowing each students' health status

D. Grouping students with unequal competitive levels

24. Which of the following actions does not promote safety?

A. Allowing students to wear the current style of shoes

B. Presenting organized activities

C. Inspecting equipment and facilities

D. Instructing skill and activities properly

25. An instructor notices that class participation is much lower than expected. By making changes in equipment and rules, the instructor applied which of the following concepts to enhance participation?

A. Homogeneous grouping

B. Heterogeneous grouping

C. Multi-activity designs

D. Activity modification

26. **Using tactile clues is a functional adaptation that can assist which type of students?**

    A. Deaf students

    B. Blind students

    C. Asthmatic students

    D. Physically challenged students

27. **Which of the following is not a skill assessment test to evaluate student performance?**

    A. Harrocks Volley

    B. Rodgers Strength Test

    C. Iowa Brace Test

    D. AAHPERD Youth Fitness Test

28. **All of the following are methods to evaluate the affective domain except:**

    A. Adams Prosocial Inventory

    B. Crowell Personal Distance Scale

    C. Blanchard Behavior Rating Scale

    D. McCloy's Prosocial Behavior Scale

29. **Educators can evaluate the cognitive domain by all of the following methods except:**

    A. Norm-Referenced Tests

    B. Criterion Referenced Tests

    C. Standardized Tests

    D. Willis Sports Inventory Tests

30. **Coordinated movements that project a person over an obstacle is:**

    A. Jumping

    B. Vaulting

    C. Leaping

    D. Hopping

31. **Using the same foot to take off from a surface and land is which locomotor skill?**

    A. Jumping

    B. Vaulting

    C. Leaping

    D. Hopping

32. Which nonlocomotor skill entails movement around a joint where two body parts meet?

   A. Twisting

   B. Swaying

   C. Bending

   D. Stretching

33. A sharp change of direction from one's original line of movement is which nonlocomotor skill?

   A. Twisting

   B. Dodging

   C. Swaying

   D. Swinging

34. Which manipulative skill uses the hands to stop the momentum of an object?

   A. Trapping

   B. Catching

   C. Striking

   D. Rolling

35. Playing "Simon Says" and having students touch different body parts applies which movement concept?

   A. Spatial Awareness

   B. Effort Awareness

   C. Body Awareness

   D. Motion Awareness

36. Which movement concept involves students making decisions about an object's positional changes in space?

   A. Spatial Awareness

   B. Effort Awareness

   C. Body Awareness

   D. Motion Awareness

37. Applying the mechanical principles of balance, time, and force describes which movement concept?

   A. Spatial Awareness

   B. Effort Awareness

   C. Body Awareness

   D. Motion Awareness

38. Having students move on their hands and knees, move on lines, and/or hold shapes while moving develops which quality of movement?

    A. Balance

    B. Time

    C. Force

    D. Inertia

39. Students that paddle balls against a wall or jump over objects with various heights are demonstrating which quality of movement?

    A. Balance

    B. Time

    C. Force

    D. Inertia

40. Having students move in a specific pattern while measuring how long they take to do so develops which quality of movement?

    A. Balance

    B. Time

    C. Force

    D. Inertia

41. There are two sequential phases to the development of spatial awareness. What is the order of these phases?

    A. Locating more than one object in relation to each object; the location of objects in relation to one's own body in space.

    B. The location of objects in relation to one's own body in space; locating more than one object in relation to one's own body.

    C. Locating more than one object independent of one's body; the location of objects in relation to one's own body.

    D. The location of objects in relation to one's own body in space; locating more than one object in relation to each object and independent of one's own body.

42. Equilibrium is maintained as long as:

    A. Body segments are moved independently.

    B. The center of gravity is over the base of support

    C. Force is applied to the base of support.

    D. The center of gravity is lowered.

43. Which of the following does not enhance equilibrium?

A. Shifting the center of gravity away from the direction of movement.

B. Increasing the base of support.

C. Lowering the base of support.

D. Increasing the base of support and lowering the center of support.

44. All of the following affect force except:

A. Magnitude

B. Energy

C. Motion

D. Mass

45. For a movement to occur, applied force must overcome inertia of an object and any other resisting forces. What concept of force does this describe?

A. Potential energy

B. Magnitude

C. Kinetic energy

D. Absorption

46. The energy of an object to do work while recoiling is which type of potential energy?

A. Absorption

B. Kinetic

C. Elastic

D. Torque

47. Gradually decelerating a moving mass by utilization of smaller forces over a long period of time is:

A. Stability

B. Equilibrium

C. Angular force

D. Force absorption

48. The tendency of a body/object to remain in its present state of motion unless some force acts to change it is which mechanical principle of motion?

A. Acceleration

B. Inertia

C. Action/Reaction

D. Linear motion

49. The movement response of a system depends not only on the net external force, but also on the resistance to movement change. Which mechanical principle of motion does this definition describe?

A. Acceleration

B. Inertia

C. Action/Reaction

D. Air Resistance

50. Which of the following mechanical principles of motion states that every motion has a similar, contrasting response?

A. Acceleration

B. Inertia

C. Action/Reaction

D. Centripetal force

51. What is the proper order of sequential development for the acquisition of locomotor skills?

A. Creep, crawl, walk, jump, run, slide, gallop, hop, leap, skip; step-hop.

B. Crawl, walk, creep, slide, walk, run, hop, leap, gallop, skip; step-hop.

C. Creep, crawl, walk, slide, run, hop, leap, skip, gallop, jump; step-hop.

D. Crawl, creep, walk, run, jump, hop, gallop, slide, leap, skip; step-hop.

52. Having students pretend they are playing basketball or trying to catch a bus develops which locomotor skill?

A. Galloping

B. Running

C. Leaping

D. Skipping

53. Having students play Fox and Hound develops:

A. Galloping

B. Hopping

C. Stepping-hopping

D. Skipping

54. Having students take off and land with both feet together develops which locomotor skill?

A. Hopping

B. Jumping

C. Leaping

D. Skipping

55. What is the proper sequential order of development for the acquisition of nonlocomotor skills?

A. Stretch, sit, bend, turn, swing, twist, shake, rock & sway, dodge; fall.

B. Bend, stretch, turn, twist, swing, sit, rock & sway, shake, dodge; fall.

C. Stretch, bend, sit, shake, turn, rock & sway, swing, twist, dodge; fall.

D. Bend, stretch, sit, turn, twist, swing, sway, rock & sway, dodge; fall.

56. Activities such as pretending to pick fruit off a tree or reaching for a star develop which non-locomotor skill?

A. Bending

B. Stretching

C. Turning

D. Twisting

57. Picking up coins, tying shoes, and petting animals develop this nonlocomotor skill.

A. Bending

B. Stretching

C. Turning

D. Twisting

58. Having students collapse in their own space or lower themselves as though they are a raindrop or snowflake develops this nonlocomotor skill.

A. Dodging

B. Shaking

C. Swinging

D. Falling

59. Which is the proper sequential order of development for the acquisition of manipulative skills?

A. Striking, throwing, bouncing, catching, trapping, kicking, ball rolling; volleying.

B. Striking, throwing, kicking, ball rolling, volleying, bouncing, catching; trapping.

C. Striking, throwing, catching, trapping, kicking, ball rolling, bouncing; volleying.

D. Striking, throwing, kicking, ball rolling, bouncing; volleying.

60. Having students hit a large balloon with both hands develops this manipulative skill.

A. Bouncing

B. Striking

C. Volleying

D. Trapping

61. Progressively decreasing the size of a target that balls are projected at develops which manipulative skill.

A. Throwing

B. Trapping

C. Volleying

D. Kicking

62. Hitting a stationary object while in a fixed position, then incorporating movement, develops this manipulative skill.

A. Bouncing

B. Trapping

C. Throwing

D. Striking

63. A subjective, observational approach to identifying errors in the form, style, or mechanics of a skill is accomplished by:

A. Product assessment

B. Process assessment

C. Standardized norm-referenced tests

D. Criterion-referenced tests

64. **What type of assessment objectively measures skill performance?**

    A. Process assessment

    B. Product assessment

    C. Texas PE Test

    D. Iowa Brace Test

65. **Process assessment does not identify which of the following errors in skill performance.**

    A. Style

    B. Form

    C. End result

    D. Mechanics

66. **Determining poor performance of a skill using process assessment can best be accomplished by:**

    A. Observing how fast a skill is performed.

    B. Observing how many skills are performed.

    C. Observing how far or how high a skill is performed.

    D. Observing several attributes comprising the entire performance of a skill.

67. **Which of the following principles is not a factor to assess to correct errors in performance for process assessment?**

    A. Inertia

    B. Action/Reaction

    C. Force

    D. Acceleration

68. **Which of the following methods measures fundamental skills using product assessment?**

    A. Criterion-referenced tests

    B. Standardized norm-referenced tests

    C. Both A and B

    D. Neither A nor B

69. **Product assessment measures all of the following except:**

    A. How the student performs the mechanics of a skill.

    B. How many times the student performs a skill.

    C. How fast the student performs a skill.

    D. How far or high the student performs a skill.

70. Instructors can evaluate skill level of achievement in archery by:

A. Giving students a written exam on terminology.

B. Having students demonstrate the correct tension of arrow feathers.

C. Totaling a student's score obtained on the target's face.

D. Time how long a student takes to shoot all arrows.

71. Instructors can determine skill level achievement in golf by:

A. The number of "birdies" that a student makes.

B. The number of "bogies" a student makes.

C. The score obtained after several rounds

D. The total score achieved throughout the school year.

72. Instructors can determine skill level achievement in swimming by:

A. How long a student can float

B. How many strokes it takes a student to swim a specified distance.

C. How long a student can stay under the water without moving.

D. How many times a student can dive in five minutes.

73. Instructors can assess skill level achievement in bowling by:

A. Calculating a student's average score.

B. Calculating how many gutter-balls the student threw.

C. Calculating how many strikes the student threw.

D. Calculating how many spares the student threw.

74. **Although they are still hitting the target, the score of some students practicing archery has decreased as the distance between them and the target has increased. Which of the following adjustments will improve their scores?**

   A. Increasing the velocity of their arrows.

   B. Increasing the students' base of support.

   C. Increasing the weight of the arrows.

   D. Increasing the parabolic path of the arrows.

75. **Some students practicing basketball are having difficulty with "free throws," even though the shots make it to and over the hoop. What adjustment will improve their "free throws?"**

   A. Increasing the height of release (i.e. jump shot).

   B. Increasing the vertical path of the ball.

   C. Increasing the velocity of the release.

   D. Increasing the base of support.

76. **An archery student's arrow bounced off the red part of the target face. What is the correct ruling?**

   A. No score.

   B. Re-shoot arrow.

   C. 7 points awarded.

   D. Shot receives same score as highest arrow shot that did not bounce off the target.

77. **A student playing badminton believed that the shuttlecock was going to land out-of-bounds. The shuttlecock landed on the line. What is the correct ruling?**

   A. The shuttlecock is out-of-bounds.

   B. The shuttlecock is in-bounds.

   C. The point is replayed.

   D. That player is charged with a feint.

78. A mechanical pinsetter accidentally knocked down the only bowling pin left standing for a spare attempt after clearing all the other pins knocked down by the first ball thrown. What is the correct ruling?

A. Foul

B. Spare

C. Frame is replayed

D. No count for that pin

79. The ball served in racquetball hits the front line and lands in front of the short line. What is the ruling?

A. Fault

B. Reserve

C. Out-of-bounds

D. Fair ball

80. Two opposing soccer players are trying to gain control of the ball when one player "knees" the other. What is the ruling?

A. Direct free kick

B. Indirect free kick

C. Fair play

D. Ejection from the game

81. Two students are playing badminton. When receiving the shuttlecock, one student consistently stands too deep in the receiving court. What strategy should the server use to serve the shuttlecock?

A. Smash serve

B. Clear serve

C. Overhead serve

D. Short serve

82. A basketball team has an outstanding rebounder. In order to keep this player near the opponent's basket, which strategy should the coach implement?

A. Pick-and-Roll

B. Give-and-Go

C. Zone defense

D. Free-lancing

83. When a defensive tennis player needs more time to return to his position, what strategy should he apply?

A. Drop shot

B. Dink shot

C. Lob shot

D. Down-the-line shot

84. An overhead badminton stroke used to hit a fore-hand-like overhead stroke that is on the backhand side of the body is a(n):

   A. Around-the-head-shot

   B. Down-the-line shot

   C. Lifting the shuttle

   D. Under hand shuttle

85. A maneuver when an offensive player passes to a teammate and then immediately cuts in toward the basket for a return pass is:

   A. Charging

   B. Pick

   C. Give-and-go

   D. Switching

86. A bowling pin that remains standing after an apparently perfect hit is a:

   A. Tap

   B. Turkey

   C. Blow

   D. Leave

87. A soccer pass from the outside of the field near the end line to a position in front of the goal is a:

   A. Chip

   B. Settle

   C. Through

   D. Cross

88. A volleyball that opponents simultaneously contact and momentarily hold above the net is a(n):

   A. Double fault

   B. Play over

   C. Overlap

   D. Held ball

89. Volleyball player LB on team A digs a spiked ball. The ball deflects off LB's shoulder. What is the ruling?

   A. Fault

   B. Legal hit

   C. Double foul

   D. Play over

90. A teacher who modifies and develops tasks for a class is demonstrating knowledge of which appropriate behavior in physical education activities.

    A. Appropriate management behavior

    B. Appropriate student behavior

    C. Appropriate administration behavior

    D. Appropriate content behavior

91. To enhance skill and strategy performance for striking or throwing objects, for catching or collecting objects, and for carrying and propelling objects, students must first learn techniques for:

    A. Offense

    B. Defense

    C. Controlling objects

    D. Continuous play of objects

92. Which of the following is not a type of tournament?

    A. Spiderweb

    B. Pyramid

    C. Spiral

    D. Round Robin

93. Which of the following is not a type of meet?

    A. Extramural

    B. Intramural

    C. Interscholastic

    D. Ladder

94. An instructor used a similar movement from a skill learned in a different activity to teach a skill for a new activity. The technique used to facilitate cognitive learning was:

    A. Conceptual thinking

    B. Transfer of learning

    C. Longer instruction

    D. Appropriate language

95. A teacher rewards students for completing tasks. Which method is the teacher using to facilitate psychomotor learning?

    A. Task/Reciprocal

    B. Command/Direct

    C. Contingency/Contract

    D. Physical/Reflex

96. All of the following are Systematic Observational Evaluations except:

A. Reflective Recording

B. Event Recording

C. Duration Recording

D. Self Recording

97. The ability for a muscle(s) to repeatedly contract over a period of time is:

A. Cardiovascular endurance

B. Muscle endurance

C. Muscle strength

D. Muscle force

98. The ability to change rapidly the direction of the body is:

A. Coordination

B. Reaction time

C. Speed

D. Agility

99. Students are performing the vertical jump. What component of fitness does this activity assess?

A. Muscle strength

B. Balance

C. Power

D. Muscle endurance

100. Students are performing trunk extensions. What component of fitness does this activity assess?

A. Balance

B. Flexibility

C. Body Composition

D. Coordination

101. Working at a level that is above normal is which exercise training principle?

A. Intensity

B. Progression

C. Specificity

D. Overload

102. **Students on a running program to improve cardio-respiratory fitness apply which exercise principle.**

    A. Aerobic

    B. Progression

    C. Specificity

    D. Overload

103. **Adding more reps to a weightlifting set applies which exercise principle.**

    A. Anaerobic

    B. Progression

    C. Overload

    D. Specificity

104. **Which of the following does not modify overload?**

    A. Frequency

    B. Perceived exertion

    C. Time

    D. Intensity

105. **Using the Karvonean Formula, compute the 60% - 80% THR for a 16-year old student with a RHR of 60.**

    A. 122-163 beats per minute

    B. 130-168 beats per minute

    C. 142-170 beats per minute

    D. 146-175 beats per minute

106. **Using Cooper's Formula, compute the THR for a 15 year old student.**

    A. 120- 153 beats per minute

    B. 123-164 beats per minute

    C. 135-169 beats per minute

    D. 147-176 beats per minute

107. **Prior to activity, students perform a 5-10 minute warm-up. Which is not recommended as part of the warm-up?**

    A. Using the muscles that will be utilized in the following activity.

    B. Using a gradual aerobic warm-up.

    C. Using a gradual anaerobic warm-up.

    D. Stretching the major muscle groups to be used in the activity.

108. Which is not a benefit of warming up?

A. Releasing hydrogen from myoglobin.

B. Reducing the risk of musculoskeletal injuries.

C. Raising the body's core temperature in preparation for activity.

D. Stretching the major muscle groups to be used in the activity.

109. Which is not a benefit of cooling down?

A. Preventing dizziness.

B. Redistributing circulation.

C. Removing lactic acid.

D. Removing myoglobin.

110. Activities to specifically develop cardiovascular fitness must be:

A. Performed without developing an oxygen debt

B. Performed twice daily.

C. Performed every day.

D. Performed for a minimum of 10 minutes.

111. Overloading for muscle strength includes all of the following except:

A. Raising heart rate to an intense level.

B. Lifting weights every other day.

C. Lifting with high resistance and low reps.

D. Lifting 60% to 90% of assessed muscle strength.

112. Which of the following applies the concept of progression?

A. Beginning a stretching program every day.

B. Beginning a stretching program with 3 sets of reps.

C. Beginning a stretching program with ballistic stretching.

D. Beginning a stretching program holding stretches for 15 seconds and work up to holding stretches for 60 seconds.

113. Which of following overload principles does not apply to improving body composition?

A. Aerobic exercise three times per week.

B. Aerobic exercise at a low intensity.

C. Aerobic exercise for about an hour.

D. Aerobic exercise in intervals of high intensity.

114. Which of the following principles of progression applies to improving muscle endurance?

A. Lifting weights every day.

B. Lifting weights at 20% to 30% of assessed muscle strength.

C. Lifting weights with low resistance and low reps.

D. Lifting weights starting at 60% of assessed muscle strength.

115. Aerobic dance develops or improves each of the following skills or health components except...

A. Cardio-respiratory function

B. Body composition

C. Coordination

D. Flexibility

116. Rowing develops which health or skill related component of fitness?

A. Muscle endurance

B. Flexibility

C. Balance

D. Reaction time

117. Calisthenics develops all of the following health and skill related components of fitness except:

A. Muscle strength

B. Body composition

C. Power

D. Agility

118. Which health or skill related components of fitness is developed by rope jumping?

    A. Muscle Force

    B. Coordination

    C. Flexibility

    D. Muscle strength

119. Swimming does not improve which health or skill related component of fitness?

    A. Cardio-respiratory function

    B. Flexibility

    C. Muscle strength

    D. Foot Speed

120. Data from a cardio-respiratory assessment can identify and predict all of the following except:

    A. Functional aerobic capacity

    B. Natural over-fatness

    C. Running ability

    D. Motivation

121. Data from assessing _____ identifies an individual's potential of developing musculoskeletal problems and an individual's potential of performing activities of daily living.

    A. Flexibility

    B. Muscle endurance

    C. Muscle strength

    D. Motor performance

122. A 17-year-old male student performed 20 sit-ups, ran a mile in 8 minutes, and has a body fat composition of 17%. Which is the best interpretation of his fitness level?

    A. Average muscular endurance, good cardiovascular endurance; appropriate body fat composition.

    B. Low muscular endurance, average cardiovascular endurance; high body fat composition.

    C. Low muscular endurance, average cardiovascular endurance; appropriate body fat composition.

    D. Low muscular endurance, low cardiovascular endurance; appropriate body fat composition.

123. **Based on the information given in the previous question, what changes would you recommend to improve this person's level of fitness?**

    A. Muscle endurance training and cardiovascular endurance training.

    B. Muscle endurance training, cardiovascular endurance training, and reduction of caloric intake.

    C. Muscle strength training and cardio-vascular endurance training.

    D. No changes necessary.

124. **An obese student's fitness assessments were poor for every component of fitness. Which would you recommend first?**

    A. A jogging program.

    B. A weight lifting program.

    C. A walking program.

    D. A stretching program.

125. **Which of the following body types is the most capable of motor performance involving endurance?**

    A. Endomorph

    B. Ectomorph

    C. Mesomorph

    D. Metamorph

126. **Which is not a sign of stress?**

    A. Irritability

    B. Assertiveness

    C. Insomnia

    D. Stomach problems

127. **Which is not a common negative stressor?**

    A. Loss of significant other

    B. Personal illness or injury.

    C. Moving to a new state.

    D. Landing a new job.

128. **Which of the following is a negative coping strategy for dealing with stress?**

    A. Recreational diversions

    B. Active thinking

    C. Alcohol use

    D. Imagery

129. **The most important nutrient the body requires, without which life can only be sustained for a few days, is:**

    A. Vitamins

    B. Minerals

    C. Water

    D. Carbohydrates

130. **With regard to protein content, foods from animal sources are usually:**

    A. Complete

    B. Essential

    C. Nonessential

    D. Incidental

131. **Fats with room for two or more hydrogen atoms per molecule-fatty acid chain are:**

    A. Monounsaturated

    B. Polyunsaturated

    C. Hydrosaturated

    D. Saturated

132. **An adequate diet to meet nutritional needs consists of:**

    A. No more than 30% caloric intake from fats, no more than 50 % caloric intake from proteins, and at least 20% caloric intake from carbohydrates.

    B. No more than 30% caloric intake from fats, no more than 40% caloric intake from proteins, and at least 30% caloric intake from carbohydrates.

    C. No more than 30% caloric intake from fats, no more than 15% caloric intake from proteins, and at least 55% caloric intake from carbohydrates.

    D. No more than 30 % caloric intake from fats, no more than 30% caloric intake from proteins, and at least 40% caloric intake from carbohydrates.

133. **Maintaining body weight is best accomplished by:**

    A. Dieting

    B. Aerobic exercise

    C. Lifting weights

    D. Equalizing caloric intake relative to output

134. Most high-protein diets:

A. Are high in cholesterol

B. Are high in saturated fats

C. Require vitamin and mineral supplements

D. All of the above

135. Which one of the following statements about low-calorie diets is false?

A. Most people who "diet only" regain the weight they lose.

B. They are the way most people try to lose weight.

C. They make weight control easier.

D. They lead to excess worry about weight, food, and eating.

136. Physiological benefits of exercise include all of the following except:

A. Reducing mental tension

B. Improving muscle strength

C. Cardiac hypertrophy

D. Quicker recovery rate

137. Psychological benefits of exercise include all of the following except:

A. Improved sleeping patterns

B. Improved energy regulation

C. Improved appearance

D. Improved quality of life

138. Which of the following conditions is not associated with a lack of physical activity?

A. Atherosclerosis

B. Longer life expectancy

C. Osteoporosis

D. Certain cancers

139. Which of the following pieces of exercise equipment best applies the physiological principles?

A. Rolling machine

B. Electrical muscle stimulator

C. Stationary Bicycle

D. Motor-driven rowing machine

Answer Key

1.	B	36.	A	71.	C	106.	B
2.	C	37.	B	72.	B	107.	C
3.	D	38.	A	73.	A	108.	A
4.	D	39.	C	74.	D	109.	D
5.	B	40.	B	75.	B	110.	A
6.	A	41.	D	76.	C	111.	A
7.	D	42.	B	77.	B	112.	D
8.	A	43.	A	78.	D	113.	A
9.	C	44.	D	79.	A	114.	B
10.	B	45.	B	80.	A	115.	D
11.	B	46.	C	81.	D	116.	A
12.	D	47.	D	82.	C	117.	C
13.	B	48.	B	83.	C	118.	B
14.	A	49.	A	84.	A	119.	D
15.	C	50.	C	85.	C	120.	B
16.	A	51.	D	86.	A	121.	A
17.	D	52.	B	87.	D	122.	C
18.	A	53.	A	88.	D	123.	A
19.	C	54.	B	89.	B	124.	C
20.	A	55.	C	90.	D	125.	B
21.	C	56.	B	91.	C	126.	B
22.	B	57.	A	92.	C	127.	D
23.	D	58.	D	93.	D	128.	C
24.	A	59.	B	94.	B	129.	C
25.	D	60.	C	95.	C	130.	A
26.	B	61.	A	96.	A	131.	B
27.	A	62.	D	97.	B	132.	C
28.	D	63.	B	98.	D	133.	D
29.	D	64.	B	99.	C	134.	D
30.	B	65.	C	100.	B	135.	C
31.	D	66.	D	101.	D	136.	A
32.	C	67.	C	102.	C	137.	B
33.	B	68.	C	103.	B	138.	B
34.	B	69.	A	104.	B	139.	C
35.	C	70.	C	105.	D		

Rationales with Sample Questions

1. **The Greek's best known early contribution to the profession Physical Education was:**

   A. The Pentathlon
   B. The Olympics
   C. The Pankration
   D. Acrobatics

(B.) The Olympics are a premiere athletic meeting that originated in ancient Greece and still exists in modern times. The Greeks held the games in ancient times on the plain of Olympia in Greece every four years. Greek citizens put aside political and religious differences as athletes from all of the Greek cities and districts competed in the Olympics. The games included patriotic and religious rituals as well as athletic contests. The winners received high honors.

2. **A major event in the history of physical education occurred among the Romans. Which of the following did the Romans identify?**
   A. Severe physical training
   B. Harmonious development of the body, mind, and spirit
   C. The worth of physical education was dignified
   D. Physical training only for warriors

(C.) The Romans first established the worth of physical education for its own sake. Answers A and D describe the Spartans, who emphasized severe physical training for warriors. Answer B describes the Athenians, who valued the harmonious development of mind, body, and spirit.

3. **President Eisenhower was alerted to the poor fitness levels of American youths. How was the poor physical conditioning of youths discovered in the Eisenhower Administration?**
   A. By WWII Selective Service Examination
   B. By organizations promoting physical fitness
   C. By the Federal Security Agency
   D. By the Kraus-Webber Tests

(D.) This is one of the programs that President Dwight Eisenhower implemented during his presidency. Using a test devised by Drs. Hans Kraus and Sonja Weber of New York Presbyterian Hospital, Bonnie began testing children in Europe, Central America, and the United States. The Kraus-Weber test involved six simple movements and took 90 seconds to administer. It compared US children to European children in the realms of strength and flexibility. The fitness emphasis in schools started by Kraus-Weber declined in the 1970s and early 1980s. The President's Council on Physical Fitness and Sports was one result of the Kraus-Weber test results.

4. **In 1956, the AAHPER Fitness Conferences established:**
   A. The President's Council on Youth Fitness
   B. The President's Citizens' Advisory Committee
   C. The President's Council on Physical Fitness
   D. A and B

(D., A., and B.) The **President's Council on Youth Fitness** was founded on July 16, 1956 to encourage American children to be healthy and active after a study indicated that American youths were less physically fit than European children. President Eisenhower created the President's Council on Youth Fitness with cabinet-level status. The Executive Order specified "one" objective. The first Council identified itself as a "catalytic agent" concentrating on creating public awareness. A President's Citizens-Advisory Committee on Fitness of American Youth was confirmed to give advice to the Council.

5. **The physical education philosophy based on experience is:**
   A. Naturalism
   B. Pragmatism
   C. Idealism
   D. Existentialism

(B.) Pragmatism, as a school of philosophy, is a collection of different ways of thinking. Given the diversity of thinkers and the variety of schools of thought that have adopted this term over the years, the term pragmatism has become almost meaningless in the absence of further qualification. Most of the thinkers who describe themselves as pragmatists indicate some connection with practical consequences or real effects as vital components of both meaning and truth.

6. **The modern physical education philosophy that combines beliefs from different philosophies is:**
   A. Eclectic
   B. Humanistic
   C. Individualism
   D. Realism

(A.) Eclectics are so-called philosophers who attach themselves to no system in particular. Instead, they select what, in their judgment, is true out of the other philosophes. In antiquity, the Eclectic philosophy is that which sought to unite into a coherent whole, the doctrines of Pythagoras, Plato, and Aristotle. There is eclecticism in art as well as philosophy. The term was applied to an Italian school which aimed at uniting the excellence of individual intellectual masters.

7. A physical education teacher emphasizes healthy attitudes and habits. She conducts her classes so that students acquire and interpret knowledge and learn to think/analyze, which is necessary for physical activities. The goals and values utilized and the philosophy applied by this instructor is:
    A. Physical Development Goals and Realism Philosophy
    B. Affective Development Goals and Existentialism
    C. Motor Development Goals and Realism Philosophy
    D. Cognitive Development Goals and Idealism Philosophy

(D.) Educators use cognitive development goals to describe the act of teaching children in a manner that will help them develop as personal and social beings. Concepts that fall under this term include social and emotional learning, moral reasoning/cognitive development, life-skills education, health education, violence prevention, critical thinking, ethical reasoning, and conflict resolution and mediation. This form of education involves teaching children and teenagers such values as honesty, stewardship, kindness, generosity, courage, freedom, justice, equality, and respect. Idealism is an approach to philosophical inquiry that asserts direct and immediate knowledge can only be had as ideas or mental pictures. We can only know the objects that are the basis of these ideas indirectly.

8. Social skills and values developed by activity include all of the following except:
    A. Winning at all costs
    B. Making judgments in groups
    C. Communicating and cooperating
    D. Respecting rules and property

(A.) Winning at all costs is not a desirable social skill. Instructors and coaches should emphasize fair play and effort over winning. Answers B, C, and D are all positive skills and values developed in physical activity settings.

9. Activities that enhance team socialization include all of the following except:
    A. Basketball
    B. Soccer
    C. Golf
    D. Volleyball

(C.) Golf is mainly an individual sport. Though golf involves social interaction, it generally lacks the team element inherent in basketball, soccer, and volleyball.

10. Through physical activities, John has developed self-discipline, fairness, respect for others, and new friends. John has demonstrated which of the following?
    A. Positive cooperation psycho-social influences
    B. Positive group psycho-social influences
    C. Positive individual psycho-social influences
    D. Positive accomplishment psycho-social influences

(B.) Through physical activities, John developed his social interaction skills. Social interaction is the sequence of social actions between individuals (or groups) that modify their actions and reactions due to the actions of their interaction partner(s). In other words, they are events in which people attach meaning to a situation, interpret what others mean, and respond accordingly. Through socialization with other people, John feels the influence of the people around him.

11. Which of the following psycho-social influences is not negative?
    A. Avoidance of problems
    B. Adherence to exercise
    C. Ego-centeredness
    D. Role conflict

(B.) The ability of an individual to adhere to an exercise routine due to her/his excitement, accolades, etc. is not a negative psycho-social influence. Adherence to an exercise routine is healthy and positive.

12. Which professional organization protects amateur sports from corruption?
    A. AIWA
    B. AAHPERD
    C. NCAA
    D. AAU

(D.) The Amateur Athletic Union (AAU) is one of the largest non-profit, volunteer sports organizations in the United States. A multi-sport organization, the AAU dedicates itself exclusively to the promotion and development of amateur sports and physical fitness programs. Answer C may be a tempting choice, but the NCAA deals only with college athletics.

13. Which professional organization works with legislatures?
A. AIWA
B. AAHPERD
C. ACSM
D. AAU

(B.) AAHPERD, or American Alliance for Health, Physical Education, Recreation and Dance, is an alliance of 6 national associations. AAHPERD is the largest organization of professionals supporting and assisting those involved in physical education, leisure, fitness, dance, health promotion, and education, as well as all other specialties related to achieving a healthy lifestyle. AAHPERD is an alliance designed to provide members with a comprehensive and coordinated array of resources, support, and programs to help practitioners improve their skills and in turn, further the health and well-being of the American public.

14. Research in physical education is published in all of the following periodicals except the:
A. School PE Update
B. Research Quarterly
C. Journal of Physical Education
D. YMCA Magazine

(A.) Each school has a PE Update that publishes their own periodicals about physical activities. It aims at helping the students to catch-up on what is happening around them. The school produces this update to encourage their students to become more interested in all of the physical activities that they offer. School PE Updates, however, do not include research findings.

15. The most effective way to promote the physical education curriculum is to:
A. Relate physical education to higher thought processes
B. Relate physical education to humanitarianism
C. Relate physical education to the total educational process
D. Relate physical education to skills necessary to preserve the natural environment

(C.) The government treats the physical education curriculum as one of the major subjects. Because of all of the games that we now participate in, many countries have focused their hearts and set their minds on competing with rival countries. Physical education is now one of the major, important subjects and instructors should integrate physical education into the total educational process.

16. The affective domain of physical education contributes to all of the following except:
A. Knowledge of exercise, health, and disease
B. Self-actualization
C. An appreciation of beauty
D. Good sportsmanship

(A.) The affective domain encompasses emotions, thoughts, and feelings related to physical education. Knowledge of exercise, health, and disease is part of the cognitive domain.

17. A physical education instructor anticipates and prevents potential injuries, watches for hidden injuries, and takes an injury evaluation of the entire class. Which of the following strategies to prevent injuries is the teacher demonstrating?
A. Maintaining hiring standards
B. Proper use of equipment
C. Proper procedures for emergencies
D. Participant screening

(D.) In order for the instructor to know each student's physical status, she takes an injury evaluation. Such surveys are one way to know the physical status of an individual. It chronicles past injuries, tattoos, activities, and diseases the individual may have or had. It helps the instructor to know the limitations of each individual. Participant screening covers all forms of surveying and anticipation of injuries.

18. Which of the following is not a consideration for the selection of a facility?
A. Community involvement
B. Custodial staff
C. Availability to women, minorities, and the handicapped
D. Bond issues

(A.) While community involvement positively impacts the communities where individuals live and work, it is not a major consideration in facility selection. Factors that are more important are staffing, accessibility, and financial considerations.

19. Which of the following is not a class-management technique?
A. Explaining procedures for roll call, excuses, and tardiness
B. Explaining routines for changing and showering
C. Explaining conditioning
D. Promoting individual self-discipline

(C.) Explaining conditioning is not a class management technique. It is an instructional lesson.

20. Long-term planning is essential for effective class management. Identify the management techniques not essential to long-term planning.
A. Parental observation
B. Progress evaluation
C. Precise activity planning
D. Arrangements for line markings

(A.) While it is important that a child have support from his/her parents, parental observation is not an essential consideration in long-term planning. Progress evaluation, precise activity planning, and arranging line markings are all essential management techniques for long-term planning.

21. Although Mary is a paraplegic, she wants to participate in some capacity in the physical education class. What federal legislative act entitles her to do so?
A. PE 94-142
B. Title IX
C. PL 94-142
D. Title XI

(C.) It is the purpose of Act PL 94-142 to assure that all handicapped children have available to them, within the time periods specified in section 612(2), (B.), a free, appropriate public education that emphasizes special education and related services designed to meet their unique needs, to assure that the rights of handicapped children and their parents/guardians are protected, to assist states and localities to provide for the education of all handicapped children, and to assess and assure the effectiveness of efforts to educate handicapped children.

22. A legal wrong resulting in a direct or an indirect injury is:
A. Negligence
B. A Tort
C. In loco parentis
D. Legal liability

(B.) A tort is damage, injury, or a wrongful act done willfully, negligently, or in circumstances involving strict liability, but not involving breach of contract, for which the injured party can bring a civil suit.

23. All of the following actions help avoid lawsuits except:
   A. Ensuring equipment and facilities are safe
   B. Getting exculpatory agreements
   C. Knowing each students' health status
   D. Grouping students with unequal competitive levels

(D.) Grouping students with unequal competitive levels is not an action that can help avoid lawsuits. Such a practice could lead to injury because of the inequality in skill, size, and strength.

24. Which of the following actions does not promote safety?
   A. Allowing students to wear the current style of shoes
   B. Presenting organized activities
   C. Inspecting equipment and facilities
   D. Instructing skill and activities properly

(A.) Shoes are very important in physical education and the emphasis on current shoe styles does not promote safety because they focus more on the look of the clothing, rather than functionality.

25. An instructor notices that class participation is much lower than expected. By making changes in equipment and rules, the instructor applied which of the following concepts to enhance participation?
   A. Homogeneous grouping
   B. Heterogeneous grouping
   C. Multi-activity designs
   D. Activity modification

(D.) Activity modification involves changing rules and equipment to fit the needs of students of different ability levels and physical development levels. Activity modification can encourage participation by making games and activities more enjoyable and allowing for more student success.

26. Using tactile clues is a functional adaptation that can assist which type of students?
   A. Deaf students
   B. Blind students
   C. Asthmatic students
   D. Physically challenged students

(B.) Blind people use tactile clues to identify colors. Instructors should use tactile clues to help students see or hear targets by adding color, making them larger, or moving them closer. It will help cooperation in a creative way.

27. **Which of the following is not a skill assessment test to evaluate student performance?**
    A. Harrocks Volley
    B. Rodgers Strength Test
    C. Iowa Brace Test
    D. AAHPERD Youth Fitness Test

(A.) Harrocks Volley is a volleyball code for a popular player named James.

28. **All of the following are methods to evaluate the affective domain except:**
    A. Adams Prosocial Inventory
    B. Crowell Personal Distance Scale
    C. Blanchard Behavior Rating Scale
    D. McCloy's Prosocial Behavior Scale

(D.) McCloy's Prosocial Behavior scale provided one of the earliest discussions on the influence of participation in sports and on the development of socially desirable character traits. Not surprisingly, large voids still exist in the knowledge about athletes' moral reasoning. One area that has thus far received little attention by social psychologists is the relationship between sport involvement, moral development, and aggression.

29. **Educators can evaluate the cognitive domain by all of the following methods except:**
    A. Norm-Referenced Tests
    B. Criterion Referenced Tests
    C. Standardized Tests
    D. Willis Sports Inventory Tests

(D.) The Willis Sports Inventory Test is the tally of all wins and losses of the popular basketball player, Willis.

30. **Coordinated movements that project a person over an obstacle is:**
    A. Jumping
    B. Vaulting
    C. Leaping
    D. Hopping

(B.) Vaulting is the art of acrobatics on horseback. Vaulting is an internationally recognized, competitive sport that is growing in popularity. At the most basic level vaulting enhances riding skills. At any skill-level, this ancient dance between horse and rider deepens the sense of balance, timing, and poise for the rider, as well as a sensitivity to and respect for the horse-rider relationship. Participants can vault in competition individually or on a team of 8 people with up to 3 people on the horse at once.

31. Using the same foot to take off from a surface and land is which locomotor skill?
A. Jumping
B. Vaulting
C. Leaping
D. Hopping

(D.) Hopping is a move with light, bounding skips or leaps. Basically, it is the ability to jump on one foot.

32. Which nonlocomotor skill entails movement around a joint where two body parts meet?
A. Twisting
B. Swaying
C. Bending
D. Stretching

(C.) Bending is a deviation from a straight-line position. It is also means to assume a curved, crooked, or angular form or direction, to incline the body, to make a concession, yield, to apply oneself closely, or to concentrate (e.g., *she bent to her task)*.

33. A sharp change of direction from one's original line of movement is which nonlocomotor skill?
A. Twisting
B. Dodging
C. Swaying
D. Swinging

(B.) Dodging is the ability to avoid something by moving or shifting quickly aside.

34. Which manipulative skill uses the hands to stop the momentum of an object?
A. Trapping
B. Catching
C. Striking
D. Rolling

(B.) The ability to use the hands to catch an object is a manipulative skill. Catching stops the momentum of an object. A successful catch harnesses the force of the oncoming object to stop the object's momentum.

35. **Playing "Simon Says" and having students touch different body parts applies which movement concept?**
    A. Spatial Awareness
    B. Effort Awareness
    C. Body Awareness
    D. Motion Awareness

(C.) Body Awareness is a method that integrates European traditions of movement and biomedical knowledge with the <u>East Asian</u> traditions of movement (e.g. <u>Tai chi</u> and <u>Zen meditation</u>).

36. **Which movement concept involves students making decisions about an object's positional changes in space?**
    A. Spatial Awareness
    B. Effort Awareness
    C. Body Awareness
    D. Motion Awareness

(A.) Spatial awareness is an organized awareness of objects in the space around us. It is also an awareness of our body's position in space. Without this awareness, we would not be able to pick food up from our plates and put it in our mouths. We would have trouble reading, because we could not see the letters in their correct relation to each other and to the page. Athletes would not have the precise awareness of the position of other players on the field and the movement of the ball, which is necessary to play sports effectively.

37. **Applying the mechanical principles of balance, time, and force describes which movement concept?**
    A. Spatial Awareness
    B. Effort Awareness
    C. Body Awareness
    D. Motion Awareness

(B.) Effort Awareness is the knowledge of balance, time, and force and how they relate to athletic movements and activities.

38. Having students move on their hands and knees, move on lines, and/or hold shapes while moving develops which quality of movement?
A. Balance
B. Time
C. Force
D. Inertia

(A.) Balance is one of the <u>physiological</u> <u>senses</u>. It allows <u>humans</u> and <u>animals</u> to <u>walk</u> without falling. Some animals are better at this than humans. For example, a <u>cat</u> (as a <u>quadruped</u> using its <u>inner ear</u> and <u>tail</u>) can walk on a thin <u>fence</u>. All forms of equilibrioception are essentially the detection of acceleration.

39. Students that paddle balls against a wall or jump over objects with various heights are demonstrating which quality of movement?
A. Balance
B. Time
C. Force
D. Inertia

(C.) Force is the capacity to do work or create physical change, energy, strength, or active power. It is a classical **force** that causes a free body with <u>mass</u> to <u>accelerate</u>. A net (or resultant) force that causes such acceleration may be the non-zero additive sum of many different forces acting on a body.

40. Having students move in a specific pattern while measuring how long they take to do so develops which quality of movement?
A. Balance
B. Time
C. Force
D. Inertia

(B.) Time is a sequential arrangement of all events or the interval between two events in such a sequence. We can discuss the concept of time on several different levels: physical, psychological, philosophical, scientific, and biological. Time is the non-spatial continuum in which events occur, in apparently irreversible succession, from the past through the present to the future.

41. There are two sequential phases to the development of spatial awareness. What is the order of these phases?
   A. Locating more than one object to each object; the location of objects in relation to one's own body in space.
   B. The location of objects in relation to ones' own body in space; locating more than one object in relation to one's own body.
   C. Locating more than one object independent of one's body; the location of objects in relation to one's own body.
   D. The location of objects in relation to one's own body in space; locating more than one object in relation to each object and independent of one's own body.

(D.) The order of the two sequential phases to develop spatial awareness are as follows: the location of objects in relation to one's own body in space, and locating more than one object in relation to each object and independent of one's own body.

42. Equilibrium is maintained as long as:
   A. Body segments are moved independently.
   B. The center of gravity is over the base of support
   C. Force is applied to the base of support.
   D. The center of gravity is lowered.

(B.) Equilibrium is a condition in which all acting influences are canceled by others, resulting in a stable, balanced, or unchanging system. It allows <u>humans</u> and <u>animals</u> to <u>walk</u> without falling. An object maintains equilibrium as long as its center of gravity is over its base of support.

43. Which of the following does not enhance equilibrium?

   A. Shifting the center of gravity away from the direction of movement.

   B. Increasing the base of support.

   C. Lowering the base of support.

   D. Increasing the base of support and lowering the center of support.

(A.) Equilibrium is a state of balance. When a body or a system is in equilibrium, there is no net tendency toward change. In mechanics, equilibrium has to do with the forces acting on a body. When no force acts to make a body move in a line, the body is in translational equilibrium. When no force acts to make the body turn, the body is in rotational equilibrium. A body in equilibrium while at rest is in static equilibrium. Increasing the base of support, lowering the base of support, and increasing the base of support and lowering the center of support all enhance equilibrium by balancing forces.

44. All of the following affect force except:
   A. Magnitude
   B. Energy
   C. Motion
   D. Mass

(D.) Mass is a property of a <u>physical</u> object that quantifies the amount of <u>matter</u> and <u>energy</u> it contains. Unlike <u>weight</u>, the mass of something stays the same regardless of location. Every object has a unified body of matter with no specific shape.

45. For a movement to occur, applied force must overcome inertia of an object and any other resisting forces. What concept of force does this describe?
   A. Potential energy
   B. Magnitude
   C. Kinetic energy
   D. Absorption

(B.) Speaking of magnitude in a purely relative way states that nothing is large and nothing small. If everything in the universe increased in bulk one thousand diameters, nothing would be any larger than it was before. However, if one thing remained unchanged, all of the others would be larger than they had been. To a person familiar with the relativity of magnitude and distance, the spaces and masses of the astronomer would be no more impressive than those of the microscopist would. To the contrary, the visible universe may be a small part of an atom, with its component ions floating in the life-fluid (luminiferous ether) of some animal.

46. The energy of an object to do work while recoiling is which type of potential energy?
   A. Absorption
   B. Kinetic
   C. Elastic
   D. Torque

(C.) In <u>materials science</u>, the word <u>elastomer</u> refers to a material that is very elastic (like <u>rubber</u>). We often use the word elastic colloquially to refer to an elastomeric material such as <u>rubber</u> or cloth/rubber combinations. It is capable of withstanding stress without injury. Elastic potential energy describes the energy inherent in flexible objects.

47. **Gradually decelerating a moving mass by utilization of smaller forces over a long period of time is:**
   A. Stability
   B. Equilibrium
   C. Angular force
   D. Force absorption

(D.) Force absorption is the gradual deceleration of a moving mass by utilization of smaller forces over a long period of time.

48. **The tendency of a body/object to remain in its present state of motion unless some force acts to change it is which mechanical principle of motion?**
   A. Acceleration
   B. Inertia
   C. Action/Reaction
   D. Linear motion

(B.) Inertia (ĭnûr'shə) is a term used in physics that describes the resistance of a body to any alteration in its state of <u>motion</u>. Inertia is a property common to all matter. Galileo first observed this property and Newton later restated it. Newton's first law of motion is sometimes called the law of inertia. Newton's second law of motion states that the external force required to affect the motion of a body is proportional to that acceleration. The constant of proportionality is the <u>mass</u>, which is the numerical value of the inertia. The greater the inertia of a body, the less acceleration is needed for a given, applied force.

49. **The movement response of a system depends not only on the net external force, but also on the resistance to movement change. Which mechanical principle of motion does this definition describe?**
   A. Acceleration
   B. Inertia
   C. Action/Reaction
   D. Air Resistance

(A.) Acceleration is the change in the <u>velocity</u> of a body with respect to time. Since velocity is a <u>vector</u> quantity involving both magnitude and direction, acceleration is also a vector. In order to produce acceleration, a <u>force</u> must on a body. The magnitude of the force (*F*) must be directly proportional to both the mass of the body (*m*) and the desired acceleration (*a*), according to Newton's second law of motion (*F=ma*). The exact nature of the acceleration depends on the relative directions of the original velocity and force. A force acting in the same direction as the velocity changes only the <u>speed</u> of the body. An appropriate force, acting always at right angles to the velocity, changes the direction of the velocity but not the speed.

50. Which of the following mechanical principles of motion states that every motion has a similar, contrasting response?
A. Acceleration
B. Inertia
C. Action/Reaction
D. Centripetal force

(C.) The principle of action/reaction is an assertion about the nature of motion from which we can determine the trajectory of an object subject to forces. The path of an object yields a stationary value for a quantity called the **action**. Thus, instead of thinking about an object accelerating in response to applied forces, one might think of them as picking out the path with a stationary action.

51. What is the proper order of sequential development for the acquisition of locomotor skills?
   A. Creep, crawl, walk, jump, run, slide, gallop, hop, leap, skip; step-hop.
   B. Crawl, walk, creep, slide, walk, run, hop, leap, gallop, skip; step-hop.
   C. Creep, crawl, walk, slide, run, hop, leap, skip, gallop, jump; step-hop.
   D. Crawl, creep, walk, run, jump, hop, gallop, slide, leap, skip; step-hop.

(D.)

LOCOMOTOR SKILL: A skill that utilizes the feet and moves you from one place to another.

CRAWL: A form of locomotion where the person moves in a prone position with the body resting on or close to the ground or on the hands and knees.

CREEP: A slightly more advanced form of locomotion in which the person moves on the hands and knees.

WALK: A form of locomotion in which body weight is transferred alternately from the ball (toe) of one foot to the heel of the other. At times one foot is on the ground and during a brief phase, both feet are on the ground. There is no time when both feet are off the ground.

RUN: A form of locomotion much like the walk except that the tempo and body lean may differ. At times one foot is on the ground and during a brief phase both feet are off the ground. There is no time when both feet are on the ground simultaneously.

JUMP: A form of locomotion in which the body weight is projected from one or two feet and lands on two feet. Basic forms: for height, from height, distance, continuous, and rebounding.
HOP: A form of locomotion in which the body is projected from one foot to the same foot.

GALLOP: A form of locomotion that is a combination of an open step by the leading foot and a closed step by the trailing foot. The same foot leads throughout. The rhythm is uneven.

SLIDE: The same action as the gallop except that the direction of travel is sideways instead of forward. The rhythm is uneven.

LEAP: An exaggerated running step. There is a transfer of weight from one foot to the other and a phase when neither foot is in contact with the ground.

SKIP: A locomotor skill that combines a hop and a step (walk or run). The rhythm is uneven.

52. Having students pretend they are playing basketball or trying to catch a bus develops which locomotor skill?
    A. Galloping
    B. Running
    C. Leaping
    D. Skipping

(B.) Playing basketball involves near constant running up and down the court. In addition, chasing is a good example to use with children to illustrate the concept of running.

53. Having students play Fox and Hound develops:
    A. Galloping
    B. Hopping
    C. Stepping-hopping
    D. Skipping

(A.) Fox and Hound is an activity that emphasizes rapid running. The form of the exercise most closely resembles a gallop, especially in rhythm and rapidity. It can develop or progress at an accelerated rate.

54. Having students take off and land with both feet together develops which locomotor skill?
    A. Hopping
    B. Jumping
    C. Leaping
    D. Skipping

(B.) Jumping is a skill that most humans and many animals share. It is the process of getting one's body off of the ground for a short time using one's own power, usually by propelling oneself upward via contraction and then forceful extension of the legs. One can jump up to reach something high, jump over a fence or ditch, or jump down. One can also jump while dancing and as a sport in track and field.

55. What is the proper sequential order of development for the acquisition of nonlocomotor skills?
    A. Stretch, sit, bend, turn, swing, twist, shake, rock & sway, dodge; fall.
    B. Bend, stretch, turn, twist, swing, sit, rock & sway, shake, dodge; fall.
    C. Stretch, bend, sit, shake, turn, rock & sway, swing, twist, dodge; fall.
    D. Bend, stretch, sit, turn, twist, swing, sway, rock & sway, dodge; fall.

(C.) Each skill in the progression builds on the previous skills.

56. **Activities such as pretending to pick fruit off a tree or reaching for a star develop which non-locomotor skill?**
    A. Bending
    B. Stretching
    C. Turning
    D. Twisting

(B.) Stretching is the activity of gradually applying <u>tensile</u> force to lengthen, strengthen, and lubricate <u>muscles</u>, often performed in anticipation of <u>physical exertion</u> and to increase the range of motion within a <u>joint</u>. Stretching is an especially important accompaniment to activities that emphasize controlled muscular strength and flexibility. These include <u>ballet</u>, <u>acrobatics</u> or <u>martial arts</u>. Stretching also may help prevent <u>injury</u> to <u>tendons</u>, <u>ligaments</u>, and muscles by improving muscular <u>elasticity</u> and reducing the stretch reflex in greater ranges of motion that might cause injury to tissue. In addition, stretching can reduce <u>delayed onset muscle soreness</u> (DOMS).

57. **Picking up coins, tying shoes, and petting animals develop this nonlocomotor skill.**
    A. Bending
    B. Stretching
    C. Turning
    D. Twisting

(A.) Bending is the action of moving the body across a skeletal joint. In each of the sample activities, one must bend from the waist or knees to reach a low object.

58. **Having students collapse in their own space or lower themselves as though they are a raindrop or snowflake develops this nonlocomotor skill.**
    A. Dodging
    B. Shaking
    C. Swinging
    D. Falling

(D.) Falling is a major cause of personal injury in athletics. Athletic participants must learn how to fall in such a way as to limit the possibility of injury.

59. **Which is the proper sequential order of development for the acquisition of manipulative skills?**
    A. Striking, throwing, bouncing, catching, trapping, kicking, ball rolling; volleying.
    B. Striking, throwing, kicking, ball rolling, volleying, bouncing, catching; trapping.
    C. Striking, throwing, catching, trapping, kicking, ball rolling, bouncing; volleying.
    D. Striking, throwing, kicking, ball rolling, bouncing; volleying.

(B.) Striking, throwing, kicking, ball rolling, volleying, bouncing, catching, and trapping is the proper sequential order of development for the acquisition of manipulative skills. Each skill in this progression builds on the previous skill.

60. **Having students hit a large balloon with both hands develops this manipulative skill?**
    A. Bouncing
    B. Striking
    C. Volleying
    D. Trapping

(C.) In a number of ball games, a volley is the ball that a player receives and delivers without touching the ground. The ability to volley a ball back and forth requires great body control and spatial awareness.

61. **Progressively decreasing the size of a target that balls are projected at develops which manipulative skill.**
    A. Throwing
    B. Trapping
    C. Volleying
    D. Kicking

(A.) Children develop throwing skills (the ability to propel an object through the air with a rapid movement of the arm and wrist) by projecting balls at progressively smaller targets.

62. **Hitting a stationary object while in a fixed position, then incorporating movement, develops this manipulative skill.**
    A. Bouncing
    B. Trapping
    C. Throwing
    D. Striking

(D.) Striking is the process of hitting something sharply, as with the hand, the fist, or a weapon.

63. **A subjective, observational approach to identify errors in the form, style, or mechanics of a skill is accomplished by:**
    A. Product assessment
    B. Process assessment
    C. Standardized norm-referenced tests
    D. Criterion-referenced tests

(B.) Process assessment is one way to identify errors in the skills of an individual. It is one way to know the limitations and skills that every individual possesses.

64. **What type of assessment objectively measures skill performance?**
    A. Process assessment
    B. Product assessment
    C. Texas PE Test
    D. Iowa Brace Test

(B.) Product assessment measures the skills of an individual. This process is a methodical evaluation of the characteristics of your product or service in the eyes of potential users and customers. The two principle types of assessments are principle-based assessments and usability testing.

65. **Process assessment does not identify which of the following errors in skill performance?**
    A. Style
    B. Form
    C. End result
    D. Mechanics

(C.) Process assessment does not evaluate end results. Process assessment emphasizes analysis of style, form, and mechanics.

66. **Determining poor performance of a skill using process assessment can best be accomplished by:**
    A. Observing how fast a skill is performed.
    B. Observing how many skills are performed.
    C. Observing how far or how high a skill is performed.
    D. Observing several attributes comprising the entire performance of a skill.

(D.) To determine the source of the error in the poor performance of an individual, we use observations of several attributes that compromise the entire performance of a skill. Instructors should observe limitations and mistakes and determine how to best address these problems to improve future performance.

67. **Which of the following principles is not a factor to assess to correct errors in performance for process assessment?**
    A. Inertia
    B. Action/Reaction
    C. Force
    D. Acceleration

(C.) Force is not a factor to focus on in process assessment.

68. **Which of the following methods measures fundamental skills using product assessment?**
    A. Criterion-referenced tests
    B. Standardized norm-referenced tests
    C. Both A and B
    D. Neither A nor B

(C.) Criterion-referenced tests and standardized norm-referenced tests are both methods that can prove and measure skills in product assessment. They can help to prevent or lessen errors.

69. **Product assessment measures all of the following except:**
    A. How the student performs the mechanics of a skill.
    B. How many times the student performs a skill.
    C. How fast the student performs a skill.
    D. How far or high the student performs a skill.

(A.) Product assessment evaluates student performance and gives insight into how students can correct errors. Product assessment measures results. Thus, how the student performs the mechanics of a skill is not relevant to product assessment.

70. **Instructors can evaluate skill level of achievement in archery by:**
    A. Giving students a written exam on terminology.
    B. Having students demonstrate the correct tension of arrow feathers.
    C. Totaling a student's score obtained on the target's face.
    D. Time how long a student takes to shoot all arrows.

(C.) **Archery** is the practice of using a <u>bow</u> to shoot <u>arrows</u>. Totaling a student's score is the only method, of the possible choices, that evaluates skill level. Choices A and B test knowledge and choice D is an arbitrary measure.

71. Instructors can determine skill level achievement in golf by:
   A. The number of "birdies" that were made.
   B. The number of "bogies" that were made.
   C. The score obtained after several rounds.
   D. The total score achieved throughout the school year.

(C.) Instructors can determine skill level in golf by evaluating a golfer's score after several rounds. The number of bogies or birdies is not necessarily indicative of skill level because they are isolated events (i.e. the score on one hole). The player who consistently scores the lowest likely has the most impressive golf skills. Therefore, a player's score is the best way to determine his/her skill level. Finally, several rounds is a sufficient sample to determine skill level. An entire year's worth of scores is not necessary.

72. Instructors can determine skill level achievement in swimming by:
   A. How long a student can float.
   B. How many strokes it takes to swim a specified distance.
   C. How long a student can stay under the water without moving.
   D. How many times a student can dive in five minutes.

(B.) Instructors can determine skill level in swimming by counting the strokes a swimmer takes when covering a certain distance. The arm movement, the strength, and the tactic to move quickly gives the swimmer an ability to swim faster. The ability to float, stay under water, and dive quickly are not relevant to swimming ability.

73. Instructors can assess skill level achievement in bowling by:
   A. Calculating a student's average.
   B. Calculating how many gutter-balls were thrown.
   C. Calculating how many strikes were thrown.
   D. Calculating how many spares were thrown.

(A.) Instructors can determine the skill level of a bowler by calculating the student's average game score. There is a possibility that some coincidences take place (e.g., bowling a strike). To check the consistency, we determine the average instead of looking at only the score from a single game.

74. **Although they are still hitting the target, the score of some students practicing archery has decreased as the distance between them and the target has increased. Which of the following adjustments will improve their scores?**
   A. Increasing the velocity of their arrows.
   B. Increasing the students' base of support.
   C. Increasing the weight of the arrows.
   D. Increasing the parabolic path of the arrows.

(D.) Increasing the parabolic path of the arrows will increase accuracy and precision at greater distances.

75. **Some students practicing basketball are having difficulty with "free throws," even though the shots make it to and over the hoop. What adjustment will improve their "free throws?"**
   A. Increasing the height of release (i.e. jump shot).
   B. Increasing the vertical path of the ball.
   C. Increasing the velocity of the release.
   D. Increasing the base of support.

(B.) In this case, increasing the vertical path of the ball will help the students make more free throws. Increased vertical path provides greater margin for error, allowing the ball to drop more easily through the hoop. Increasing the velocity cannot work due to common sense. Finally, increasing the height of release and base of support are not viable options in this case because the students are having no problem getting the ball to the basket.

76. **An archery student's arrow bounced off the red part of the target face. What is the correct ruling?**
   A. No score.
   B. Re-shoot arrow.
   C. 7 points awarded.
   D. Shot receives same score as highest arrow shot that did not bounce off the target.

(C.) When an arrow bounces off the red area of a target, the archer receives 7 points, the value of the shot had the arrow stuck in the target.

77. **A student playing badminton believed that the shuttlecock was going to land out-of-bounds. The shuttlecock landed on the line. What is the correct ruling?**
   A. The shuttlecock is out-of-bounds.
   B. The shuttlecock is in-bounds.
   C. The point is replayed.
   D. That player is charged with a feint.

(B.) If a shuttlecock lands on the line, it is inbounds by the rules of badminton.

78. **A mechanical pinsetter accidentally knocked down the only bowling pin left standing for a spare attempt, after clearing all the other pins knocked down by the first ball thrown. What is the correct ruling?**
   A. Foul
   B. Spare
   C. Frame is replayed
   D. No count for that pin

(D.) When the mechanical pin setter touches a pin and knocks it down, there is no count for the pin because the pin fell because of mechanical fault and the player had nothing to do with it. The other pins count and there is no foul for the player.

79. **The ball served in racquetball hits the front line and lands in front of the short line. What is the ruling?**
   A. Fault
   B. Reserve
   C. Out-of-bounds
   D. Fair ball

(A.) If a served ball falls in front of the short line, it is a fault according to a rule that states that a ball must fall within the short line frame at the time of serving. It is not out-of-bounds, as it is still within the limits of the pitch. However, it is also not a fair ball due to the service rule.

80. **Two opposing soccer players are trying to gain control of the ball when one player "knees" the other. What is the ruling?**
   A. Direct free kick
   B. Indirect free kick
   C. Fair play
   D. Ejection from a game

(A.) Assuming that the soccer player didn't intentionally hit the other player's knee, the result would be a direct free kick. If the foul was intentional, the referee can eject the offender from the game. Minor offenses and offenses not involving contact result in indirect free kicks.

81. **Two students are playing badminton. When receiving the shuttlecock, one student consistently stands too deep in the receiving court. What strategy should the server use to serve the shuttlecock?**
    A. Smash serve
    B. Clear serve
    C. Overhead serve
    D. Short serve

(D.) The short serve would give land short in the court so the opponent would not be able to reach the shuttlecock. Therefore, the short serve would win the point. A clear or overhead serve enables the opponent to hit the shuttlecock and continue the game. A smash serve runs a higher risk of falling out-of-bounds. Neither of these scenarios are goals of the server.

82. **A basketball team has an outstanding rebounder. In order to keep this player near the opponent's basket, which strategy should the coach implement?**
    A. Pick-and-Roll
    B. Give-and-Go
    C. Zone defense
    D. Free-lancing

(C.) A zone defense, where each player guards an area of the court rather than an individual player, allows an outstanding rebounder to remain near the basket. The give-and-go, pick-and-roll, and free-lancing are offensive strategies that do not affect rebounding.

83. **When a defensive tennis player needs more time to return to his position, what strategy should he apply?**
    A. Drop shot
    B. Dink shot
    C. Lob shot
    D. Down-the-line shot

(C.) When a tennis player is off the court and needs time to return to his position, the player should play a lob shot. Down-the-line shots and drop shots are offensive shots and are too risky in this situation. The dink shot would allow the opponent to take control of the point.

84. **An overhead badminton stroke used to hit a forehand-like overhead stroke that is on the backhand side of the body is called:**
    A. Around-the-head-shot
    B. Down-the-line shot
    C. Lifting the shuttle
    D. Under hand shuttle

(A.) A shot played from the backhand side and over the head is known as an around-the-head shot. It is played when the shuttlecock is high and cannot be reached any other way.

85. **A maneuver when an offensive player passes to a teammate and then immediately cuts in toward the basket for a return pass is:**
    A. Charging
    B. Pick
    C. Give-and-go
    D. Switching

(C.) In the game of basketball, a give-and-go is an offensive play where a player passes to a teammate and immediately cuts toward the basket for a return pass. Charging is an offensive foul, a pick is a maneuver to free up a teammate for a pass or shot, and switching is a defensive maneuver.

86. **A bowling pin that remains standing after an apparently perfect hit is called a:**
    A. Tap
    B. Turkey
    C. Blow
    D. Leave

(A.) A bowling pin that remains standing, even after a perfect shot, is known as a tap. Other options, like turkeys and blows, are not relevant to the standing pin.

87. **A soccer pass from the outside of the field near the end line to a position in front of the goal is called:**
    A. Chip
    B. Settle
    C. Through
    D. Cross

(D.) Any long pass from the sides of the field toward the middle is a cross, since the hitter hits it across the field. A chip is a high touch pass or shot. A through pass travels the length of the field through many players. Finally, settling is the act of controlling the ball after receiving a pass.

88. **A volleyball that is simultaneously contacted above the net by opponents and momentarily held upon contact is a(n)**:
    A. Double fault
    B. Play over
    C. Overlap
    D. Held ball

(D.) In volleyball, if two players simultaneously contact the ball above the net, the ball is a held ball.

89. **Volleyball player LB on team A digs a spiked ball. The ball deflects off of LB's shoulder. What is the ruling?**
    A. Fault
    B. Legal hit
    C. Double foul
    D. Play over

(B.) Since the spiked ball does not touch the ground and instead deflects off LB's shoulder, it is a legal hit. In order for a point to end, the ball must touch the ground. In this instance, it does not.

90. **A teacher who modifies and develops tasks for a class is demonstrating knowledge of which appropriate behavior in physical education activities.**
    A. Appropriate management behavior
    B. Appropriate student behavior
    C. Appropriate administration behavior
    D. Appropriate content behavior

(D.) In this case, the teacher is demonstrating knowledge of a behavior in reference to physical activity. It is known as appropriate content behavior. The other options are not related to physical activities.

91. **To enhance skill and strategy performance for striking or throwing objects, for catching or collecting objects, and for carrying and propelling objects, students must first learn techniques for:**
    A. Offense
    B. Defense
    C. Controlling objects
    D. Continuous play of objects

(C.) For enhancing the catching, throwing, carrying, or propelling of objects, a student must learn how to control the objects. The control gives the player a sense of the object. Thus, offense, defense, and continuous play come naturally, as they are part of the controlling process.

92. Which of the following is not a type of tournament?
   A. Spiderweb
   B. Pyramid
   C. Spiral
   D. Round Robin

(C.) A spiral is not a type of tournament.

93. Which of the following is not a type of meet?
   A. Extramural
   B. Intramural
   C. Interscholastic
   D. Ladder

(D.) A ladder is not a type of meet.

94. An instructor used a similar movement from a skill learned in a different activity to teach a skill for a new activity. The technique used to facilitate cognitive learning was:
   A. Conceptual thinking
   B. Transfer of learning
   C. Longer instruction
   D. Appropriate language

(B.) Using a previously used movement to facilitate a new task is a transfer of learning. The individual relates the past activity to the new one, enabling him/her to learn it more easily. Conceptual thinking is related to the transfer of learning, but it does not give the exact idea. Rather, it emphasizes the history of all learning.

95. A teacher rewards students for completing tasks. Which method is the teacher using to facilitate psychomotor learning?
   A. Task/Reciprocal
   B. Command/Direct
   C. Contingency/Contract
   D. Physical/Reflex

(C.) Since the teacher is rewarding the student, the contingency/contract method is in place. The command/direct method involves the interaction between student and teacher when the student fails to fulfill the requirements.

96. All of the following are Systematic Observational Evaluations except:
   A. Reflective Recording
   B. Event Recording
   C. Duration Recording
   D. Self Recording

(A.) Reflective recording is not a type of systematic observational evaluation. Event, duration, and self recordings are all methods used in systematic observational evaluations.

97. The ability for a muscle(s) to repeatedly contract over a period of time is:
   A. Cardiovascular endurance
   B. Muscle endurance
   C. Muscle strength
   D. Muscle force

(B.) Muscle endurance gives the muscle the ability to contract over a period of time. Muscle strength is a prerequisite for the endurance of muscle. Cardiovascular endurance involves aerobic exercise.

98. The ability to change rapidly the direction of the body is:
   A. Coordination
   B. Reaction time
   C. Speed
   D. Agility

(D.) Agility is the ability of the body to change position quickly. Reaction time, coordination, and speed are not the right words to describe the ability to move quickly, as we always say that the goalkeeper is agile.

99. Students are performing the vertical jump. What component of fitness does this activity assess?
   A. Muscle strength
   B. Balance
   C. Power
   D. Muscle endurance

(C.) Vertical jumping assesses the power of the entire body. It shows the potential of the legs to hold the upper body and the strength in the joints of the legs. Balance and muscle strength are secondary requirements. Power automatically ensures these secondary requirements.

100. **Students are performing trunk extensions. What component of fitness does this activity assess?**
   A. Balance
   B. Flexibility
   C. Body Composition
   D. Coordination

(B.) The core component of trunk extensions is flexibility. Trunk extensions also indicate the body's capacity for full expansion and emphasizes areas such as the stomach, arms, and shoulder joints.

101. **Working at a level that is above normal is which exercise training principle?**
   A. Intensity
   B. Progression
   C. Specificity
   D. Overload

(D.) Overloading is exercising above normal capacities. Intensity and progression are supporting principles in the process of overload. Overloading can cause serious issues within the body, either immediately or after some time.

102. **Students on a running program to improve cardio-respiratory fitness apply which exercise principle.**
   A. Aerobic
   B. Progression
   C. Specificity
   D. Overload

(C.) Running to improve cardio-respiratory fitness is an example of specificity . Specificity is the selection of activities that isolate a specific body part or system. Aerobics is also a good option, but it deals with the entire body, including areas not specific to cardio-respiratory fitness.

103. **Adding more reps to a weightlifting set applies which exercise principle.**
   A. Anaerobic
   B. Progression
   C. Overload
   D. Specificity

(B.) Adding more repetitions (reps) to sets when weightlifting is an example of progression. Adding reps can result in overload, but the guiding principle is progression.

104. Which of the following does not modify overload?
   A. Frequency
   B. Perceived exertion
   C. Time
   D. Intensity

(B.) Time extension, frequency of movement, and intensity are all indicators of overload. However, exertion is not a good indicator of overload, because measuring exertion is subjective and difficult to monitor.

105. Using the Karvonean Formula, compute the 60% - 80% THR for a 16-year old student with a RHR of 60.
   A. 122-163 beats per minute
   B. 130-168 beats per minute
   C. 142-170 beats per minute
   D. 146-175 beats per minute

(D.)

$220 - 16$ (age) $= 204$, $204 - 60$ (RHR) $= 144$, $144 \times .60$ (low end of heart range) $= 86$, $86 + 60$ (RHR) $= \mathbf{146}$ **(bottom of THR)**

$220 - 16$ (age) $= 204$, $204 - 60$ (RHR) $= 144$, 144×0.80 (high end of heart range) $= 115$, $115 + $ (RHR) $= \mathbf{175}$ **(top of THR)**

146-175 beats per minute is the 60%-80% THR.

106. Using Cooper's Formula, compute the THR for a 15-year old student.
   A. 120-153 beats per minute
   B. 123-164 beats per minute
   C. 135-169 beats per minute
   D. 147-176 beats per minute

(B.) 123-164 beats per minute.

107. Prior to activity, students perform a 5-10 minute warm-up. Which is not recommended as part of the warm-up?
   A. Using the muscles that will be utilized in the following activity.
   B. Using a gradual aerobic warm-up.
   C. Using a gradual anaerobic warm-up.
   D. Stretching the major muscle groups to be used in the activity.

(C.) Warm-up is always necessary, but it should not be an anaerobic warm-up. The muscle exercises, the stretching, and even the aerobics are all helpful and athletes should complete these exercises within the normal breathing conditions. In fact, athletes should focus more closely on proper breathing. Athletes should engage in anaerobic stretching after activity, when muscles are loose and less prone to injury.

108. Which is not a benefit of warming up?
   A. Releasing hydrogen from myoglobin.
   B. Reducing the risk of musculoskeletal injuries.
   C. Raising the body's core temperature in preparation for activity.
   D. Stretching the major muscle groups to be used in the activity.

(A.) Warm-up can reduce the risk of musculoskeletal injuries, raise the body's temperature in preparation for activity, and stretch the major muscle groups. However, a warm-up does not release hydrogen from myoglobin. Myoglobin binds oxygen, not hydrogen.

109. Which is not a benefit of cooling down?
   A. Preventing dizziness.
   B. Redistributing circulation.
   C. Removing lactic acid.
   D. Removing myoglobin.

(D.) Cooling down helps the body to regain blood circulation and to remove lactic acid. It also prevents dizziness, which may occur after extensive exercises. The only thing that cooling down does not support is removing myoglobin. However, it can help myoglobin get a strong hold in the muscles.

110. Activities to specifically develop cardiovascular fitness must be:
   A. Performed without developing an oxygen debt
   B. Performed twice daily.
   C. Performed every day.
   D. Performed for a minimum of 10 minutes.

(A.) The development of cardiovascular fitness is not dependent on specific time limits or routine schedules. Participants should perform aerobic activities without developing an oxygen debt.

111. Overloading for muscle strength includes all of the following except:
   A. Lifting heart rate to an intense level.
   B. Lifting weights every other day.
   C. Lifting with high resistance and low reps.
   D. Lifting 60% to 90% of assessed muscle strength.

(A.) Overloading muscle strength is possible by lifting the weights every other day or by lifting weights with high resistance and low repetition. Overloading does not cause or require an intense increase in heart rate. However, overloading has many other possibilities.

112. Which of the following applies the concept of progression?
   A. Beginning a stretching program every day.
   B. Beginning a stretching program with 3 sets of reps.
   C. Beginning a stretching program with ballistic stretching.
   D. Beginning a stretching program holding stretches for 15 seconds and work up to holding stretches for 60 seconds.

(D.) Progression is the process of starting an exercise program slowly and cautiously before proceeding to more rigorous training. Answer D is the only answer that exemplifies progression.

113. Which of following overload principles does not apply to improving body composition?
   A. Aerobic exercise three times per week.
   B. Aerobic exercise at a low intensity.
   C. Aerobic exercise for about an hour.
   D. Aerobic exercise in intervals of high intensity.

(A.) To improve body composition, a person should engage in aerobic exercise daily, not three times per week. However, an individual can do aerobics for at least half an hour daily, he/she can exercise at a low intensity, or he/she can train with intervals of high intensity.

114. Which of the following principles of progression applies to improving muscle endurance?
   A. Lifting weights every day.
   B. Lifting weights at 20% to 30% of assessed muscle strength.
   C. Lifting weights with low resistance and low reps.
   D. Lifting weights starting at 60% of assessed muscle strength.

(B.) To improve muscle endurance, a person should lift weights at 20 to 30% of the assessed muscle strength. Lifting weights daily is counterproductive because it does not allow for adequate rest. In addition, lifting at 60% of the assessed muscle strength can damage the muscle.

115. Aerobic dance develops or improves each of the following skills or health components except...
A. Cardio-respiratory function
B. Body composition
C. Coordination
D. Flexibility

(D.) Aerobic dance does not develop flexibility, as flexibility results from stretching and not aerobic exercise. Ballet dancing, however, does develop flexibility. Aerobic dance develops cardio-respiratory function due to the unusual body movements performed. It also improves body composition and coordination due to the movement of various body parts.

116. Rowing develops which health or skill related component of fitness?
A. Muscle endurance
B. Flexibility
C. Balance
D. Reaction time

(A.) Rowing helps develop muscle endurance because of the continuous arm movement against the force of the water. However, flexibility, balance, and reaction time are not important components of rowing. Rowing also develops the lower abdominal muscles while the individual is in the sitting position when rowing.

117. Calisthenics develops all of the following health and skill related components of fitness except:
A. Muscle strength
B. Body composition
C. Power
D. Agility

(C.) Calisthenics is a sport that actually helps to keep a body fit in by combining gymnastic and aerobic activities. Calisthenics develop muscle strength and agility and improves body composition. However, calisthenics do not develop power because they do not involve resistance training or explosiveness.

118. **Which health or skill related component of fitness is developed by rope jumping?**
    A. Muscle Force
    B. Coordination
    C. Flexibility
    D. Muscle strength

(B.) Rope jumping is a good mental exercise and it improves coordination. Many athletes (e.g. boxers, tennis players) jump rope to improve coordination and quickness. Muscle strength is secondary to that.

119. **Swimming does not improve which health or skill related component of fitness?**
    A. Cardio-respiratory function
    B. Flexibility
    C. Muscle strength
    D. Foot Speed

(D.) Swimming involves every part of the body. It works on the cardio-respiratory system and it develops flexibility because of the intense body movement in the water. It also improves muscle strength as swimmers must move their bodies against the force of water. Increased foot speed is not an outcome of swimming.

120. **Data from a cardio-respiratory assessment can identify and predict all of the following except:**
    A. Functional aerobic capacity
    B. Natural over-fatness
    C. Running ability
    D. Motivation

(B.) The data from cardio-respiratory assessment can identify and predict running ability, motivation, and functional aerobic capacity. However, it cannot predict natural over-fatness, as natural over-fatness is a part of the human body. It is not artificially developed like running ability and motivation.

121. **Data from assessing _____ identifies an individual's potential of developing musculoskeletal problems and an individual's potential of performing activities of daily living.**
    A. Flexibility
    B. Muscle endurance
    C. Muscle strength
    D. Motor performance

(A.) Flexibility.

122. **A 17-year-old male student performed 20 sit-ups, ran a mile in 8 minutes, and has a body fat composition of 17%. Which is the best interpretation of his fitness level?**
    A. Average muscular endurance, good cardiovascular endurance; appropriate body fat composition.
    B. Low muscular endurance, average cardiovascular endurance; high body fat composition.
    C. Low muscular endurance, average cardiovascular endurance; appropriate body fat composition.
    D. Low muscular endurance, low cardiovascular endurance; appropriate body fat composition.

(C.) A 17-year-old male who performs 20 sit-ups, runs a mile in 8 minutes and has 17% fat composition has low muscular endurance, average cardiovascular endurance, and appropriate fat composition. 20 sit-ups is a relatively low number. An 8-minute mile is an average time for a 17-year-old male. Finally, a body fat composition of 17% is appropriate.

123. **Based on the information given in the previous question, what changes would you recommend to improve this person's level of fitness?**
    A. Muscle endurance training and cardiovascular endurance training.
    B. Muscle endurance training, cardiovascular endurance training, and reduction of caloric intake.
    C. Muscle strength training and cardio-vascular endurance training.
    D. No changes necessary.

(A.) The person requires both muscle endurance and cardiovascular training while keeping the other bodily intakes normal. An appropriate program would include moderate weightlifting and regular aerobic activity.

124. **An obese student's fitness assessments were poor for every component of fitness. Which would you recommend first?**
    A. A jogging program.
    B. A weight lifting program.
    C. A walking program.
    D. A stretching program.

(C.) An obese person should begin by walking and then progress to jogging. Weightlifting and stretching are not as important initially. They are also dangerous because the student may not have the ability to complete such strenuous tasks safely.

125. Which of the following body types is the most capable of motor performance involving endurance?
A. Endomorph
B. Ectomorph
C. Mesomorph
D. Metamorph

(B.) Characteristically, ectomorphs are lean and slender with little body fat and musculature. Ectomorphs are usually capable of performing at high levels in endurance events.

126. Which is not a sign of stress?
A. Irritability
B. Assertiveness
C. Insomnia
D. Stomach problems

(B.) Assertiveness is not a sign of stress. Irritability, insomnia, and stomach problems are all related to stress.

127. Which is not a common negative stressor?
A. Loss of significant other
B. Personal illness or injury.
C. Moving to a new state.
D. Landing a new job.

(D.) Landing a new job is generally not a cause of worry or stress. In fact, it is a positive event. Personal illness, loss of a significant other, or moving to a strange state can cause negative stress.

128. Which of the following is a negative coping strategy for dealing with stress?
A. Recreational diversions
B. Active thinking
C. Alcohol use
D. Imagery

(C.) The use of alcohol is a negative coping strategy for dealing with stress. Alcohol causes the brain to lose the stressful data thus soothing the individual, but it can be highly detrimental in the long run. Positive ways to deal with stress include active thinking, imagery, and recreational diversions.

129. The most important nutrient the body requires, without which life can only be sustained for a few days, is:
   A. Vitamins
   B. Minerals
   C. Water
   D. Carbohydrates

(C.) Although the body requires vitamins, minerals, and carbohydrates to achieve proper growth and shape, water is essential. Without it, the body gets dehydrated and death is a possibility. Water should be pure, as seawater can cause kidney failure and death.

130. With regard to protein content, foods from animal sources are usually:
   A. Complete
   B. Essential
   C. Nonessential
   D. Incidental

(A.) Animal protein is complete, meaning it provides all of the amino acids that the human body requires. Although animal meat is not essential to a person's diet, it is an excellent source of protein.

131. Fats with room for two or more hydrogen atoms per molecule-fatty acid chain are:
   A. Monounsaturated
   B. Polyunsaturated
   C. Hydrosaturated
   D. Saturated

(B.) Polyunsaturated fatty acids contain multiple carbon-carbon double bonds. Thus, there is room for two or more hydrogens. Polyunsaturated fats are healthier than saturated fats.

132. An adequate diet to meet nutritional needs consists of:
   A. No more than 30% caloric intake from fats, no more than 50 % caloric intake from proteins, and at least 20% caloric intake from carbohydrates.
   B. No more than 30% caloric intake from fats, no more than 40% caloric intake from proteins, and at least 30% caloric intake from carbohydrates.
   C. No more than 30% caloric intake from fats, no more than 15% caloric intake from proteins, and at least 55% caloric intake from carbohydrates.
   D. No more than 30 % caloric intake from fats, no more than 30% caloric intake from proteins, and at least 40% caloric intake from carbohydrates.

(C.) General guidelines for nutritionally sound diets are 30% caloric intake from fats, no more than 15% caloric intake from proteins, and at least 55% caloric intake from carbohydrates.

133. Maintaining body weight is best accomplished by:
   A. Dieting
   B. Aerobic exercise
   C. Lifting weights
   D. Equalizing caloric intake relative to output

(D.) The best way to maintain a body weight is by balancing caloric intake and output. Extensive dieting (caloric restriction) is not a good option as this would result in weakness. Exercise is part of the output process that helps balance caloric input and output.

134. Most high-protein diets:
   A. Are high in cholesterol
   B. Are high in saturated fats
   C. Require vitamin and mineral supplements
   D. All of the above

(D.) High-protein diets are high in cholesterol, saturated fats, and they require vitamin and mineral supplements.

135. Which one of the following statements about low-calorie diets is false?
   A. Most people who "diet only" regain the weight they lose.
   B. They are the way most people try to lose weight.
   C. They make weight control easier.
   D. They lead to excess worry about weight, food, and eating.

(C.) People who participate in low-calorie diets do not control their weight easily. They must work more and utilize their bodies in many other ways (e.g., walking) to keep themselves fit.

136. Physiological benefits of exercise include all of the following except:
   A. Reducing mental tension
   B. Improving muscle strength
   C. Cardiac hypertrophy
   D. Quicker recovery rate

(A.) Physical exercises can help improve muscle strength by making the body move and they can help provide quicker recovery between exercise sessions and from injuries. However, physical activity does not directly relieve mental tension. It might reduce tension temporarily, but chances are the tension will persist.

137. **Psychological benefits of exercise include all of the following except:**
   A. Improved sleeping patterns
   B. Improved energy regulation
   C. Improved appearance
   D. Improved quality of life

(B.) The psychological benefits of exercise include improved sleeping patterns, improved appearances, and an improved quality of life. Improved energy regulation is a physical benefit, not a psychological one.

138. **Which of the following conditions is not associated with a lack of physical activity?**
   A. Atherosclerosis
   B. Longer life expectancy
   C. Osteoporosis
   D. Certain cancers

(B.) A lack of physical activity can contribute to atherosclerosis, osteoporosis, and certain cancers. Conversely, regular physical activity can contribute to longer life expectancy.

139. **Which of the following pieces of exercise equipment best applies the physiological principles?**
   A. Rolling machine
   B. Electrical muscle stimulator
   C. Stationary Bicycle
   D. Motor-driven rowing machine

(C.) A stationary bicycle is the best option to support the body physically as it includes all of the operations related to an individual's body (e.g., movement of legs, position of arms, back exercise, stomach movement). Electrical muscle stimulators are very dangerous as they can cause muscles to loosen too much. Other machines may provide an unnecessarily extensive workout that is dangerous for muscle.

Sample Written Assignment #1

This sample written assignment consists of a brief scenario followed by a sequence of questions or topics to discuss. You should draft an essay of 150-300 words addressing all of the topics or questions. It is important that you organize your response and demonstrate a thorough understanding of the subject matter. Content is more important than writing style, though poor grammar, punctuation, spelling, and sentence structure can detract from your response.

Use the information below to complete the exercise that follows.

Evan is a 10-year-old fifth grade student who recently completed a physical fitness evaluation in his physical education class. Evan was able to perform 6 push-ups and no pull-ups. He completed the mile run in 6:58. The evaluation also showed that Evan had below average flexibility.

Evan is a physically active child, participating in tennis and soccer outside of school. Evan is a very talented athlete looking to improve his performance in his sporting activities. Evan is also a very reserved, shy child who does not make friends easily or interact much with other children. In addition, Evan's parents feel Evan is an unusually gifted tennis player and should stop playing soccer to focus on tennis.

Based on your knowledge of physical fitness construct a written response that addresses the following:

- interpret the results of Evan's fitness evaluation; determine the components of fitness that Evan needs to address

- identify two age-appropriate fitness activities that will help Evan achieve his goals

- advise Evan's parents on their desire to have Evan focus on tennis taking into account the social and psychological aspects of participation in sports and fitness activities

Strong Response to the Sample Written Assignment #1

The results of Evan's physical fitness assessment show that he has a high level of cardiovascular endurance (good mile run time), a low level of muscular endurance (poor results on push-up and pull-up test), and a low level of flexibility. Thus, a fitness program for Evan should focus on developing muscular endurance and flexibility. In addition, because Evan participates in soccer and tennis, he likely receives more than enough aerobic activity in these aerobically intensive sports.

Flexibility and muscular endurance are important, and often overlooked, aspects of tennis and soccer. Thus, developing these areas will improve Evan's athletic performance. Because Evan is only 10-years-old, I would recommend he engage in body support exercises, rather than resistance training exercises, to increase his muscular endurance. Such exercises include push-ups, pull-ups, sit-ups, lunges, and squats. I would not recommend weight training for a 10-year-old because lifting weights is dangerous and possibly detrimental for developing bodies. Evan should also engage in a regular stretching program after his tennis and soccer practices and matches. Stretching improves flexibility and stretching after physical activity is safest and most effective.

Finally, I would advise Evan's parents that he should continue to play both soccer and tennis. Sport specialization is not necessary at Evan's age to maximize performance and asking Evan to give up soccer could have other detrimental effects. Because Evan is shy and reserved, the social aspects of a team sport like soccer are important to his development. Participation in team sports promotes the development of social skills, leadership, teamwork, and interpersonal relationships. Evan will benefit from such interaction with other children and will improve his self-esteem, especially because he is a talented player. While tennis is an excellent sport, it is mainly an individual sport, and the opportunity for socialization and the development of friendships is limited.

Sample Written Assignment #2

This sample written assignment requires you to respond to a question about human health and development. You should draft an essay of 150-300 words addressing the topic. It is important that you organize your response and demonstrate a thorough understanding of the subject matter. Content is more important than writing style, though poor grammar, punctuation, spelling, and sentence structure can detract from your response.

Participation in physical activities can enhance the development of many social skills. Choose <u>one</u> of the following social skills enhanced by physical activity: collaboration/cooperation/teamwork, loyalty, compassion/consideration for others, leadership, valuing/respecting diversity and individual differences.

- **discuss how participation in physical activity can affect the development of the social skill you chose**

- **identify strategies for encouraging development of the skill in the physical education classroom**

- **discuss how the acquired skill will benefit students later in life**

Strong Response to Sample Written Assignment #2

Participation in physical activities and sports can greatly enhance the development of collaboration, cooperation, and teamwork skills. Many physical activities require some degree of cooperation, most notably team sports. Team sports require participants to work together to achieve a common goal. Participants learn to pool the talents and minimize the weaknesses of different team members. Students will quickly learn that individualism can destroy the team concept and damage the team's performance. In addition, students will learn that a lack of respect or dissension between teammates will hurt the team. Students will learn to respect their teammates, value their contributions, and encourage them to perform their best.

Physical educators can encourage development of teamwork skills by including team-oriented activities in their lesson plans. Common examples include basketball, softball, volleyball, and soccer. In addition, instructors should watch closely for and discipline students that blatantly disrupt the team concept by bullying or belittling teammates.

Teamwork, collaboration, and cooperation skills are important in many walks of life. Students will use teamwork skills in their academic careers, in the workplace, and at home. For example, many academic classes from elementary school through college require group work. Most jobs require employees to work with others to achieve goals. Finally, we can view a family unit as a team. Students will have to play many roles on their family team (e.g. child, sibling, spouse, and parent) throughout their lives.

XAMonline, INC. 21 Orient Ave. Melrose, MA 02176

Toll Free number 800-301-4647

TO ORDER Fax 781-662-9268 OR www.XAMonline.com

ILLINOIS TEACHER CERTIFICATION SYSTEM - ICTS - 2006

PO#   Store/School:

Address 1:

Address 2 (Ship to other):

City, State Zip

 Credit card number_____-_____-_____-_____   expiration_____

EMAIL _____

PHONE   FAX

13# ISBN 2007	TITLE	Qty	Retail	Total
978-1-58197-977-0	ICTS Assessment of Professional Teaching- Birth to Grade 3 102			
978-1-58197-976-3	ICTS Basic Skills 096			
978-1-58197-996-1	ICTS Elementary-Middle Grades 110			
978-1-58197-997-8	ICTS Elementary-Middle Grades 110 Sample Questions			
978-1-58197-981-7	ICTS English Language Arts 111			
978-1-58197-991-6	ICTS Family and Consumer Sciences 172			
978-1-58197-987-9	ICTS Foreign Language- French Sample Test 127			
978-1-58197-988-6	ICTS Foreign Language- Spanish 135			
978-1-58197-992-3	ICTS Library Information Specialist 175			
978-1-58197-983-1	ICTS Mathematics 115			
978-1-58197-989-3	ICTS Physical Education 144			
978-1-58197-995-4	ICTS Principal 186			
978-1-58197-993-0	ICTS Reading Specialist 176			
978-1-58197-994-7	ICTS School Counselor 181			
978-1-58197-978-7	ICTS Science- Biology 105			
978-1-58197-979-4	ICTS Science- Chemistry 106			
978-1-58197-980-0	ICTS Science- Earth and Space Science 108			
978-1-58197-984-8	ICTS Science: Physics 116			
978-1-58197-982-4	ICTS Social Science- History 114			
978-1-58197-985-5	ICTS Social Science- Political Science 117			
978-1-58197-986-2	ICTS Social Science- Psychology 118			
978-1-58197-975-6	ICTS Special Education General Curriculum Test 163			
978-1-58197-990-9	ICTS Visual Arts Sample Test 145			

		SUBTOTAL	
FOR PRODUCT PRICES GO TO **WWW.XAMONLINE.COM**		Ship	$8.25
		TOTAL	

LaVergne, TN USA
18 November 2010
205323LV00001B/25/A